ReFocus: The Films of Pedro Costa

ReFocus: The International Directors Series

Series Editors: Robert Singer, Stefanie Van de Peer and Gary D. Rhodes

ReFocus is a series of contemporary methodological and theoretical approaches to the interdisciplinary analyses and interpretations of international film directors, from the celebrated to the ignored, in direct relationship to their respective culture—its myths, values, and historical precepts—and the broader parameters of international film history and theory. The series provides a forum for introducing a broad spectrum of directors, working in and establishing movements, trends, cycles and genres including those historical, currently popular, or emergent, and in need of critical assessment or reassessment. It ignores no director who created a historical space—either in or outside of the studio system—beginning with the origins of cinema and up to the present. *ReFocus* brings these film directors to a new audience of scholars and general readers of Film Studies.

Titles in the series include:

ReFocus: The Films of Susanne Bier
Edited by Missy Molloy, Mimi Nielsen, and Meryl Shriver-Rice

ReFocus: The Films of Corneliu Porumboiu
Monica Filimon

ReFocus: The Films of Francis Veber
Keith Corson

ReFocus: The Films of Andrei Tarkovsky
Sergei Toymentsev

ReFocus: The Films of Jia Zhangke
Maureen Turim and Ying Xiao

ReFocus: The Films of Xavier Dolan
Edited by Andrée Lafontaine

ReFocus: The Films of Pedro Costa: Producing and Consuming Contemporary Art Cinema
Nuno Barradas Jorge

edinburghuniversitypress.com/series/refocint

ReFocus:
The Films of Pedro Costa

Producing and Consuming Contemporary
Art Cinema

Nuno Barradas Jorge

EDINBURGH
University Press

Edinburgh University Press is one of the leading university presses in the UK. We publish academic books and journals in our selected subject areas across the humanities and social sciences, combining cutting-edge scholarship with high editorial and production values to produce academic works of lasting importance. For more information visit our website: edinburghuniversitypress.com

© Nuno Barradas Jorge, 2020, 2021

Edinburgh University Press Ltd
The Tun—Holyrood Road
12(2f) Jackson's Entry
Edinburgh EH8 8PJ

First published in hardback by Edinburgh University Press 2020

Typeset in 11/13 Ehrhardt MT by
IDSUK (DataConnection) Ltd, and
printed and bound by CPI Group (UK) Ltd

A CIP record for this book is available from the British Library

ISBN 978 1 4744 4453 8 (hardback)
ISBN 978 1 4744 4454 5 (paperback)
ISBN 978 1 4744 4455 2 (webready PDF)
ISBN 978 1 4744 4456 9 (epub)

The right of Nuno Barradas Jorge to be identified as the author of this work has been asserted in accordance with the Copyright, Designs and Patents Act 1988, and the Copyright and Related Rights Regulations 2003 (SI No. 2498).

Contents

List of Figures	vi
Acknowledgements	viii
Introduction	1
1 Cinema's 'Primitive Beauty': Pedro Costa's Artistic Formation and the Making of *Blood* (1989)	12
2 Negotiating Filmmaking: Adaptation, Location and *Docufiction*	32
3 Digital Filmmaking at the Interstices	53
4 Critical Reception and the International Film Festival	69
5 Between the Black Box and the White Cube	90
6 Renegotiating Circulation: Retrospectives and DVD Releases	110
7 A 'Document of Documents': Authorship, Intertextuality and Politics in *Horse Money* (2014)	128
Conclusion	148
Filmography	152
Bibliography	154
Index	165

Figures

1.1–1.3	Stylistic correlations with classical cinema in *Blood* (1989): the evocation of the work of Nicholas Ray, Jacques Tourneur and of *Night of the Hunter* (1955)	15
1.4	Still of *Blood* (1989), featuring Pedro Hestnes and Inês de Medeiros. This was one of the images used to promote the film during its domestic commercial release in 1990	29
2.1 and 2.2	Stills of the initial scenes of *Casa de Lava* (1994), featuring footage of the Fogo Island volcano eruption shot by Orlando Ribeiro in 1951	33
2.3	Resolving spatial restrictions through *mise en scène*: still of *Bones* (1997) featuring Vanda Duarte, Isabel Ruth and Mariya Lipkina	51
4.1	'Family photo': Jean-Marie Straub, Pedro Costa and Danièle Huillet in 2001	77
5.1 and 5.2	Pedro Costa's two-screen video installation *Daughters of Fire* (2013), displayed at the São Roque Church	91
5.3	Double-screen narrative compositions of *Little Boy Male, Little Girl Female* (2005)	99
5.4	An exception in Costa's coherent filmic universe: still from *The End of a Love Affair* (2003), featuring Gustavo Sumpta	101
5.5	Still from *Tarrafal* (2007): Zé Alberto's deportation notice as a 'cursed document' similar to the ones used in Tourneur's *Night of the Demon* (1957)	102

7.1	Still from *Horse Money* (2014): the appearance of the iconic Chaimite armoured vehicle serves as a narrative device both for a historical setting and for Ventura's achronological subjective condition	136
7.2 and 7.3	The epistolary device as narrative juxtaposition between films: Mariana (Inês de Medeiros) reads the letter destined for Edite (Edith Scob) in *Casa de Lava* (1994); Vitalina (Vitalina Varela) reads the letter penned by Ventura in *Horse Money* (2014)	138
7.4	Still from *Horse Money* (2014): Vitalina Varela's off-screen personal documents and objects are used as filmic props to reinstate her identity on screen	140

Acknowledgements

This book initially took shape as a PhD dissertation started in 2011, a research project reworked and extensively rewritten over the following years. My debts, therefore, go back a long way. I would like first to express my sincere gratitude to my former supervisors at the University of Nottingham, Mark Gallagher and Julian Stringer, who not only guided me through the entire doctoral process but also generously provided me with motivation, advice and inspiration during the writing of this volume. Thanks also to Lúcia Nagib, who pointed out to me the potential of my initial study and encouraged me to carry it further. I am also particularly grateful to Catherine Attwood for the lively conversations, patience and meticulous copy-editing.

I am also pleased to acknowledge the support and advice offered by the staff and postgraduate community at Nottingham. I am truly grateful to my colleagues at the Department of Cultural, Media and Visual Studies, particularly to Roberta Pearson who has been, over the years, truly supportive of the long-term endeavour of which this book is now the result. Special thanks also go to James Mansell, Ian Brookes and Andrew Goffey. I also thank my former PhD colleagues Daniel King, Juyeon Bae, Sriparna Ray, Aaron Calbreath-Frasieur, Melissa Shani Brown, Mag Yung-Wen and Yu-Peng Lin. My gratitude also extends to Iain Robert Smith, Caroline Edwards, Emma Crawford, Pedro Sobral Pombo, Alec Millward and Filipe Francisco. Their support at different stages of this project provided me with confidence and emotional backing.

I wish to express my gratitude to Pedro Costa, for the information provided during two interviews in 2012 and 2013 and during several email exchanges over the years. I am also thankful to Francisco Villa-Lobos for providing me with information about the production of *In Vanda's Room*, *Colossal Youth* and *Change Nothing*. Likewise, this book also benefited greatly from information provided by many film professionals whom I met or conversed with via email over the years. I wish to thank Abel Ribeiro Chaves (OPTEC Filmes), Patrícia Saramago, Cláudia Tomaz, Jörg Schneider (Das Kleine Fernsehspiel, ZDF), Daniel del-Negro, Cláudia Rita Oliveira, Chris Barwick (Second Run), Craig Keller (Masters of Cinema), Pedro Borges (Midas Filmes), Ji-Hoon Jo (JIFF), Yano Kazuyuki (Cinematrix) and Teresa Villaverde. Many thanks also to Valérie Massadian and Richard Dumas for their generosity in allowing me to reproduce their photographs on the cover of the book and in Chapter 4, respectively. I am also grateful for the information and resources offered by Teresa Barreto Borges (Cinemateca Portuguesa), Mariana Pimentel (Instituto do Cinema e do Audiovisual), Isabel de Carvalho (RTP), Francisco Ferreira, the Calouste Gulbenkian Foundation and the library staff at the Glasgow School of Art. Thanks are also due to the School of Modern Languages and Cultures and the Graduate School at Nottingham, whose research travel grants in 2012 and 2013, respectively, allowed me to carry out research in Lisbon during the initial stages of this project.

Special thanks also go to everyone at Edinburgh University Press, especially to Gillian Leslie, Richard Strachan and the *ReFocus: The International Directors Series* team, Robert Singer, Stefanie Van de Peer and Gary D. Rhodes. Thank you for your patience, generous guidance and constant encouragement. My gratitude is extended to the anonymous EUP readers for their comments and suggestions regarding the book's initial proposal.

Portions of this book have been previously published as an article and as book chapters. A section of Chapter 2 appeared in a different form as 'Pedro Costa on the Island of the Dead: Distant Referencing and the Making of *Casa de Lava*' in *Adaptation*, vol. 7, issue 3 (2014). I would like to thank the editors and anonymous reviewers from Oxford University Press for their invaluable comments. Two sections of Chapter 5 appeared initially in a chapter included in *Slow Cinema* (2016, Edinburgh University Press), edited by Tiago de Luca and myself, and in a chapter included in *Portugal's Global Cinema*, edited by Mariana Liz (2018, I. B. Tauris, used with the permission of Bloomsbury Publishing Plc). I am extremely grateful to Tiago and Mariana for their productive comments.

Finally, I would like to thank my wife, Maria Manuela Marinho de Castro, for her dedicated and unconditional support over the years, and to Jaime, for bringing light to my life. This work is dedicated to you both.

Introduction

Pedro Costa is one of the most distinctive filmmakers in contemporary global art cinema. Since the late 1980s, he has directed a body of work that is easy to recognise but difficult to explain. From the outset, the visual, thematic and narrative characteristics of his *oeuvre* convey an evolving yet coherent filmic universe which is at once austere, highly stylised and cryptic. The making of his films likewise suggests the stoicism and artistry of an uncompromising filmmaking ethos. From the late 1990s onwards, Costa's films have been produced through a digital video low-budget filmmaking process which relies on protracted collaborations with non-professional actors recruited largely from the poor suburbs of Lisbon. Inevitably, reception discourses around the Portuguese filmmaker commonly make a bridge between the aesthetic characteristics and the production conditions of his films. Costa is commonly characterised as an obsessive and slow filmmaker, fiercely independent and having a mercurial relationship with producers.

Over the years, Costa has become one of the most internationally celebrated Portuguese filmmakers, alongside his compatriots Manoel de Oliveira, João César Monteiro and, more recently, Miguel Gomes and João Pedro Rodrigues. Whilst accruing critical esteem and the support of a burgeoning international fan base, Costa's exposure remains limited to cinephile fringes around the art-house and film festival circuits. Moreover, and as with other contemporary filmmakers catering mostly to boutique cinephiles, his creative output also finds receptive audiences on a variegated international circuit composed of academic-related venues, art galleries and museums. Costa's reception, however, remains mixed and his films provoke praise and derision in equal measures. He is considered by French film criticism to be one of Europe's leading directors and he generates passionate responses among Japanese art-house audiences. Yet his films seem to leave Anglo-American film critics indifferent for the most part, and at times exasperated. The attention Costa receives from film scholars and the appreciation expressed by some revered filmmakers – Jacques Rivette, Jean-Marie Straub and Danièle Huillet – reveals his almost canonical status. Such a position, however, seems to provoke further accusations commonly levied by some critics that his work is cinema for a cinephile elite, excessively formalist and incompressible by nature.

This brief contextualisation of Pedro Costa positions him as an ambiguous creative agent who epitomises tensions between film aesthetics, production practices and forms of consumption which currently animate discussions about contemporary global art cinema. This volume takes the above considerations further by examining authorial and production processes adopted by the Portuguese filmmaker over the years and the reception and consumption practices around his films. This does not mean that it eschews any consideration of textual, aesthetic and thematic dimensions of his work. On the contrary, here I suggest that these characteristics are informed by the possibilities and conditions shaping an evolving artistic practice which is manifested at different stages of film production and consumption. The aim of this volume is, therefore, to provide both a comprehensive historical account and a critical examination of Costa's authorship practices and film aesthetics by addressing the central importance of the production and consumption contexts of his films. I discuss Pedro Costa as a creative agent whose film aesthetics are, firstly, imprinted in the materiality of the production process of his films and, secondly, become refined and redefined at the level of consumption through first-person strategical value negotiations and in collective evaluating and discursive practices.

In this respect, the book dialogues with film criticism and scholarly interpretations of the Portuguese filmmaker's work, although it takes a different approach to its study. The discussion about Costa mostly takes place in the pages of the specialised film-related press, in academic edited collections and journal articles. Film critics and scholars such as Thom Andersen, Chris Fujiwara, James Quandt, Jonathan Rosenbaum, Jacques Lemière and Adrian Martin, among many others, have contributed extensively to the study of the thematic, aesthetic and political dimensions of Costa's *oeuvre*. Initially dispersed through several publications, some of this literature has been subsequently reissued in the Portuguese language collection *Cem mil cigarros: os filmes de Pedro Costa*, edited by Ricardo Matos Cabo (2009). French scholar and philosopher Jacques Rancière similarly offers an illuminating reflection on Costa's cinema in *The Emancipated Spectator* (2008) and in other subsequent writings by looking particularly into the problematic dialogue between film aesthetics and their possible political readings. More recently, monographs such as *Questi fiori malati: Il cinema di Pedro Costa* by Michael Guarneri and *Aprender bellas palabras* by María del Pilar Gavilanes (both 2017), as well as the collection *Pedro Costa* edited by Malte Hagener and Tina Kaiser (2016), offer relevant debate on the rich aesthetic, thematic and textual formulations visible in Costa's cinema. Scholarly discussions focused on these qualities also transpire in other volumes only partially dedicated to the analysis of Costa's work, such as Volker Panteburg's *Ränder des kino – Godard, Wiseman, Benning, Costa* (2010), Antony Fiant's *Pour un cinéma contemporain soustractif* and Ira Jaffe's *Slow Movies: Countering the Cinema of Action*, the latter two published in 2014.

These works attest to the productive debates around this filmmaker. Yet I argue that there is a lack of comprehensive and extensive discussion concerning the different production contexts which have shaped Costa's work since his directorial debut. This is so even if we consider that some of the literature mentioned above offers analysis of practices of production around his cinema. While different in their approach, and with some exceptions, these examples pay only limited attention to the intricate dialogue between film aesthetics and production. Moreover, most of this scholarly material overlooks the contexts in which the multifaceted circulation of Costa's work takes place. Pertinently, a central argument sustaining the approach of this book is that Pedro Costa's filmic universe – understood here as a confluence of textual, thematic, narrative and audiovisual stylistic characteristics – is linked to constantly changing intricacies of film production and to the evolving forms of exhibition and distribution supporting contemporary art cinema.

Further contextualisation is needed here to assess this convergence between production and consumption. Pedro Costa was born in 1959 into a middle class Lisbon family with professional links to television and radio. During his mid-teens he was influenced by the left wing political idealism and cultural excitement brought by the Revolution of 25 April 1974, which ended forty-eight years of dictatorship. Costa's interests at the time were mostly centred on music. He soon became a participant in Lisbon's emerging punk rock subculture, while also acquiring a personal interest in cinema and photography. In the late 1970s, and after dropping out of an undergraduate course in History at the University of Lisbon, Costa enrolled in the Escola Superior de Teatro e Cinema (Lisbon Theatre and Film School). While still a student, he gained professional experience as an assistant in numerous film productions. He also started planning what would become his first feature film, *O Sangue* (*Blood*, 1989).

Costa's impressively stylised black and white directorial debut is animated by a constellation of aesthetic influences such as the filmmakers Robert Bresson and Jacques Tourneur (to name but two). The making of *Blood* also reflects the humble production framework and lack of exhibition opportunities that characterised Portuguese cinema in the 1980s. Costa's subsequent projects, *Casa de Lava* (also known as *Down to Earth*, 1994)[1] and *Ossos* (*Bones*, 1997), offer contrasts with both the aesthetic and the production conditions of his first work. *Casa de Lava* and *Bones* reflect an evolution in filmic style less concerned with artifice, a preoccupation which Costa subsequently developed further. Produced by influential producer Paulo Branco, the making of these two films came to rely on infrastructures offered by the European co-production model. The production and financial conditions informing these two films made possible the enhancement of Costa's authorial and directorial practices. They also placed on him expectations as to how his films would be tied to the production values and aesthetic formations which characterise contemporary European cinema.

Costa's response to these expectations was a steering away from the film industry processes which made possible his previous works, by abandoning time-constraint routines, large-scale shooting crews and the use of 35mm film. Instead, he adopted a low-budget filmmaking blueprint characterised by the use of digital video and small-scale collaborative practices, which merged professional and non-professional divisions of labour. The initial result of this blueprint is *No Quarto da Vanda* (*In Vanda's Room*, 2000), a film that relies heavily on the participation of non-professional actor Vanda Duarte and several other inhabitants of Fontainhas, an impoverished neighbourhood in Lisbon, now demolished. The film is exemplary as regards the intricate and conjoined relation between production and aesthetics. Its small-scale and prolonged shooting made possible a close depiction of the lives of a group of permanent and temporary residents at this location. These conditions are clearly imprinted in the aesthetic of the film, which merges documentary and fiction. Pertinently, this filmic style is a result of Costa's evolving aesthetic formulations, but also of an attentive and patient artistic practice which considers the advantages and limitations provided by the use of digital video.

This interweaving of film production and aesthetics is taken further in *Juventude em Marcha* (*Colossal Youth*, 2006) and *Cavalo Dinheiro* (*Horse Money*, 2014), as well as a group of short films directed between 2007 and 2012. This body of work is characterised aesthetically by a studied scenic minimalism and filmic deceleration, conveyed by long takes and fragmented and elliptical narratives. In different ways, these works discuss an interstitial position between the documental and the fictionalised to give expression to a thematic universe centred on non-professional actors whose lives are tied to a Portuguese postcolonial context. Such aesthetic and thematic qualities are intertwined with the production of these works, as these reflect the refinement of a filmmaking practice significantly supported by the use of digital video. A short digression is necessary here to point out that this dialogue between aesthetics and production is not exclusive to the above-named films, but also concerns projects which do not reflect such themes. These include *Où gît votre sourire enfoui?* (*Where Does Your Hidden Smile Lie?*, 2001) and the two iterations of *Ne Change Rien* (*Change Nothing*, 2005 and 2009), which this book also discusses. Moreover, the filmic universe transmitted by *Colossal Youth* and *Horse Money* is greatly informed by the authorial collaboration between Costa and non-professional actor José Tavares Borges, commonly known as Ventura, who came from Cape Verde to Lisbon in the early 1970s. Currently such collaboration is also extended to another Cape Verdean non-professional actor, Vitalina Varela, who participated in *Horse Money* and in *Vitalina Varela* (2019; in post-production at the time of writing).

The collaborative working practices maintained by Costa also extend to other works situated outside the boundaries of theatrical exhibition. From the early 2000s onwards, Costa has engaged in artistic practices such as video installations which are often produced to be exhibited at art galleries with the works of other artists with whom he collaborates. An example of this collaboration is the long-time creative partnership between Costa and Portuguese artist Rui Chafes, initiated in the mid-2000s and still ongoing. This creative practice serves as an illustration of a possible collaborative environment maintained by Costa over the years, as well as of ongoing dialogues between the 'black box' of cinema exhibition and the 'white cube' of the art gallery. Moreover, Costa's video installations call attention to a creative agency which increasingly negotiates between production and exhibition. Therefore, this book also looks at how consumption is also a constitutive part of production processes. Costa's agency as a filmmaker does not simply impact on creative and production practices but is also dispensed through tactical negotiations designed to respond to the dynamics of exhibition and circulation supporting contemporary global art cinema. Costa actively, and increasingly, engages with a network of variegated exhibition venues and circulation networks outside the film festival, as well as those placed at the limits of traditional art-house theatrical exhibition. These networks come to impact on authorial processes and production practices maintained by the filmmaker while also making possible complementary professional activities and artistic consecration at an international level. When possible, Costa deals directly with the international distribution companies responsible for the DVD and, more recently, Blu-ray editions of his films. These practices reflect an increasing authority in film circulation, yet these are also dependent on different contextual strata formed by art cinema institutions and by social networks with both formal and informal inflections.

These different contexts of production and consumption invite reflection on how Costa maintains a professional practice which responds to the multiple and ambiguous mechanisms supporting *art cinema*. Both historical and contemporary understandings of this term call upon a constellation of different forms of authorial expression, production practices and cultural formations situated at the reception stage, which makes it as much inclusive as unclear. Scholarly literature progressed far beyond the analysis of film aesthetics and personal creative intent initially invoked by the term, as defined in David Bordwell's seminal article 'The Art Cinema as a Mode of Film Practice' (1979). Film scholars came to focus attention instead on the institutions in which the production and circulation of art cinema takes place and on the variegated cultural contexts, taste formations and notions of symbolic value encapsulated by it (see, for example, Wilinsky 2001; Betz 2003; James 2005; Galt and Schoonover 2010; Andrews 2013).

Possible definitions or redefinitions of the term art cinema, as well as any of its possible derivatives, are outside the remit of this book. I consider it pertinent to mention, nonetheless, that my approach to the term takes its initial cues from Pierre Bourdieu's understanding of the workings of the field of cultural production, as it theorises the dynamic process between the mechanisms of production and circulation of cultural goods and the attribution of prestige. As Bourdieu reminds us, artistic practices function as an apparent 'negation' of norms of economic capital; these practices rely first and foremost on the accumulation of 'symbolic capital', a form of 'economic or political capital that is disavowed, mis-recognised and thereby recognised' – a capital that, potentially and eventually, can revert to forms of economic gain (1980: 261–2). To some extent this 'Bourdieusian' approach reflects the arguments of yet another seminal article devoted to art cinema, Steve Neale's 'Art Cinema as Institution' (1981). These value transactions take place within an infrastructure which supports a 'commodity-dominated' mode of 'production, distribution and exhibition' operating at national and international levels (Neale 1981: 15). As a creative agent, Pedro Costa adapts to these different contexts shaping the art cinema institution, through his directorial and authorial role, but also as a figure negotiating economic and symbolic forms of value. His films illustrate clearly these different scopes of the art cinema infrastructure as they traverse national, pan-European and global contexts of production, as well as different value transactions included in them. Equally, his films are produced and circulated through a network of public and private cultural institutions and small and medium-scale companies, and consumed within different cultural and subcultural constituencies.

Therefore, I also extend my attention to the synergic or overlapping interests of different creative and commercial agents around the production and consumption of Costa's work. I should point out, however, that my understanding of art cinema as institution is far more inclusive and nuanced than initially perceived in Neale's discussion. Art cinema as institution has been constantly reconfigured, even challenged, through diverse yet overlapping contemporary frameworks of production and consumption that negotiate their role within what Janet Harbord designates as 'film cultures' (2002: 44–5). Filmic texts that were once considered within contained aesthetic and thematic categories come to share a web of circulation catering to different but overlapping cinephile communities. This porous cinephile culture is also relevant when looking at the roles of different agents supporting the economy of prestige around art film. While Harbord's formulation of film cultures particularly concerns film consumption, such versatile cultural formations transcend this context. Communities and institutions within distribution and exhibition of art cinema – the international film festival and art-house circuits, but also the art gallery, fan constituencies and academia – are also, in a broad sense, producers. As discussed in this book, these circles do not simply dispense forms of symbolic value but also, in some instances, collaborate in production and consumption activities.

The creative agency of Pedro Costa inevitably calls our attention to authorial mediations taking place in film production and consumption broadly, and in contemporary art cinema in particular. Theoretical approaches to *auteurism* and the role of the *auteur* alternate between notions of independent individual creative agency and their social, cultural and industrial contours. Traditionally these terms have served to sustain discursive notions such as authenticity, creative independence and authorial control, particularly in the context of historical European art film traditions (Bordwell [1979] 2002a: 97; see also Kovács 2007: 218; Sayad 2014: xvi–xvii). On the other hand, however, the film *auteur* came to be defined as less a creative authority and more a commercial and ideological figure, used to organise 'audience reception' and 'bound to distribution and marketing aims that identify and address potential cult status' (Corrigan 1991: 103, 136; also Staiger 2003: 45–6). This approach proves instructive to the discussions offered in this book, particularly with regards to the power that this figurative presence acquires in mediating between symbolic and economic value. Thus my understanding of authorship concerns the mediation of often collective creative and production processes, as well as value negotiations taking place at the level of consumption. Accordingly, this study avoids the use of historically and ideologically conditioned terms such as *auteurism* and *auteur* and considers, instead, both the social and discursive nature of authorship which takes place within Costa's filmmaking practices.

This volume argues for the multifaceted strategic competence that Pedro Costa refined over the years. The approach followed here is to organise the understanding of such strategic competence as an evolving working process or, in other words, as a narrative of production. The term narrative of production offers a possible definition of the constantly negotiated artistic and labour practices carried on by Costa within a variety of contexts – authorial, industrial, economic, cultural and social – which often merge between professional and personal spheres. This narrative, moreover, is informed by Costa's numerous interviews and other public disclosures. In these the filmmaker insistently comments on his aversion to the cumbersome and expensive industrial processes supporting contemporary cinema, while explaining how he establishes an alternative to such means of production. Moreover, these explanations often include information about his collaborative practices with non-professional actors, and consider their political context and social conditions. These public disclosures provide us with valuable understanding of the material conditions of the making of Costa's films, as well as their possible political contours. Yet these also constitute what John Caldwell calls a form of 'industrial reflexivity', in which knowledge provided by creative agents is always constructed discursively, often within self-reflection and sense-making narratives (2008: 3–5).

I consider both the factual and discursive dimensions of this narrative of production by offering analysis of material sourced through several of Costa's public disclosures, as well as information obtained during two personal interviews with the filmmaker which took place in Lisbon in 2012 and 2013. Complementing this evidence, this book also benefited greatly from personal communications with several film professionals who either participated in the production and distribution of Costa's works or who are currently involved in professional collaborative practices with the filmmaker. The discussion offered here is enhanced by my communications with, among others, film producers Francisco Villa-Lobos (Contracosta Produções), Abel Ribeiro Chaves (OPTEC Filmes) and Jörg Schneider (ZDF), film professionals and former Costa collaborators Cláudia Tomaz and Patrícia Saramago, and film distributors Chris Barwick (Second Run), Pedro Borges (Midas Filmes), Craig Keller (Eureka! Masters of Cinema) and Kazuyuki Yano (Animatrix).

ReFocus: The Films of Pedro Costa discusses Costa's narrative of production by tracing chronologically the evolving professional practices created and sustained by the Portuguese filmmaker, while also examining how their discursive delineations sustain negotiations of symbolic capital at the consumption stages of his work. The initial three chapters position Costa in relation to the different modes of production that made possible his films from the late 1980s to the early 2000s. Chapter 1 discusses Costa's personal and professional development during the 1970s and 1980s. The discussion offered here concerns how formative experiences came to inform aesthetic preoccupations displayed in his directorial debut, *Blood*, as well as to reflect industrial, social and cultural contexts of the film's production. Costa's personal and professional development was shaped by Lisbon's youth cultures enjoying political freedoms and cultural openness resulting from the Revolution of 25 April 1974. This climate was particularly reflected in the output of a new generation of filmmakers emerging in the 1980s, as well as in their passionate cinephilia, collaborative practices and pragmatic professional ethos. The making of *Blood* reflects such historical characteristics, while also exemplifying the constraints shaping Portuguese cinema at the time. This first chapter also examines the initial domestic reception of the film, providing further context to Costa's role as an emerging filmmaker.

Chapter 2 contextualises Pedro Costa's transition from a young director working within the constraints of Portuguese national cinema to an emergent European filmmaker enjoying a more efficient and substantial co-production framework, such as the one offered by the influential producer Paulo Branco. This chapter traces Costa's authorship process of *Casa de Lava* and the production of *Bones*. In it I highlight two main aspects that became present in Costa's *oeuvre*. The first is the evolution from an authorial process shaped by cinephilia-informed influences to a form of creative practice which, while still considering these influences, becomes increasingly attentive to the social and political contexts present at the shooting locations of both films. Reflecting this characteristic, the second aspect concerns the increasingly tense relationship between creative practice and the means of production sustaining the making of these two films.

Considering the latter aspect, Chapter 3 offers a comprehensive discussion of the making of *In Vanda's Room*. Here I contextualise Costa's rejection of the filmmaking model previously used in the making of *Casa de Lava* and *Bones*. As already mentioned, Costa's fourth feature film relies significantly on the use of digital video to sustain a low-budget shooting process that merges personal and professional agency. These characteristics came to shape a filmmaking blueprint that Costa would, from then on, refine and consolidate in his subsequent works. *In Vanda's Room* can surely be considered the filmmaker's most radical approach to filmmaking, particularly with regards to its shooting process. Unsurprisingly, the film is commonly analysed as the result of a personal endeavour which privileges creative independence and artisanal practices steering away from film industry norms. Such notions constitute part of the narratives around the making of the film, which are conveyed by Costa during interviews and commonly redeployed by film critics, scholars and fans. As this chapter explains, however, the film is as much a result of a low scale digital video artisanal practice as it is of production negotiations commonly observed in European film co-productions. Examining this interstitial quality, this chapter offers a fresh insight into the making of *In Vanda's Room* by also scrutinising its finance and post-production processes, overlooked in previous academic and non-academic literature about the film.

The following chapters establish a rapport between the production of Pedro Costa's works and their reception, circulation and consumption. Chapter 4 investigates symbolic and economic value formations surrounding both Costa and his films. It focuses mostly on the reception of *Colossal Youth* to assess nuanced and, at times, dissonant statuses of artistic consecration taking place on the international film festival circuit, and conferred through film criticism. Such analysis considers various forms of prestige generated at the reception level, particularly with regard to the role of film criticism in situating Costa's work under particular filmic and cinephile-related taste and cultural categories. Accordingly, the chapter examines controversies surrounding *Colossal Youth* and its characterisation as a 'difficult' art film and as an example of 'Slow Cinema'. This chapter also discusses *Where Does Your Hidden Smile*

Lie?, which documents the work process of French filmmakers Jean-Marie Straub and Danièle Huillet. As explained, this documentary became a vehicle for including Costa within particular film lineages. Lastly, Chapter 4 offers further readings of different forms of capital at stake in the international film festival by examining the economic and symbolic value synergies which made possible the production of *A Caça ao Coelho com Pau* (*The Rabbit Hunters*), a 2007 short film commissioned by the Jeonju Digital Project.

Chapter 5 looks at others of Costa's commissioned works by discussing numerous video installations created and displayed within the international art gallery circuit. The chapter contextualises the approximation of the art gallery to cinema, a medium which increasingly overlaps aesthetic and production processes with contemporary artistic practices. As I argue in this chapter, the analysis of Costa's video installations offers a further context to the intertwinement between aesthetics, production and consumption observed elsewhere in his filmic output. These works for the 'white cube' rely on aesthetic, authorial and production characteristics that bond them to those exclusively produced for the 'black box'. This chapter provides comparisons between these works and short films directed by Costa between 2007 and 2012, such as *The Rabbit Hunters, Tarrafal* (also produced in 2007), *O Nosso Homem* (*Our Man*, 2010) and *Lamento da Vida Jovem* (*Sweet Exorcism*, 2012).

This inclusion in the art gallery circuit also calls our attention to Costa's increasing effort to expand the circulation of his creative output outside the international film festival and art-house circuits. Chapter 6 examines this endeavour by looking into production and distribution practices conducted by the filmmaker since the mid-2000s. As regards production, the chapter contextualises the making of *Change Nothing*, initially a short film released in 2005 and later reworked as a feature film in 2009. This period corresponds to the end of a partnership between Costa and producer Francisco Villa-Lobos and the beginning of a collaboration with Portuguese production company OPTEC Filmes. This change also affected the distribution of Costa's films. Concerning this, the chapter looks at international film retrospectives and numerous DVD and Blu-ray releases from the mid-2000s onwards. It examines the implications of a creative agency which is not confined to authorial practices but also visibly impacts upon consumption. Thus, the chapter explains how Costa maintains a close dialogue between professional endeavour (reflected not just in creative terms, but also in production processes) and commercial demand. This dialogue is particularly observed in Costa's participation in special screenings and retrospectives, and in his close supervision of materials for the home video market.

Chapter 7 is also dedicated to Costa's authorial presence, albeit differently. The last chapter of the monograph goes back to Costa's evolving authorial process, initially discussed in the first two chapters, by centring its attention on 2014 feature film *Horse Money*. Here I offer a context for its production process, but my main focus is to scrutinise Costa's current authorial practices. This chapter considers the different levels of intertextuality animating Costa's cinema, particularly with regards to the inclusion of different documents and the reworking of personal stories lived by some of his non-professional collaborators. As regards this latter aspect, the chapter sheds light on the ambiguous nature of authorship, understanding it as a creation process that is as much dependent on individual authority as it is indebted to collaborative practices. Both textually and contextually, *Horse Money* is the result of a long-term creative relationship with non-professional actor Ventura. Thus I draw comparisons between this film and previous works directed by Costa, and particularly *Colossal Youth*, in which the actor also had a significant creative role. The chapter extends its analysis to the creative role of Vitalina Varela. Varela's participation in *Horse Money* enhances collaborative practices currently maintained by Costa while also providing possible clues to upcoming projects. The intertextual and collaborative practices informing *Horse Money*, moreover, come to reflect possible political aspects transmitted by Costa's filmic universe. Returning to the discussions initially opened in Chapter 2, this final chapter concludes by looking at some of the critical debates around *Horse Money*, which are particularly animated by possible political readings transmitted by Costa's films.

It can be tentatively argued that the critical reception of *Horse Money* gives expression to the complex interchanges between film aesthetics and modes of production that sustain Pedro Costa's filmic universe. The possible political contours of this universe are both contingent on, but also reflected within, a narrative of production which is attentive to all material aspects of production and consumption. *ReFocus: The Films of Pedro Costa* discusses the diverse factors and permutations informing Costa's *oeuvre*, understood here as a result of creative processes and collaborative practices which are expanded at different production stages and which enable different forms of consumption. Costa's cinema can be understood as idiosyncratic, both in aesthetic and production terms. Yet it also constitutes a pertinent example of the multifaceted and nuanced production and consumption mechanisms taking place within a variety of circuits sustaining contemporary art cinema, some of which this book aims to analyse.

NOTE

1. This book uses *Casa de Lava*, as the most recently adopted title of the film in its international distribution.

CHAPTER I

Cinema's 'Primitive Beauty': Pedro Costa's Artistic Formation and the Making of *Blood* (1989)

Pedro Costa's directorial debut, *O Sangue* (*Blood*, 1989), had its Portuguese theatrical release in December 1990, after its world premiere at the 1989 Venice Film Festival. The film, depicting the lives of young characters who try to keep their juvenile innocence amidst the violence of the adult world, was in tune with the creative preoccupations of a new generation of Portuguese filmmakers rising to prominence in the mid to late 1980s. Yet *Blood* was also a somewhat curious filmic artefact, visibly and deliberately reclaiming an inheritance from a cinema located in the past – historically and in discursive terms. Its numerous filmic citations, expressive black and white photography, and fragmented narrative exuberantly reveal Costa's early filmic influences, drawing as it does on an aesthetic family that combines the image poetics, narrative mechanisms and thematic preoccupations of filmmakers such as Robert Bresson, Jacques Tourneur and Nicholas Ray among others.

These stylistic properties situate the film in an artistic endeavour rooted in a 'libidinal, emotional, and affective attachment' expressed by cinephilia (Hagener and de Valck 2008: 19). Foregrounding such manifest stylistic qualities, the film's press release describes it as: 'bring[ing] back the primitive beauty of a cinema which still believes in the purity and rigor of its images, and in the simpler and stronger feelings that animate its characters' (Atalanta Filmes 1990). Even if covertly, such a description provides us with clues as to how the aesthetics of *Blood* seemed to offer a distinctive approach to the filmic formulas observed in Portuguese cinema at the time. As Sofia Sampaio argues, its narrative and themes allowed for numerous readings around cinema's 'universal values' and 'archetypes', to the detriment of its local and national particularities (2013: 475). Yet, and as Sampaio's study comprehensively demonstrates, these qualities also clearly express a geographical, historical and political materiality particularly rooted in the context of late twentieth-century Portugal.

The particularities of this context can be further examined by looking at the production process and creative choices that culminated in the release of the film in 1990. The making of *Blood* is entwined in the industrial and circulation constraints that shaped 1980s Portuguese art cinema. As a first work, its production reflects a professional framework sustained by a pragmatic attitude toward filmmaking and collaborative practices shared among young Portuguese filmmakers at the time. An examination of the film also needs to consider the professional network that supported its production and, moreover, the discursive formations that help position it within the context of Portuguese contemporary cinema. *Blood* is a combination of thematic and stylistic influences, production processes and aesthetic discourses taking shape at its reception stage. I scrutinise how these different facets – film style, production and reception – reflect both Costa's early personal and professional development and a filmmaking practice which negotiates between past cinematic traditions and contemporary social factors.

CINEPHILIA AND AESTHETIC INHERITANCE

Costa's first feature film is included in a group of first works which reveal, in different ways, the anxieties of a generation growing up in the turbulent years after the 1974 Revolution. *Blood* shares a thematic universe depicting teenage angst, fragmented families and inter-generational conflicts with other first feature films such as *Três Menos Eu* (*Three Less Me*, dir. João Canijo, 1988), *Uma Pedra no Bolso* (*Tall Stories*, dir. Joaquim Pinto, 1988), *Xavier* (dir. Manuel Mozos, initially produced in the mid-1980s, concluded in 1992 and released commercially in 2003), *A Idade Maior* (*Alex*, dir. Teresa Villaverde, 1991), and *Nuvem* (dir. Ana Luísa Guimarães, 1992). While sharing thematic characteristics with these films, *Blood* stands out from the majority of Portuguese works of this period in terms of its filmic style. From the outset, its black and white cinematography, uncommon at the time in Portuguese cinema, created a mark of distinction. Moreover, the film conveys a filmic and narrative style deliberately drawing on aesthetic relationships with historical cinemas, which is distinct from the first works listed above. This distinction is noted, even considering the manifest cinephilia in the creative output of some of these 1980s first-time directors.[1]

In contemporary cinema, aesthetic relationships are manifested via explicit textual correlations 'expressed through narrative and thematic similarity as well as aspects of visual style, editing and sound' (Gallagher 2013: 47). As further argued by Gallagher, aesthetic relationships are mostly 'articulated and contextualized' through discursive 'sense-making activities' situated at both the production and reception stages of filmic texts (2013: 47–8). In these terms, *Blood* reveals aesthetic relationships articulated in terms of artistic options which impacted on its stylistic intertextuality and, subsequently, informed its critical reception. A description of *Blood* allows for a further discussion of such intertextual qualities. The film depicts the struggle of three young characters, Vicente (Pedro Hestnes), in his late teens, his ten-year-old brother Nino (Nuno Ferreira) and Vicente's girlfriend Clara (Inês de Medeiros), who works in the school attended by Nino. The two brothers try to function as a family, without a mother and with their critically ill father (Henrique do Canto e Castro) frequently absent. After their father's death (Vicente's possible act of parricide is never depicted yet implied), and assisted by Clara, Vicente and Nino try to carry on living without any adult supervision. This new family arrangement, however, soon comes to an end when their uncle (Luís Miguel Cintra) arrives and takes Nino away. At the same time, Vicente has to deal with the increasing aggressiveness of his late father's former criminal associates (played by Henrique Viana and Luís Santos), with whom he had been working on a financial scam. Unable to reclaim money taken by Vicente's father, the associates resort to kidnapping Vicente. The film concludes with the efforts of the separated brothers to break free from their respective captivities, and Clara's efforts to find them. This narrative finds correspondences in films thematically centred on childhood and adolescent experiences and struggles to escape adult authority. Themes and key narrative moments in *Blood* resonate with scenes in films such as *Night of the Hunter* (dir. Charles Laughton, 1955), *They Live by Night* (dir. Nicholas Ray, 1948), *Mouchette* (dir. Robert Bresson, 1967) and others (see, for example, Azoury 2009; da Costa 2009: 19). These appropriations are also present in its meticulous *mise en scène* compositions and shadowy monochrome cinematography (Figures 1.1–1.3). It is also worth noting that some of these films were important to the pre-production process of *Blood*. According to Inês de Medeiros (who plays the character of Clara in the film), works such as *They Live by Night*, *Night of the Hunter* and Bresson's *Au Hasard Balthazar* (1966) were shown by Costa to the cast, as part of the character planning (Coutinho 2009: 9).

The black and white cinematography of *Blood* emphasises the tense and melancholic feelings present in its narrative and themes, allowing for the identification of further aesthetic links. Taking place around the period between Christmas and New Year's Eve, *Blood* in no way reflects this festive time of year. Instead, it transmits a troubled atmosphere marked by broken family ties, generational tensions and ghostly absences. The first part of the film is set in an unnamed rural town near Lisbon, where the main characters live. It divides its action between an almost oneiric daylight scenery – the woods around the

Figures 1.1–1.3 Stylistic correlations with classical cinema in *Blood* (1989): the evocation of the work of Nicholas Ray, Jacques Tourneur and of *Night of the Hunter* (1955)

town are presented as a mysterious place of children's play – and a night-time setting, in which imminent threats posed by adult issues loom. The monochrome palette accentuates these differences, presenting the daytime locations as bright, even if austere. By contrast, the night scenes are rendered in a dramatic chiaroscuro, heightened by dominant shadows and a lack of *mise en scène* clarity. The second part of the film, set in Lisbon, portrays the confinement of Nino and Vicente and Clara's search for the two brothers. Composed mostly of night scenes, this narrative segment depicts the city as a place constantly threatened by shadows, reinforcing the main characters' feelings of loss and confusion after their forced separation. Drifting through the city streets, the characters become part of shadow-filled backgrounds, casting a ghostly presence which adds yet more uncertainty to the already fragmented narrative of the film.

The intertextual correlations observed in the filmic and narrative style of *Blood* find their origin in Costa's early cinephilic attachments. As Bénard da Costa rightly puts it, Costa 'didn't invent a new black and white, [nor a] new love [or] ghost story' (da Costa 2009: 19). Elaborating on Costa's cinephilia-informed work, Jonathan Rosenbaum notes that the film combines different cinematic moments. Rosenbaum argues that *Blood* 'already announces the essence of Pedro Costa's cinema by declaring every shot an event, regardless of whether or not we can understand it in relation to some master narrative' (2010a: 191). In another article, Rosenbaum further defines Costa's event-driven narrative when characterising his whole *oeuvre* as one portraying 'fully realized moments, secular epiphanies', instead of depicting 'stories' or 'characters in the literary sense' (2010b: 204). As far as *Blood* is concerned, these filmic moments come to shape a narrative structure which circumvents traditional continuity mechanisms. As expressed by Costa, this moment-driven narrative gives primacy to the *raccord* (the connection between shots) sustaining his belief that 'what happens between shots is what is important' (Moutinho and Lobo 1997: 66). The film is structured around the ambiguity and complexity of blood relationships, as its title announces. We are not presented with any mention of Vincente and Nino's absent mother, nor are we able to clearly determine whether or not Vincente commits parricide. Similarly, the end of the film does not provide clues as to the eventual fate of any of the main characters.

The predominance of the filmic moment in *Blood* is indebted to a cinephilia-informed authorial process, which collects and assembles moments with particular sentimental associations and uses them as a narrative mechanism. The use of such cinematic moments, combined with carefully crafted *mise en scène* compositions would later become, as Rosenbaum points out, Costa's authorial markers. These authorial markers acquire further meaning at the level of reception. As Adrian Martin suggests, Costa's cinema is a vehicle of a 'cinephile experience' which allows comparisons with both past and contemporary films (2009: 3). Martin argues, however, that such influences are different from contemporary cinema's 'quotations', or 'postmodern games of allusion, parody and re-working'; instead, he categorises Costa's intertextual correlations as a personal 'signature':

> [t]he poetics of certain filmmakers have been so deeply internalised, we may say so deeply lived (in the imaginary realm) by Costa, that a unique palimpsest has been formed at the intersection of all these visions, all these worlds, all these memories: his signature is that knotted thicket, too tangled, fused and transformed to ever be cleanly separated, now, into its various separate source elements. (Martin 2009: 3)

Martin's proposition is relevant in positioning Pedro Costa as a legitimate heir to an aesthetic inheritance which is reflected at the production and reception stages. It is pertinent to examine how this legacy took shape, by looking into other contextual factors related to the cultural environment of the years immediately following the 25 April 1974 Revolution.

PEDRO COSTA'S PERSONAL AND PROFESSIONAL DEVELOPMENT

Portugal in the mid to late 1970s was defined by constant political, social and cultural changes. The democratic process originated by the 1974 Revolution made possible a new political and social freedom, as well as a newfound cultural openness. The end of the authoritarian regime also triggered the end of censorship of cultural, political and press activities soon after April 1974, later officially consolidated by the 1976 Portuguese Constitution. This lifting allowed access to, and circulation of, an extensive range of cultural goods which were previously considered politically or morally subversive. The sudden unrestricted availability of cinematic works once banned or previously released with (sometimes extensive) cuts propelled several exhibition initiatives which responded to the needs of existing art-house communities, as well as helping to educate new generations of cinephiles.

A multitude of filmic texts would coexist under a web of circulation catering to distinct but overlapping 'film cultures', cinephile communities that would imprint new social and cultural configurations on specific locations (see Harbord 2002: 44–5; Schober 2013: 62). Central to Lisbon's post-revolutionary growth in cinephile expression were the film cycles and retrospectives held by the Calouste Gulbenkian Foundation soon after 1974 and at the Portuguese Cinematheque in the late 1970s and early 1980s (de Pina 1986: 206). Costa recalls the importance of these film cycles and retrospectives to a vibrant community that formed around the screenings in the Gulbenkian Foundation's large auditorium, and the 'overwhelming experience' of watching American cinema classics and Mizoguchi films as part of a large and expressive audience (personal interview, Costa 2012). This enthusiastic engagement with cinema was complemented by the Portuguese Cinematheque, which ran a series of retrospective programmes showing the filmographies of Fritz Lang, John Ford, Yasujirō Ozu and Roberto Rossellini, among others. As filmmaker Teresa Villaverde pointed out to me, these retrospectives had a decisive 'formative role' in the post-revolution generation of filmmakers (personal interview, Villaverde 2012). These initiatives allowed access to a constellation of contemporary and classic cinema traditions rarely or never exhibited in Portugal. Inevitably, these film cycles would visibly impact on Villaverde's initial work, as well as that of many of her colleagues growing up in Lisbon during the 1970s and 1980s. More than just inhabiting particular exhibition locations, these initiatives were also centred on revered and influential figures. Crucial to these film exhibition initiatives in both institutions was the role of the intellectual, film critic and programmer João Bénard da Costa. Like many other young Lisbon cinephiles, Pedro Costa enjoyed the films he discovered at these successive cycles programmed by Bénard da Costa. These screenings were complemented by the passionate discussions generated among Costa's friends and older cinephiles by the works of Jean-Marie Straub and Danièle Huillet, Robert Bresson and Jean-Luc Godard. Bénard da Costa's influence on the formation of both cinephiles and future cinema professionals was not just confined to these initiatives. He was also a lecturer at the Lisbon Theatre and Film School until 1980 and soon after occupied roles in the direction of the Portuguese Cinematheque until his death in 2009.

This burgeoning cinephilia was located at the intersection between Lisbon's film cultures and other informal cultural associations newly permitted in post-revolution Portugal. Like many urban teenagers and young adults, Costa participated in the various forms of cultural and political expression taking place in Lisbon during the 1970s. These cultural formations were shaped by the left-wing political idealism of the time and the rebellious attitude epitomised by an emerging first wave of Portuguese punk rock. As Costa explained to me, apart from the intense schedule of movie-going, many of his daily routines would consist of 'listening [to records] loudly' in his and his friends' bedrooms, and engaging in the constant political street agitation observed in Lisbon at the time (Costa 2012). As he further explains, in a conversation with Cyril Neyrat:

> I've lived, in the prime of youth, the [1974] revolution, the discovery of politics, [. . .] and, at the same time, [. . .] discovered Wire, Godard, The Clash, poetry, [. . .] all the films by Danièle [Huillet] and Jean Marie [Straub], the first films by Ozu and Ford, [which I] watched thanks to João Bénard da Costa. (Costa et al. 2012: 17)

This intersection of different formative influences equipped Costa with a variety of references that would be later reflected not just in his first feature film, but also in his subsequent works. These initial influences would be further developed when Costa started attending the Lisbon Theatre and Film School in the late 1970s. At the time, and since its foundation in 1973, the educational values of the school were mostly informed by the theoretical concerns of film professionals who participated in the 1960s Portuguese new wave. Known as *Cinema Novo*, this new wave was characterised by an anti-commercial production ethos to support an austere filmic style thematically preoccupied with Portuguese identity. These characteristics would later acquire dogmatic contours, as announced by the controversial title 'Portuguese School' (Baptista 2010: 3–4; Lemière 2006: 737).

In pedagogical terms, this austere filmmaking would be translated into an orthodoxy that, though nuanced, was not particularly appealing to many of the students at the Lisbon Theatre and Film School. As Costa recalls, the school's 'obscurantist theory, "bourgeois" as we called it at the time' was initially 'insufferable'; instead, Costa was mostly interested in the practical side of filmmaking (Costa 2012; see also Gandolfi 2013). This interest in the practicalities of filmmaking was, however, soon complemented by the theoretical teachings of the charismatic filmmaker, poet and film theorist António Reis. Reis lectured in the film school from 1977 until shortly before his death in 1991. Fellow film school lecturer and *Blood* producer José Bogalheiro points out that Reis's approach to teaching was that of an 'anti-academic radical' (Moutinho and Lobo 1997: 56). This attitude presented an alternative to the school's staid theoretical orthodoxy. As Costa similarly argues, 'Reis was more "punk" than us, so to speak, far more extreme than we were' (Costa 2012). In practical terms, Reis's teaching instilled in his students a careful attention to detail and called their attention to the possibilities of filmic assemblage between different forms of artistic expression. Reis's former student Daniel Del-Negro recalls:

> [Reis] wasn't truly a 'filmmaker', above all he was an image poet. He didn't teach [technical aspects of filmmaking], he mostly called our attention to relations between images (normally small details of movement or shape), and their readings. (Del-Negro 2012)

This form of relational reading equipped many of Reis's former students, Costa included, with a creative method which incorporated different visual influences into a personal filmic language. Reis's teachings were complemented by screenings at the school which included films directed by Roberto Rossellini, F. W. Murnau, Jean-Luc Godard and Robert Bresson, among others (Moutinho and Lobo 1997: 64).

Reis's influence on the artistic formation of Pedro Costa was not confined to his lectures in film school but extended to the teacher's filmmaking practice. As his teachings, Reis's filmmaking revealed a radical engagement with 'everyday life poetics', similar to the kind of political engagement observed in punk rock (Moutinho and Lobo 1997: 67). His films, frequently co-directed with Margarida Cordeiro, would become paradigms of austere filmmaking – aesthetically, technically, and economically. *Jaime* (1974), *Trás-os-Montes* (1976), *Ana* (1985) and *Rosa de Areia* (1989) would have a lasting impact on Costa and other filmmakers of his generation, such as Vítor Gonçalves and Joaquim Pinto (the latter collaborated with Reis and Cordeiro on *Trás-os-Montes*). These films also provide inspiration to successive generations of Portuguese filmmakers. This influence is also extended to Reis's younger former students João Pedro Rodrigues and Joaquim Sapinho, and others. This impact would later be recognised through the theorisation of what Haden Guest calls 'The School of Reis'. This term appears in film criticism soon after the film retrospective with the same title which took place at the Harvard Film Archive in 2012 and, subsequently, at the Anthology Film Archives and at UCLA Film and Television Archive.[2]

Costa's early steps would tentatively reclaim such an intransigent aesthetic commitment and passionately pragmatic approach to filmmaking. *Trás-os-Montes*, for instance, transmits a blend of documentary and fiction and an entanglement between everyday life and folktales presented without any narrative separation (Lim 2012: 102; Barroso and Ribas 2008: 144). This entanglement between the documented and the represented would later be given clear expression in Costa's subsequent films *Casa de Lava*, *Bones* and *In Vanda's Room*. Reis and Cordeiro's filmmaking practice, moreover, was carried through low budgets and with small crews. This practice would similarly be reflected in the production ethos maintained by Costa from the late 1990s onwards.

'ABSOLUTE BEGINNERS'

The personal and artistic formation of Costa and his colleagues at the Lisbon Theatre and Film School additionally reflected the ethos of youth cultures around urban and in suburban Lisbon. These youth cultures would gravitate towards the city's alternative artistic communities, gathering at the bohemian Bairro Alto neighbourhood. Known for a nightlife that catered to a range of different subcultural constituencies, Bairro Alto was near to the film school, but also to the Portuguese Cinematheque and Lisbon School of Fine Arts. These communities created an environment shaped by cross-pollinations between music, fashion, visual and performance arts and cinema. As pointed out by filmmaker Manuel Mozos, this informal convergence of different young artists meeting in the social spaces of Bairro Alto, would prove decisive in encouraging collaborative practices that sustained the production of many first film works during the 1980s (Mourinha 2009: 11).

This climate of supportive interdependence helped to minimise the impact of the lack of reliable technical and financing infrastructures which have been a constant in Portuguese cinema (see Lemière 2006: 731; de Pina 1986: 215; da Costa 1996: 11–22). The prospects faced by young film professionals starting their careers in the mid-1980s and early 1990s reflected this lack of structural investment. Financial support for film production was confined to a small number of annual grants provided by the Instituto Português de Cinema (Portuguese Cinema Institute, IPC henceforth). At the time, beginners had to compete for these grants with already established filmmakers; the funding allocated specifically for first film works provided by this institution was not established until the mid-1990s (Barroso and Ribas 2008: 148). This funding was augmented by support from other institutions, such as the RTP (Rádio e Televisão de Portugal – the Portuguese public broadcasting corporation), and the Calouste Gulbenkian Foundation. This support was vital yet inadequate to finance Portuguese cinema. Moreover, technical infrastructures for production and post-production were limited and expensive.

Domestic film exhibition conditions reflected similar limitations. The opportunities for commercially releasing a first film were restricted. As film critic Augusto M. Seabra pointed out at the time, the exhibition of Portuguese film was mostly confined to the Portuguese Cinematheque and to a small and unstable (mostly urban) art-house circuit (1987: 130). These difficulties were eased thanks to a cohesive network formed by young filmmakers. Their dedication to filmmaking is articulated by journalist Teresa Carmo, in an extensive article about the new generation of Portuguese filmmakers emerging in the 1980s; according to the journalist, these 'absolute beginners' possessed a 'fanatical' passion for filmmaking, even if facing reduced career prospects (Carmo 1991: 25). Perhaps because of this ethos, the period between 1986 and 1992 is highly significant in terms of the number and variety of first works in Portuguese cinema. This period saw the emergence of a considerable number of first feature films directed by former students of the Lisbon Theatre and Film School, as well as self-taught film professionals such as Rita Azevedo Gomes, Teresa Villaverde and João Canijo.

Additionally, and like most of these young film professionals, Pedro Costa benefited from the prolific film production environment that existed in Portugal from the early 1980s onwards. The hectic activity of film producer Paulo Branco and the financial support generated by the European co-production model created opportunities for these young professionals to obtain practical skills. Some of these filmmakers initiated their professional activity in Portuguese and international productions, working on films directed by Manoel de

Oliveira, João César Monteiro, Raúl Ruiz, Wim Wenders, Werner Schroeter and Alain Tanner, among others. Costa himself worked in assistant production roles in Wenders's *Der Stand der Dinge* (*The State of Things*, 1982) and in *À Flor do Mar* (dir. João César Monteiro, 1986). By the mid-1980s, he began to find regular work as an assistant director. In this role, he worked on films such as *Duma Vez Por Todas* (1986), directed by former fellow film student Joaquim Leitão, *Um Adeus Português* (*A Portuguese Farewell*, dir. João Botelho, 1986) and *Agosto* (*August*, dir. Jorge Silva Melo, 1988). During the production of the latter film Costa met actor Pedro Hestnes, who would subsequently participate in *Blood* (Alves 1990: 28).

The prolificacy of this production environment extended to first filmic works. Reflecting the workings of a supportive informal network, many of the technical staff and cast involved on those films also collaborated on first works directed by emerging filmmakers. Some of these young professionals, moreover, started small-scale independent production units such as G.E.R. (Grupo de Estudos e Realizações, founded by Joaquim Pinto), Azul, or Trópico Filmes. While mostly ephemeral, these companies nonetheless served as a blueprint for a burgeoning number of production enterprises which would sustain Portuguese art film in the following decade. The production company Azul, founded by Daniel Del-Negro and Vítor Gonçalves in 1980, supported the production of the former's first feature film, *Atlântida: do outro lado do espelho* (*Atlântida*, 1985), and the latter's *Uma Rapariga no Verão* (*A Girl in Summer*, 1986). Both films were collaborative efforts between students and former students of the Lisbon Film School such as directors Manuel Mozos and Joaquim Leitão, as well as Pedro Caldas and José Bogalheiro. Towards the end of the production of *A Girl in Summer*, disagreements between Del-Negro and Gonçalves led to the formation of another company, Trópico Filmes. Founded in the mid-1980s, this production outfit was the result of collaboration between Gonçalves, Pedro Costa, Pedro Caldas, José Bogalheiro and Ana Luísa Guimarães. The company would go on to complete *A Girl in Summer* and later support the production of *Blood* and Guimarães's first feature film, *Nuvem* (*Clouds*, 1992).[3]

A Girl in Summer came to epitomise the conditions of Portuguese cinema production at the time. The making of this film reflects the pragmatic ethos that would later also sustain the production of *Blood*. Apart from numerous collaborators, the central production crew in Gonçalves's first feature film were Del-Negro (cinematography), Costa (assistant director), Caldas (sound), Bogalheiro (production) and Guimarães (film editor). With the exception of Del-Negro, all these professionals would later work on *Blood*. Starting with a grant awarded to Gonçalves by the Calouste Gulbenkian Foundation for a short film, the project soon took shape as a feature-length work. The production of the film extended over a period of three years, and was often halted due to financial issues. As Costa recalled during an interview with me, participants did not receive any payment and, consequently, the making of the film was carried out mostly during spare time from their paid jobs (2012). Apart from the production assistant roles in several films, the professionals associated with Azul and Trópico Filmes participated in numerous commissioned works. An example of these works was the children's television series *Cartas à Júlia* (*Letters to Julia*), commissioned by RTP in the mid-1980s.[4]

A Girl in Summer reflects not just production constraints but also the inefficient distribution of Portuguese film in the 1980s. Despite difficult financial and technical constraints, the creative network sustaining the production of the film made its completion possible in 1986.[5] However, the film was never released commercially and its circulation has been confined to special screenings in Portugal and, since 2012, to international retrospectives dedicated to Portuguese cinema. Similarly, Del-Negro's *Atlântida*, completed in 1985, was never released commercially and is still rarely exhibited. This lack of exposure reflected the difficulties faced by young filmmakers in a small domestic film market dominated by Hollywood productions. It is estimated that approximately 40 per cent of Portuguese films completed between 1976 and 1988 were shelved after completion, never to be released on the domestic commercial circuit (Antunes 1990: 15; see also Stanbrook 1989: 119). Unsurprisingly, the expression 'lost generation' came to be imposed on some of Costa's former colleagues, with some of these professionals struggling to maintain a regular professional activity in filmmaking (Mourinha 2009: 11).

THE MAKING OF *BLOOD*

The production of *A Girl in Summer* reflected a collaborative framework which would soon after be deployed in the making of *Blood*. Costa's first feature film was produced under the constraints of a small budget, yet it benefited from the collaborative working environment explained above. As observed by Ana Luísa Guimarães, *Blood* and the other films produced by Trópico Filmes privileged pragmatic and 'collective work' practices, which allowed these professionals to 'learn a lot about filmmaking' even if they did so under demanding conditions (Moutinho 1996: 11). As also already explained, the main technical crew of *Blood* was made up of former film students involved in *A Girl in Summer*. Later, this core team would be completed with more experienced professionals who provided decisive technical support.

Similarly, the cast combined emerging and veteran Portuguese actors. The leading roles were given to Inês de Medeiros and Pedro Hestnes. Both actors gained visibility in films directed by both young and accomplished filmmakers, and quickly became recognised names in late 1980s Portuguese art cinema. Among other films, the two actors collaborated on Joaquim Pinto's directorial debut *Tall Stories*, in *O Desejado* (*Mountains of the Moon*, 1987, directed by veteran filmmaker Paulo Rocha), and in *Tempos Difíceis* (*Hard Times*, dir. João Botelho, 1987). Hestnes also acted in Silva Melo's *August* and in *Três Menos Eu* (*Three Less Me*, 1988), the first feature film directed by João Canijo. In *Blood*, the two young actors shared acting credits with, among others, veteran actors Henrique do Canto e Castro, Luís Miguel Cintra and Isabel de Castro. These latter three actors had already enjoyed prestigious acting careers in Portuguese cinema and theatre, and are commonly associated with directors who started their professional activities during the 1960s and 1970s. Cintra, for instance, had been a regular collaborator with both Paulo Rocha and João César Monteiro since the early 1970s and also acted in several works directed by Manoel de Oliveira from the early 1980s onwards. The presence of these veteran actors gave *Blood* further cinephilic cachet. Completing the main cast was ten-year-old Nuno Ferreira, a non-professional actor recruited from a charitable institution that assists children who have no stable family support (Alves 1990: 28).

The initial stages of scriptwriting of *Blood* started during Costa's intense years of punk rock and movie-going. As Costa recalls during an interview with Mark Peranson, the initial plot of the film was centred on 'three boys, or two boys and a girl, [. . .] that obviously came from Nicholas Ray, or maybe Mizoguchi . . . ' (2010: 131). These ideas would later be reworked as part of the initial script treatment. Later, during the 1980s and parallel to his collaboration in *A Girl in Summer* and other professional activities, Costa consolidated these ideas into a script produced to comply with the funding requirements of the IPC. This was, according to the filmmaker, 'a classic script, 100 pages, huddled up with a storyboard' (Costa 2012). Funding was granted in 1987, after several submissions to the funding contests of the IPC, allowing Trópico Filmes to start the production process.[6] This financial support was later supplemented by grants from RTP and the Calouste Gulbenkian Foundation.[7] According to Costa, the total budget of *Blood* was approximately 32,000,000 Portuguese escudos (€115,000) (Alves 1990: 29). This amount was not enough to cover the production costs of the film. Somewhat easing this issue, the more experienced actors and some of the technicians did not charge any fees – a practice which, as Costa recalls, was normal for first films at the time (Costa 2012; also Peranson 2010: 132).

Another main issue in the production of *Blood* was the difficulty of shooting with black and white film. Reflecting Costa's debt to the influences that shaped his early aesthetic, this choice turned out to be challenging to execute. The technical process was expensive and required technical know-how which was not readily available. As Costa explained to me, experienced Portuguese cinema technicians who would be willing to work with black and white were not available at the time; equally, younger professionals were reluctant to deal with the risky and time-consuming production and post-production processes associated with monochrome film stock (Costa 2012). At the earlier stages, the production team had considerable difficulty in finding an experienced and skilful cinematographer who could provide an efficient, yet inexpensive, way of shooting the film. Using his network of professional contacts, Costa was able to contact Martin Schäfer. The German cinematographer had experience with monochrome film, having worked with Wim Wenders on *Im Lauf der Zeit* (*Kings of the Road*, 1976, in which he shared the cinematography credits with Robby Müller), and on *The State of Things*. Schäfer's expertise in black and white was also visibly deployed in the camera work for *Radio On* (dir. Christopher Petit, 1979), a British–German co-production with participation from Wenders as associate producer. The inclusion of Schäfer in the production team of *Blood* eased these early concerns and became decisive in producing the distinctive – and technically difficult – contrasted spotlighting visible in *Blood*.

Martin Schäfer participated in most of the shooting process that took place in late 1987, divided between Barreiro and Valada do Ribatejo (locations situated around Lisbon) and central Lisbon. Costa recalls the shooting process:

> it was a small crew [around thirty people]. The sound crew were only two people, but the image [department] had a lot of people. Perhaps not as many as it should, but the apparatus was big, with those big old floodlights. [. . .] Filming at night near the river . . . during the winter was complicated. [Martin Schäfer] had to do his best . . . and I was lucky [. . .]. The cinematography of *Blood* ended up looking like those in the old Hollywood films. (Costa 2012)

Furthermore, as Costa also explains, Schäfer's experience helped to guide the young Portuguese professionals during the shooting and post-production stages:

> Martin gave a lot to the film, he [also] helped organising the set . . . helped us a lot! We were a bit clumsy: [shooting] sometimes in one place, sometimes in another . . . he used to concentrate everything in one place. [. . .] He also gave assurance [to the film processing] at Tobis [Portuguesa]. [The lab technicians] knew he was one of Wenders' DOPs. (Costa 2012)

Blood relied substantially on Schäfer's technical competence and experience. In the interval between location shoots, however, his collaboration in the project came to a halt. Martin Schäfer died in April 1988, shortly after interrupting his work in Portugal to participate in a film project in Germany. The cinematographer left the shooting process of *Blood* unfinished, with some of the scenes of the film set in Lisbon still needing to be shot. Costa once again used his network of contacts to find experienced cinematographers who would be able to complete the production stages. Costa and the Trópico Filmes team came to rely on experienced Portuguese cinematographers Acácio de Almeida and, later, Elso Roque. The former was the cinematographer of films directed by Reis and Cordeiro and João César Monteiro during the 1970s. Acácio de Almeida also worked on several international film productions shot in Portugal, including *Dans la Ville Blanche* (*In the White City*, dir. Alain Tanner, 1983) and *La Ville des Pirates* (*City of Pirates*, dir. Raúl Ruiz, 1983) – both shot in black and white. Similarly, Elso Roque had considerable experience as a cinematographer. He worked in a significant number of films directed by Paulo Rocha from the mid-1960s onwards, and was a regular collaborator of Manoel de Oliveira from the mid-1970s. Recalling the last days of shooting, Costa explains:

> we had almost all the shooting done, only five days to go I think . . . I went to speak with Acácio de Almeida, who worked with Reis, César [Monteiro], and in [Jorge Silva Melo's *August*], in which I also worked as assistant. [. . .] Once again I was lucky. Acácio told me he would use his own team and equipment, all at a minimum cost. While working with Acácio, [the actor] Luís Miguel Cintra got ill and we had to interrupt the shooting on its final day. Unfortunately, Acácio had other work scheduled [. . .]. So I had to call another DOP, Elso Roque, who I didn't know very well. [. . .] He finished the film . . . by that time all the team had changed, except the cast and the personnel from Trópico [Filmes]. (Costa 2012)

The shooting of *Blood* was eventually concluded, despite these dramatic changes in the technical crew. Martin Schäfer's cinematography, complemented by the work of de Almeida and Roque, helped to create the recognisable gripping and sharply contrasted images of the film. The process described above, moreover, also helps to illustrate the intricate dialogue between aesthetics and production in the making of *Blood*. This dialogue gained further expression in the initial domestic reception of the film.

SITUATING *BLOOD*: DOMESTIC CIRCULATION AND CRITICAL RECEPTION

The domestic release of *Blood* is tied to changes in film circulation operating in Portugal from the late 1980s onwards. Domestic film exhibition and distribution became dominated in 1987 by Portuguese media conglomerate Lusomundo (currently NOS), when the company acquired the assets of rival cinema distributor Mundial Filmes (Seabra 1987: 130). Soon after, there was also a revitalisation of the art-house circuit, with the appearance in 1989 of the exhibition and distribution companies Atalanta Filmes and Medeia Filmes. Founded by producer Paulo Branco, in association with Miguel Ferreira and Gabriel Lopes, these companies complemented the work carried by Branco's film production company Madragoa Filmes. These new ventures privileged the exhibition and distribution of international and Portuguese art cinema, and created an exhibition platform for works of both established and emerging Portuguese filmmakers.

Between 1989 and 1992, Atalanta commercially released *Blood* as well as other first works such as Joaquim Pinto's *Tall Stories*, Teresa Villaverde's *Alex* and Guimarães's *Clouds*. This initiative may have rescued these films from the obscurity previously imposed on a number of first works produced in the mid-1980s. Moreover, they were exhibited alongside others directed by Portuguese filmmakers who had already acquired consistent international critical acclaim. Around this time, and among others, Atalanta commercially released João César Monteiro's *Recordações da Casa Amarela* (*Recollections of the Yellow House*, 1989) and Manoel de Oliveira's *'Non', ou A Vã Glória de Mandar* (*No, or the Vain Glory of Command*, 1990). The exhibition strategy used by Atalanta helped to situate these first works as part of an already critically acclaimed art cinema, helping to spread knowledge of these new filmmakers amongst domestic art-house audiences.

Atalanta responded to the needs of a young urban domestic audience receptive to both international and domestic art cinema, which emerged soon after Portugal's joining the European Union in 1986. Atalanta's marketing director at the time, Pedro Borges, calculates that there was a threefold increase in box-office numbers at screening rooms owned by the company around the first half of 1990s (quoted in da Silva 1995b: 15). *Blood* seemed to have helped to start this trend. Exhibited commercially over a period of six weeks in only two cinema studios (in Lisbon and in Coimbra, in central Portugal), the film had a domestic box-office audience that Costa estimates at approximately 20,000 (Costa 2012). While an estimate, this number is particularly expressive considering the small size of the Portuguese market, let alone the much smaller domestic art-house circuit at the time. Box-office numbers presented by Pedro Borges give us a hint that the most successful Portuguese films circulating in the Atalanta screen circuit between 1990 and 1995 had audiences of between 20,000 and 25,000 spectators (quoted in da Silva 1995b: 15).

Moreover, and as Costa suggested to me, *Blood* responded to the sensibilities of this burgeoning art-house audience:

> more than the number of spectators what happened was that there were many people [. . .] aroused by [*Blood*]. It's a kid's film, in black and white, very cinephilic. There wasn't anything like it at the time. People in the Bairro Alto *movida* would tell me that they were enthused [by the film]. (Costa 2012)

As implied by Costa, key elements of the initial domestic success of *Blood* were its cinephilia-driven style and cinematography. These aesthetic characteristics helped both audiences and film critics to situate it as exceptional within contemporary Portuguese cinema. The use of black and white creates a 'tangible cachet' of authenticity and exception in a colour-saturated contemporary media landscape (Grainge 2002: 2–3). As Bénard da Costa suggests, the cinematography of *Blood* can be seen as a form of resistance against particular commercial film strategies taking shape at the time: for instance, the controversial practice of colouring black-and-white movies operated by the Turner Broadcasting System in the late 1980s (da Costa 1990: 117–18).[8] This exceptional status sustains a discourse rooted in notions of 'primitive beauty' which harks back to particular examples of Hollywood classical cinema and historical European art film. As Costa himself points out in interviews at the time of the domestic release of *Blood*, this choice was born from reluctance to film in colour in order to avoid the processed 'standardised colour' regime observed in 1980s cinema (Alves 1990: 29). Actor Pedro Hestnes similarly argues that the black and white palette used in *Blood* allowed him to feel a filmic 'nostalgia' which was impossible to achieve in 1980s undifferentiated 'standard-colour' films (da Silva 1995a: 6).

This notion of exception was clearly present in the marketing campaign of *Blood*, which adopted refined monochrome visuals such as dramatic scene-stills of actors Pedro Hestnes and Inês de Medeiros (Figure 1.4). Printed materials promoting the film circulated through arts and entertainment sections of the daily and weekly newspapers with wide circulation in Portugal, and its trailer was exhibited on public television channels. Some of these materials highlighted Martin Schäfer's contribution to the film and his link to Wim Wenders. The press release of the film also makes evident Schäfer's importance. The cinematographer was, apart from Costa, the only member of the crew to be mentioned in its introductory text. The press release also highlights the visual aspects of the film, with only Costa and Schäfer featured in the space for biographical notes. The marketing document gives to the cinematographer a level of visibility commonly only given to the main actors. Martin Schäfer's prominence was carried over to the press reviews, either directly discussing the film's cinematography or commenting positively on its aesthetic and technical properties.

While *Blood* received a largely positive critical response, some film critics highlighted issues with its narrative qualities. One review, while enthusiastically praising the film, nonetheless pointed out that its 'fragile' plot reflects one of the 'flaws' normally observed in Portuguese cinema (Brás 1990: 52). Another claimed that the lack of a clear story did not match the film's technical and aesthetic excellence. This is an issue which, according to the reviewer, is common in a national cinema normally 'anaemic' in narrative terms (Rosado 1990: 22). These observations can be contextualised, at

Figure 1.4 Still of *Blood* (1989), featuring Pedro Hestnes and Inês de Medeiros. This was one of the images used to promote the film during its domestic commercial release in 1990

least partially, as intrinsic to a constant problematic relation between Portuguese art film and its domestic reception. Discourses commonly expressed by both mainstream audiences and cultural critics define Portuguese art film as a cinema of 'boredom', with sombre acting, de-emphasised forms of narrative, and unappealing filmic technique (Mendes 1997: 45). As Paulo Granja argues, controversies surrounding Portuguese art film define it (both historically and in contemporary terms) as a cinema that neither engages in any type of market practices nor addresses the domestic audience's need for filmic entertainment (2010: 64). These assumptions concerning Portuguese art cinema have only grown stronger since the 1980s. Filmmakers Manoel de Oliveira and João César Monteiro consolidated their reputation among international film festival audiences at the time, yet struggled to captivate the attention of domestic spectators outside the urban art-house circuit (Granja 2010: 65).

The new generation of filmmakers in which Costa is commonly included produced an artistic output which differs substantially from these two filmmakers. *Blood*, for example, contrasts with the highbrow theatrical and literary artifice of Oliveira's cinema, or the satirical and poetic personal universe created by César Monteiro. Yet it is not surprising that previous assumptions concerning lack of narrative clarity attributed to Portuguese art cinema, by audiences and critics alike, may have tainted the reception of films directed in late 1980s and early 1990s. *Blood* thus seems to occupy a singular place in such discussions. The positive reception of a small but loyal domestic art-house audience, receptive to the aesthetic of Costa's directorial debut, may have helped to dissipate (at least temporarily) some of the generalised and inequitable categorisations imposed on Portuguese art film. As one journalist remarked, *Blood* 'is a Portuguese film that doesn't look like [Portuguese cinema]' (Luz 1990: 28). Instead, film critics positioned the film as a peculiar work, reflecting a thematic and stylistic debt to a past filmic expression unrelated to contemporary Portuguese cinema.

In spite of this positioning, however, there are some film critics who approximate *Blood* to some historical Portuguese films. One article penned by film critic Augusto M. Seabra, for instance, explicitly links *Blood* to Paulo Rocha's *Os Verdes Anos* (*The Green Years*, 1963); Seabra contends that both films share similar 'youthful' expression (Seabra 1990: 18). Commonly considered the seminal work which started the Portuguese *Cinema Novo*, Rocha's directorial debut – shot in black and white and under a restrictively low budget – reflects on the rising social alienation of teenagers and young adults living in a culturally and politically isolated 1960s Portugal (Granja 2010: 62).[9] Seabra finds similarities in the cultural contexts of both films, even suggesting a possible renaissance in Portuguese cinema, similar to the one that took place in the 1960s: 'perhaps [*Blood*] will become a sign of our green years' Seabra offers (1990: 18).[10]

The comparison to a paradigmatic example of the Portuguese *Cinema Novo* further emphasises the ambiguity of the critical discourses surrounding *Blood* at the time of its domestic release. As previously mentioned, Costa's directorial debut was critically received as exceptional particularly because of stylistic choices. These qualities encourage readings of its uniqueness, seeing the film as not taking part in contemporary cinema stylistic traditions. Simultaneously, some film critics tried to point out particularities which position *Blood* as a possible forerunner of a stylistic reinvention of Portuguese national cinema. All these different yet somehow overlapping understandings imprint a further uniqueness on Costa's first film. Yet, and perhaps rather less abstrusely, these readings impart the context in which *Blood* was initially received by domestic audiences: a work deemed to be outside mainstream cinema and which responds to the cinephilic sensibilities of urban art-house audiences receptive to emerging Portuguese art film.

In broader terms, these discussions serve not just to elucidate possible early influences that would inform Pedro Costa's directorial debut, but also to reveal intricate contexts from which his early authorial and production processes emerge. *Blood* transmits stylistic characteristics which make it fairly distinct in Portuguese cinema. This exceptionality was further emphasised in its initial domestic reception. That being said, Costa's first feature film reflects the historical, political and cultural particularities of the context of its making, a context that was common to a group of Portuguese filmmakers who started their activity in the mid-1980s. While a distinctive first work, *Blood* can nevertheless be positioned as an early example of a revitalisation of Portuguese cinema during this period – a revitalisation which, retrospectively, became further visible throughout the 1990s.

NOTES

1. Another example of explicit textual links in 1980s first works is *Duma Vez por Todas* (1986), the first feature film directed by Joaquim Leitão, in which Costa also participated. Leitão's directorial debut is a *film noir* set in contemporary Lisbon, closely obeying genre conventions and with clear plot correlations with some films directed by Alfred Hitchcock in the 1950s.
2. It is relevant to point out that Reis's influence can be observed not just in the work of these younger directors but is also extended to his collaborations in works of other Portuguese filmmakers such as Manoel de Oliveira's *Acto da Primavera* (*Rite of Spring*, 1963) and Paulo Rocha's *Mudar de Vida* (*Change One's Life*, 1966). Similarly, there are multiple textual homages and citations of Reis in several works directed by João César Monteiro.
3. As explained to me by Daniel Del-Negro in a 2012 email communication, Azul was responsible for the production of *A Girl in Summer*. After disagreements between Del-Negro and Vítor Gonçalves, the rights of the film were transferred to Trópico Filmes.
4. According to Pedro Costa, in the personal interview already cited, this television series comprised twelve short films shot in 16mm. The professionals involved rotated between different professional roles, with Costa directing some of these shorts. Also according to Costa, all copies of the series are now believed lost.
5. The Azul production team (later Trópico Filmes) was assisted by short-term collaborations with other film professionals, as well as several artists. The latter included the Portuguese musicians Paulo Pedro Gonçalves and Rui Reininho (at the time members of the popular bands Heróis do Mar and GNR, respectively) and the British composer Andrew Poppy, responsible for the soundtrack. Another collaborator in *A Girl in Summer* was the film and television writer and director Luís Filipe Costa (Pedro Costa's father).
6. According to the information provided by ICA in an email communication to the author on 27 July 2012.
7. Information provided by the Calouste Gulbenkian Foundation in an email to the author on 3 August 2012.
8. For more considerations of this practice, see Grainge (2002: 1–2).
9. One of the professionals starting his film career in Rocha's film was Elso Roque, as camera assistant.
10. This connection between *Blood* and Rocha's film also emerges in the interview with Pedro Hestnes already cited, suitably titled 'The Face of the Green Years' (see da Silva 1995a).

CHAPTER 2

Negotiating Filmmaking: Adaptation, Location and *Docufiction*

The first scene of *Casa de Lava* (1994) shows the eruption of Cape Verde's Fogo Island volcano, recorded in 1951 by Portuguese geographer Orlando Ribeiro (Figures 2.1 and 2.2).[1] The inclusion of such colour-infused images signals a clear stylistic departure from the monochromatic stylised ambience of Pedro Costa's directorial debut, *Blood*. These images, taken from what was once a scientific documentary, transmit approximation to a filmic style which privileged location – both as a thematic element and a film set. The third feature film directed by Costa, *Ossos* (*Bones*, 1997), transmits similar textual and stylistic preoccupations. Partly filmed at the former Lisbon shantytown of Fontainhas, the film develops further the rapport between fiction and documentary. *Bones* depicts the lives of characters cast out of the city's mainstream social fabric. These roles are mostly played by non-professional actors recruited on location.

Though stylistically distinct from each other, *Casa de Lava* and *Bones* nevertheless express authorship processes reflecting aesthetic inheritances. *Casa de Lava* was planned around a possible adaptation of the low-budget horror film *I Walked with a Zombie*, directed by Jacques Tourneur in 1943. As for *Bones*, its non-linear narrative and decelerated aesthetic minimalism transmit a clear influence of the cinema of Robert Bresson. It is clear, however, that Cape Verde and Fontainhas were the settings which propelled Costa's attention to the creative potential of working within the multifaceted contexts of these two locations – geographical, spatial, historical and social. The locations offer what Martin Lefebvre designates as 'a doubly temporalized landscape' (2006: 29). The *docufiction* style and attention to location against which these two films are set announce, in different ways, the impact of the cinema of António Reis and Margarida Cordeiro in Costa's authorial process. Both Cape

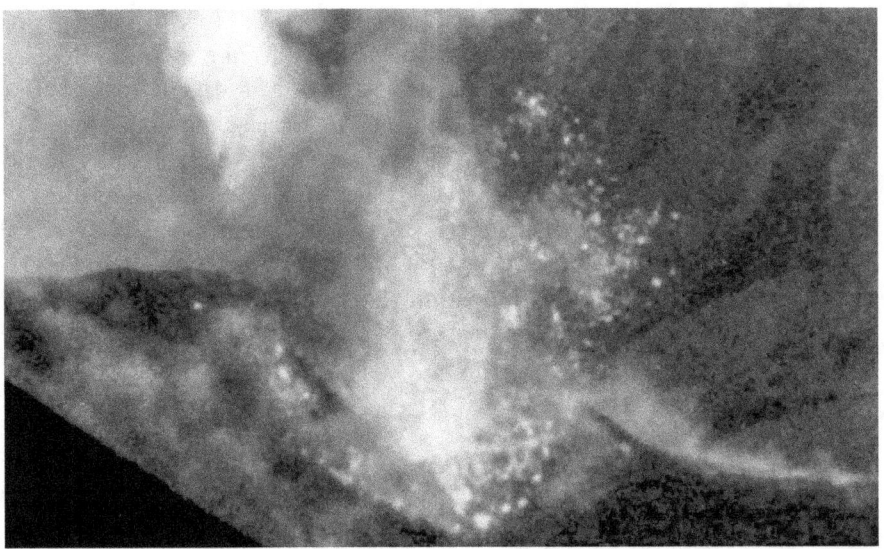

Figures 2.1 and 2.2 Stills of the initial scenes of *Casa de Lava* (1994), featuring footage of the Fogo Island volcano eruption shot by Orlando Ribeiro in 1951

Verde and Fontainhas are used as film sets where filmic narratives take place but also carry their own stratified narratives which Costa aimed to incorporate in both films.

These different aspects call our attention to the multifaceted adaptation processes informing Costa's filmmaking. Production documents of *Casa de Lava* allow us to trace the different adaptation stages of *I Walked with a Zombie* and its successive revisions, made to accommodate the nature of the shooting location. Aspects of adaptation can also be deduced from examining an artistic practice which is informed by the political and historical contexts of Cape Verde. The making of *Bones* similarly relied on the social conditions offered by the location and on the collaborative practices between Costa and its inhabitants. The making of the two films reveals a stratified and evolving process of adaptation, in which the dialogue between professional and non-professional agency assumes visible centrality. In all, *Casa de Lava* and *Bones* provide evidence of the close relation between filmic style and production values, while also giving clues to the dynamic nature of authorial control informing the cinema of Pedro Costa.

ADAPTING *I WALKED WITH A ZOMBIE*, AUTHORING *CASA DE LAVA*

Responding to an invitation by producer Paulo Branco, Costa started the process of screenwriting *Casa de Lava* soon after the domestic release of *Blood* in 1990. Initially, Costa envisaged a project that would convey a similar cinephilic universe to the one observed in his directorial debut. As explained by Costa at the time of *Casa de Lava*'s domestic release, his early ideas were a 'pastiche' of 'a romantic story, in an exotic place', which reflected the thematic universe of *I Walked with a Zombie* and the adventure films directed by Fritz Lang (Câmara 1995: 3). The importance of *I Walked with a Zombie* for the production of *Casa de Lava* is, however, both noticeable and complex. The initial authorial intent to adapt this particular filmic source would become shaped by complexities offered by production constraints and its shooting location.

Like *Casa de Lava*, *I Walked with a Zombie* negotiates forms of adaptation which consider different sources. The film epitomises the production values of the 1940s RKO Radio Pictures' horror B-movie unit, led by producer Val Lewton. The production blueprint used by this unit frequently adapted from many different sources themes and narratives to create distinct filmic storylines. The script of *I Walked with a Zombie*, credited to Curt Siodmak and Ardel Wray, takes its theme from an anecdotal account of voodoo practices in Haiti. The initial source of inspiration was the appropriately titled article 'I Met a Zombie', written by the entertainment columnist writer Inez Wallace in 1942 for *American Weekly*. Lewton used Wallace's article, imposed by RKO studio executives on the production team, as a pretext for a 'West Indian version' of Charlotte Brontë's novel *Jane Eyre* – a source that was only vaguely adapted (Fujiwara 1998: 85).

The plot of *I Walked with a Zombie* tells the story of a Canadian nurse, Betsy Connell (Frances Dee), hired to care for Jessica Holland (Christine Gordon).

Holland is the wife of the owner of a sugar plantation (Tom Conway) on the Caribbean island of Saint Sebastian, inhabited mostly by black slave descendants. Betsy soon becomes aware of the family issues which caused Jessica's unresponsive, zombie-like mental condition. This condition is later revealed as a psychological ailment caused by her tragic romantic entanglement with her brother-in-law (James Ellison). At the same time, the nurse also becomes aware of the plantation workers' voodoo practices. Eager to find a cure for Jessica's condition, and following the suggestion of her maid (Theresa Harris), Betsy takes her to be seen by a voodoo priest during a ceremony. The intervention of the voodooists, channelled mainly through the uncanny presence of the zombie Carrefour (Darby Jones), precipitates the narrative's tragic ending, with Jessica dying while trying to escape her zombie curse.

Costa's second feature film appropriates elements of this storyline, placing these in a different yet vaguely comparable postcolonial context. Set in the former Portuguese colony of Cape Verde, *Casa de Lava* is built around a Portuguese nurse, Mariana (Inês de Medeiros), and the Cape Verdean immigrant Leão (Isaach De Bankolé), who is in a coma after an accident at a construction site in Lisbon. Mariana is instructed to travel to Cape Verde with Leão, discharged from the hospital in Lisbon under mysterious circumstances, so he can be reunited with his family. Arriving on Cape Verde, the nurse soon discovers that no one seems to know Leão, and she decides to prolong her stay. Looking for some of his family members, Mariana wanders around the islands of Santiago and Fogo trying to fit in among the locals, who seem somehow uncomfortable with her quest. She nonetheless manages to get closer to Tina and Tanho, two local teenagers (played by non-professional actors Sandra do Canto Brandão and Cristiano Andrade Alves, respectively).

Mariana also meets Edite (Edith Scob) and her son (Pedro Hestnes), the only two European white residents. As the story develops we come to understand that Edite was formerly also a nurse. It is also implicit that she is the widow of a political prisoner who died in the Tarrafal prison camp, a penal colony established in the 1930s to incarcerate political activists opposed to the Portuguese dictatorship. Edite uses her resources to help the local men escape the archipelago. These men are destined soon to be working in construction sites in Lisbon, and supposed never to come back. The plot develops further when Leão wakes from his comatose state. Tensions start to grow further between Edite and Mariana, adding to the already tense relationship between the latter and some of the locals. Mariana starts to realise that Leão was supposed never to come back to a land populated by zombie-like characters waiting to leave.

While similarities in the narrative structures of *Casa de Lava* and *I Walked with a Zombie* are perceptible, Costa reworked the relations between the different characters. In Tourneur's film the narrative is sustained by the tensions between the plantation owner and his half-brother because of Jessica (and later Betsy). These tensions escalate further with the inclusion of supernatural elements. In *Casa de Lava* such tensions are transferred to the female characters, Mariana and Edite, with Leão's character replacing the role (and zombie-condition) initially conferred on Jessica. Similarly, the setting of *Casa de Lava* helps to replicate the postcolonial set of *I Walked with a Zombie*, albeit the studio-set Caribbean rich vegetation of the latter is replaced by Cape Verde's scorched landscape dominated by the presence of the Fogo Island volcano.

These differences propel further readings in terms of the filmic appropriations used in Costa's film. The *mise en scène* of *Casa de Lava* reveals similarities with another RKO production (in partnership with Berit Films), Roberto Rossellini's *Stromboli, terra di Dio* (*Stromboli*, 1950), which is set in the Sicilian volcanic island of the same name. Similarly, the outsider status of Mariana's character compares to the main female character in *Stromboli*, played by Ingrid Bergman. Both films, moreover, combine fictionalised narrative with moments of documentary nature. Film reviews written at the time of *Casa de Lava*'s domestic release point out these similarities, while omitting references to *I Walked with a Zombie*. *Público*'s film critic Luís Miguel Oliveira, for example, sees the influence of Rossellini and Robert Bresson as 'tutelary' presences in *Casa de Lava* (1995: 5). Similarly, Carlos Melo Ferreira points out the 'literal, almost excessive' references to *Stromboli* in Costa's second feature film (1995: 6).

These approximations to both *I Walked with a Zombie* and *Stromboli* instigate further readings on the nature of film adaptation and cinephilic appropriations observed in Costa's cinema. As Jonathan Rosenbaum argues, film critics seem to alternate between these two films as referential keys to interpret *Casa de Lava*:

> [s]ome people, unlike me, feel that as a reference point, *I Walked with a Zombie* provides an obstacle or distraction when it comes to appreciating *Casa de Lava* rather than a useful key that unlocks some of the film's treasures. Others feel that *Stromboli* is a more helpful reference point, whereas for me it is the Rossellini film, with its very different and less politicized form of mysticism, that provides a distraction and an obstacle, whatever its own merits. *Casa de Lava*, by contrast, poses the unanswerable question of how one can honourably or usefully behave inside a charnel house, a former slave colony. (Rosenbaum 2012: 4)

There are visible sub-textual approximations to Rossellini's work in *Casa de Lava*. Yet Rosenbaum's preference draws attention to two aspects which are central when discussing the film directed and scripted by Pedro Costa. The first one implicitly interrogates the nature of the adaptation of *I Walked with a*

Zombie assumed by Costa, which steers away from a close reading of Siodmak and Wray's screenplay. The second aspect, analysed later, is the postcolonial context offered by Cape Verde and how Costa reworks the latent political contours offered in Tourneur's film.

Looking firstly at the nature of the adaptation contained in *Casa de Lava*, it can be observed that Costa's early screenplay was developed around layered references to *I Walked with a Zombie*. One of these layers is filmic referencing, which can be contextualised under an authorial strategy informed by textual citation and homage. *Casa de Lava*, however, does not simply rely on such citations. It also depends on the acknowledgement of a filmic source (even if not mentioned in his film credits), by tacitly borrowing particular narrative elements of *I Walked with a Zombie* as starting points to achieve another filmic universe. Acknowledging the ambiguous nature of film adaptation, Jack Boozer argues that film adaptations are not just manifested in 'literal or close' readings and general narrative and thematic correspondences, but can also be informed by a 'distant referencing' to other works (2008: 9). It can be argued, for instance, that *I Walked with a Zombie* relies on thematic correspondences drawn from Wallace's article (credited as the source of the original story), as well as (an uncredited) distant referencing to Brontë's novel.

Casa de Lava employs a form of adaptation which distantly references Tourneur's film. This distant referring can be traced by looking into the different stages of production of Costa's film. Two relevant sources support this analysis. The first one is an early production document titled *Quando Ninguém Olhar Por Mim* ('When no one looks after me'; *Quando Ninguém* henceforth). This document was submitted by Branco's production company, Madragoa Filmes, for the funding contest held by the IPC in June 1991. *Quando Ninguém* includes a synopsis, a project description and an initial script treatment, all differing largely from the film later produced in 1994. The second source is a later script treatment titled *Down to Earth*, dating from 1992, containing similar information but which reveals changes to the initial project.[2] These two production documents provide details of the different stages of the production of the project, as well as offering some hints on the adaptation process centred on *I Walked with a Zombie*.

Quando Ninguém presents implicit references to Tourneur's work, both in terms of narrative structure and characterisation. The document also alludes to Tourneur's recognisable ambiguous narrative construction and use of shadowy *mise en scène*. Reflecting the plot of *I Walked with a Zombie*, the script treatment in *Quando Ninguém* focuses on the complicity between two female patients and their female nurse, and their attempts to escape an isolated rural psychiatric hospital where most of the plot takes place. The narrative tension escalates with the introduction of a young white warden and a black gardener, both of whom exhibit symptoms of an unidentified psychological disorder.

The narrative structure follows the plot of Tourneur's film by portraying the female characters as being divided between their efforts to resolve their psychological condition, and their ambiguous response to the oppressive presence of the male characters. This early script treatment indicates further similarities with narrative moments with *I Walked with a Zombie*: there are references to inactive behaviour which characterises *amour fou*, suggesting comparison to the character of Jennifer Holland. The script treatment also describes the constant presence of the sleepwalker gardener (and his subservient relationship to the warden), alluding to the zombie Carrefour. Moreover, the document describes nocturnal walks that both female patients take in the woods, again suggesting similarities with some scenes in Tourneur's film.

Quando Ninguém also provides clues to the early pre-production arrangements of *Casa de Lava*. It is clear in this production document that the initial planning of what would become Costa's second feature film was far more closely related to both filmic style and shooting locations featured in *Blood*. Furthermore, the three main actors from *Blood*, Pedro Hestnes, Inês de Medeiros and Nuno Ferreira, are also mentioned in the document. The cast list in *Quando Ninguém* also reveals the inclusion, early in the project, of Edith Scob. The presence of the French actress amounts to yet another cinephilic reference, for Scob is best known for her role as the disfigured and reclusive Christiane Génessier, in Georges Franju's notorious horror film *Les Yeux Sans Visage* (1960). Unlike *Blood*, however, the film was to be shot on 35mm colour film. Nonetheless, the numerous rainy days and night scenes scripted would perhaps help to create possible stylistic similarity between *Blood* and this film project.

Other relevant information in the early version of *Quando Ninguém* is the establishment of the initial shooting location. Film critics have assumed that the location initially chosen for *Casa de Lava* was the volcanic islands of Cape Verde, something also stated by Costa himself. This document reveals that the project was instead intended to be filmed in the same locations as *Blood* (around Ribatejo and in central Lisbon). Reflecting on Rosenbaum's observations above, it can be pointed out that some of the cinephilic relations between *Casa de Lava* and *Stromboli* became defined only after the final shooting location was established. The possibility of filming in Cape Verde emerged from another project on which Costa was working in the early 1990s. While starting to work on the follow-up to *Blood*, Costa was also invited by Paulo Branco to direct one of four television films commissioned by RTP that were thematically related to the four classical elements. This television film, which would represent 'Fire' in the tetralogy, was set on a volcanic island. According to Costa, the initial script had the potential to become 'something bigger' and he soon abandoned the project commissioned by the television channel (Luz 1994: 29).[3] The pre-production process of what would later become *Casa de Lava*, however, soon came to a halt. Having failed to initially win funding from the IPC, Paulo Branco gathered international funding for the project, while reapplying to the same institution's funding contest with a script treatment for a film titled *Terra a Terra* (of which the script treatment *Down to Earth* is the English translation). In this document the shooting location given was Cape Verde, serving as a setting depicted as a 'living hell of unbelievable beauty for tormented characters' (Madragoa Filmes 1992).

DOWN TO EARTH: SHOOTING *CASA DE LAVA*

A discussion of the making of *Casa de Lava* elucidates further the intricate process of adaptation discussed above. The film was produced by Branco's companies Madragoa Filmes (Portugal) and Gemini Films (France), and relied on funding from Portuguese and European public institutions and film financial support initiatives. Branco complemented the IPC funding, eventually granted in 1992, with other financial resources obtained through the Centre national du cinéma et de l'image animée (henceforth CNC). Later, in 1994, this funding was complemented with financial support provided by RTP. These financial arrangements reflected a production team with roles shared between mostly Portuguese and French film professionals. Similarly, the cast included de Medeiros and Hestnes, as well as Scob and the Ivorian-French actor Isaach De Bankolé.

The production process of *Casa de Lava* was marked by constant adjustments to the location and by issues arising during the shooting. The production logistics associated with filming on location in Cape Verde were particularly difficult, and added to the complexity of the co-financed project. In the early 1990s, Cape Verde offered limited filming conditions. All the shooting equipment brought from Europe had to be transported between islands on large rafts, at times during adverse weather conditions. The members of the cast and crew had to adapt to the harsh conditions and the isolation offered by the location. Furthermore, the shooting was beset by constant personal conflicts and numerous incidents on the set. As Costa recalls:

> people fell ill [. . .], half of the team had been dismissed; I had a fight with a member of the cast. [. . .] And there were [conflicts] between the Portuguese and French crew. Paulo [Branco], in Lisbon, would be constantly ringing us [to mediate issues]. [. . .] The shooting was a troubled process because of the location, but also because I pushed the situation to the limit: I decided to film near the [island of Fogo] volcano, but we had to take all the equipment up there . . . to the production crew that was very problematic . . . the road, the stones, the heat and the cold, the lack of water . . . (Costa 2012)

These difficulties were expanded by Costa's decision to abandon the script during the shooting. As he explains to Mark Peranson, this decision enables a creative process marked by constant 'improvisation' which accommodate constantly varying perceptions of the location and its inhabitants (Peranson 2010: 135). This new working method was matched by a proportional increase in the visibility of the local participants who were recruited on location, all of whom had no previous acting experience. De Bankolé's role, in particular, was changed to accommodate the inclusion of these characters, and become less visible than planned in the script. As disclosed by Costa during the interview already cited with me, De Bankolé was not fully aware that his character would spend a significant part of the film in a comatose state: 'I've extended the coma [scenes] while De Bankolé wanted to "wake up" earlier' (Costa 2012). This decision aggravated significantly the already existing tensions on the set.

A comparative analysis between the script treatment titled *Down to Earth* and the final cut of *Casa de Lava* helps to understand the changes to the initially scripted plot. The script treatment follows a relatively linear storyline around the characters of Mariana, Leão and Edite. Most of this storyline was retained in the first part of the film. Yet, this document also includes other narrative events that are either not included or that were changed in the film. The script treatment, for instance, describes the death of the two teenage characters Mariana befriended and seemed to rely upon, something only suggested in the film; the attempted murder of Mariana by Edite's son was also scripted in detail, though the scene is omitted in the narrative of the film. Similarly, the final scene in the script depicts Mariana's efforts to escape the island. This scripted scene suggests an ending similar to the one depicted in *I Walked with a Zombie*. Such an ending, however, is only alluded to in *Casa de Lava*. These changes and omissions reflect what Costa characterises as a narrative 'open structure' (Peranson 2010: 135), which evolved from the script-free daily improvisation carried on during the shooting of the film.

The changes which occurred in the shooting process of *Casa de Lava*, however, still accommodate many details that express the intended adaptation of *I Walked with a Zombie*. The plot of the film, centred on Mariana, Leão and Edite, still reflects the narrative tension observed in the work directed by Tourneur, albeit with the differences already described. Similarly, the strange zombie-like condition which affects some of the characters in *Casa de Lava* – Leão most obviously, but also Edite's son – refers to the main plot mechanism used in Siodmak and Wray's script. These similarities are patent in the initial 30 minutes of *Casa de Lava* which, as already mentioned, still follow some of the narrative moments described in the Madragoa Filmes' script treatment. The second part of the film, however, diverges into multiple subplots that move away not just from its initial narrative moments but also from the narrative sequences depicted in *I Walked with a Zombie*. Focused on the rambling walks of Mariana and the inhabitants' daily life, the second part of *Casa de*

Lava reveals the importance given by Costa to the location in which the film is set. The inclusion of scenes of documentary nature in this second part of *Casa de Lava* comes to suggest the postcolonial condition of Cape Verde.

RE-CONTEXTUALISING LOCATION

The discussion of the different contextual characteristics of Cape Verde allows further understanding of how the nature of adaptation of *I Walked with a Zombie* is conditioned by the political complexity of the location in which the narrative of *Casa de Lava* takes place. In Costa's film, Cape Verde is transformed into a film set, populated with mysterious characters that re-enact power relations and amplify the sexual tensions perceived in *I Walked with a Zombie*. Yet *Casa de Lava* also alludes to a location marked by colonial rule and shaped by postcolonial structural underdevelopment and immigration. Depicted as arid and without resources, underdeveloped and sparsely populated, the Cape Verde depicted in Costa's film also makes us aware of this location's overlapping spatial, historical and social contexts.

Like the East Indies which serves as the setting for Tourneur's film, Cape Verde offers historical and contemporary political resonances which were incorporated in the narrative of *Casa de Lava*. As Fernando Arenas argues, the work of Pedro Costa

> underscores a paradoxical and shifting dynamic of 'distant proximity' at work both in the metropole and in the islands as far as the privileged historical, cultural, and linguistic links between contemporary Cape Verde and Portugal are concerned, as a result of colonialism, widespread miscegenation in Cape Verde, a special legal and ontological status of Cape Verde within the African colonial empire and the Portuguese imaginary, in addition to mass Cape Verdean migration to Portugal and economic dependence. (Arenas 2011: 18; quotation marks as in the original)

Indeed, Arenas's notion of 'distant proximity' permeates the political context of Cape Verde. Due to its geographical position on the African Atlantic coast the archipelago was a strategic point for the Portuguese sea expansion that started in the fifteenth century and soon became central to the Atlantic slave trade. Its cosmopolitan population composed of several European and African constituencies came to reflect the ambiguities of interracial and cross-cultural mixing under colonialism. During the twentieth century, Portuguese propaganda kept to a discourse based on the idea of colonial unity, claiming that all overseas territories shared the same national identity. Cape Verde was historically ascribed an ideological significance in this colonial discourse: the territory served as 'showcase of Luso-African racial harmony', and its inhabitants enjoyed more rights than those allowed in mainland Portuguese colonies (Meintel 1984: 3). This position was kept after its independence in 1975. As Arenas explains, the country currently enjoys a special status due to:

> [its] alleged cultural proximity to Europe; its intimate historical ties with Portugal; high living standards vis-à-vis the African continent; political stability; and its shared 'ultra-peripheral status' with EU insular territories such as the Azores, Canary Islands, Guadeloupe, Madeira, and Martinique. (Arenas 2011: 7; quotation marks as in the original)

Cape Verde's interstitial position, between Africa and Europe, presented an ideal location in the early twentieth century for the establishment of the Tarrafal prison camp. The camp was initially the forced destination of some of the fiercest elements of opposition to the Portuguese dictatorship. Later, during the colonial/independence war(s) in the 1960s and early 1970s, it was used for the imprisonment of African freedom fighters and liberation movement supporters. Cape Verde is also the place of origin of a multigenerational immigrant diaspora located in Portugal, as well as distributed throughout several countries in Europe and the Americas. In an interview with film critic Vasco Câmara, Costa posits the idea that there is a correlation between Cape Verdean immigrants working on Lisbon's construction sites and the political repression symbolised by the Tarrafal prison camp. According to the filmmaker there is a concealed 'political death chain' linking these different yet equally efficient forms of oppression (Câmara 1995: 4; see also Jorge 2014: 45). This criticism is extended to what the filmmaker understands as contempt by Portuguese contemporary society for the former colonies. During the promotional event after the screening of *Casa de Lava* at the 1994 Cannes Film Festival, Costa declared to the Portuguese press that the film was an expression of the 'disgust' he felt towards Portuguese politics and society at the time (Luz 1994: 29).

Costa aims particular criticism at the Social Democrat governments of Prime Minister Aníbal Cavaco Silva, in power between 1985 and 1995. This was a period of substantial social and economic change, caused by the rapid implementation of the European Union's economic measures which deeply contrasted with the social ideals put forward by the 1974 revolution (Owen 2018: 185; see also Jorge 2014: 45–7). This period came to be characterised by infrastructural investment and public works which were largely supported by European Union funding initiatives. The construction of these infrastructures relied on a large workforce partly composed of migrant workers. Simultaneously, the 1990s was also a decade in which there was an official effort to eradicate Lisbon's impoverished auto-constructed neighbourhoods. The relocation of their former residents to newly built estates located outside urban centres reflected the preparations to host the 1998 World Exhibition (Pardue 2014: 64). This large-scale exhibition was the culmination of several initiatives helping to project Portugal's international image in relation to its European Community partners, such as the presidency of the EU in 1992 and Lisbon European Capital of Culture in 1994. The official discourse transmitted during these international initiatives insists on the legacy of the Portuguese 'Discoveries' (the Portuguese sea expansion started in the fifteenth century) as a benign process of universal 'togetherness', while omitting 'slavery' and 'colonial brutality rule' (Lemière 2009: 104).

Casa de Lava thematically conveys this problematic relationship between Portugal and its former colony. The narrative of the film is centred on Cape Verdean immigration to Portugal, while also alluding to the remnants of colonial rule. However, and as Hilary Owen points out, 'no overt or unambiguous political message' emerges from the film's narrative (2018: 186). Instead, the film projects a mysterious image of Cape Verde through a discontinuous narrative that alludes to its past and present political contexts, mixing the fictionalised plot with almost documental episodic narrative detours. As Costa explains, his perception of the place and the increasing familiarity with the local participants in the film (first during the location scouting and later during shooting) made him reconsider the narrative structure; as the filmmaker argues, this allowed him adapting to 'the land [and] the people, who contributed with their own stories, pointing to ways that the film could follow' (Lemière 2009: 100). Costa's observation indicates a form of authorial negotiation in which a potential political stance becomes manifested in the postcolonial condition observed on Cape Verde. This explanation, however, also calls our attention to the discursive contours of an authorial process of which Costa still retains significant control. The film presents numerous close-ups of the faces and bodies of the local participants, as well as stylised depictions of small compositions placed in the *mise en scène*. These scenes seem to indicate more of a fascination with the participants' condition rather than with giving narrative density to the postcolonial context of the location and its numerous implications (Owen 2018: 191–2; Arenas 2011: 136).

Costa's original fieldwork notebook, initially compiled during location scouting and research for the film, offers clues to the ambiguous role of these local participants. The inclusion of several photos of some of these non-professional actors in the notebook alludes to their increasing importance in the creative process of *Casa de Lava*. Some of these photos, however, are also studies for shots subsequently included in the film. In this regard, their nature is as much documental as it is staged. These images become elements in a multiplicity of inspirational sources taken into consideration when planning the film. They participate in an intertextual dialogue that also considers film stills: among others, images from *I Walked with a Zombie* and *Les*

Yeux Sans Visage. It also includes several newspaper clippings concerning, for example, the Tarrafal prison camp and exploitative interventions maintained by pharmaceutical companies in Africa. The patchwork of different elements contained in Costa's production notebook points to a creative process already concerned with different contextual temporalities offered by the location, and its incorporation into the fictionalised narrative of the film.

This relation between the documental and the fictionalised alludes to the influence of the cinema of António Reis and Margarida Cordeiro. *Trás-os-Montes* and *Ana*, for instance, present an intricate combination of fiction and documentary. Dennis Lim terms these two films as 'ethnofiction' and 'docufable' respectively, with their narratives composed with a 'merging of past and present, and the refusal to distinguish between the flux of life and the flux of stories' (Lim 2012: 102). These two films were filmed in, but also narratively structured by, Portugal's northeastern region of Trás-os-Montes. Presented as a doubly temporalised landscape, this region serves as both a landscape where everyday life activities occur and the settings of folktale narratives are re-enacted. Costa's noticeable aim at a realistic, albeit stylised, filmic representation mirrors these characteristics. The textual characteristics of *Casa de Lava* make evident that location serves not just as a film set but also as a non-fictional narrative and thematic entity. As discussed below, this overlapping narrative quality gains stronger expression in Costa's subsequent film, set in Fontainhas.

LETTERS TO FONTAINHAS

Bones similarly expresses the importance of location in creative and authorial processes maintained by Pedro Costa. The film further exemplifies the filmmaker's aim at a realistic depiction of the location, strengthening the connection between cinematic representation and the realities lived by its characters. Though set in Lisbon, the film is inherently tied to Cape Verde. Responding to the requests of several of the local participants in *Casa de Lava*, Costa and other film crew members returned from Cape Verde with gifts and letters destined for Cape Verdean family members and friends living in Lisbon and surrounding urban areas. As Costa recalls:

> during the last day of shooting, [. . .] they came to us with bags full of things – letters, presents, coffee, tobacco – for us to carry [to Lisbon]. The addresses were mostly [. . .] in Fontainhas, Benfica, Damaia, Estrela de África, Cova da Moura. [. . .] At that time [around 1995] these neighbourhoods were problematic but we went there and we were very well received. (Costa 2012)

Serving as an intermediary between Cape Verde and its Lisbon-based diaspora, Costa gained privileged access into neighbourhoods considered out of bounds. He became particularly fascinated by the social characteristics of Fontainhas. Through successive visits between 1995 and 1996 Costa deepened his relationship with some of Fontainhas' inhabitants, particularly with the sisters Vanda and Zita Duarte (da Silva 1997: 28).

The origins of Fontainhas are tied to the immigration context alluded to in *Casa de Lava*. This unplanned residential area was constructed clandestinely by successive waves of migrant workers coming from Portugal's interior regions and its former colonies (Figuerinhas 2011: 15). Until its phased demolition in the late 1990s, the multicultural neighbourhood housed a substantial number of African immigrants, with a high percentage of Cape Verdeans. Fernando Arenas's notion of distant proximity is, once again, suitable to define this cultural geography as a territory placed in Lisbon's geographical borders, yet alien to most Lisboners (2011: 18). As with other areas that Costa visited at the time, Fontainhas was only made visible through reports by Portuguese news media, which portrayed it as a place associated with informal economies such as drug trafficking and with violent crime. As Costa describes it:

> Fontainhas was not completely outside of Lisbon, but let's say it was on the border of Lisbon. It was a big shantytown, very dark, organized in architecture, space and colour like an African or even Arab medina – the old town. There was a very secret way in and way out. They even had guards. It was really like a fortress, a castle. I had no reason to go there before and really no one would walk in there unless they wanted to buy or sell something – often drugs. (McGilligan 2010: 82–3)

Echoing Costa's description, Arenas argues that this location, as depicted in *Bones* and later in *In Vanda's Room*, transmits 'a sense of the uncanny [. . .] combined with claustrophobia, spatial disorientation and cultural and linguistic deterritorialization' (2011: 18). Both films deeply contrast with what Mariana Liz calls the touristic 'postcard' representations of Lisbon, as offered in Wim Wenders's *Lisbon Story* (1994) – a film commissioned by Lisbon European Capital of Culture (2018b: 122–3). The inaccessibility which transpires in these films made Fontainhas close yet outside any recognisable area of Lisbon. Its location reflects a contemporary urbanity greatly influenced by the social and cultural formations emerging from Portugal's former colonial presence and from the successive social changes brought about under democracy.

In an interview with filmmaker Jean-Pierre Gorin, Costa explains that while already regularly visiting Fontainhas, he was asked by Paulo Branco to produce an initial script treatment in order to start the funding process of *Bones* (Costa and Gorin 2010). The initial storyline of the film was inspired by a newspaper report concerning a teenage mother caught when abandoning her baby in Lisbon's central train station restroom. This occurrence, as Costa admitted to me, was not directly related with Fontainhas (Costa 2012; also in Costa and Gorin 2010). Yet this episode became the central motif in a narrative set between central Lisbon and the suburban neighbourhood. The narrative of the film follows the fate of a newborn baby who is taken away by its father (Nuno Vaz) soon after the mother, Tina (Mariya Lipkina), attempts suicide. The father meets Eduarda (Isabel Ruth) while begging with the baby in the streets of Lisbon. Soon after the baby is taken to hospital due to food poisoning, Eduarda, who works as a nurse in the hospital, accommodates them in her apartment. In the meantime, Tina comes to rely on her neighbour Clotilde (Vanda Duarte), who works as a house cleaner in several apartments in central Lisbon. From this moment onwards the narrative of the film concentrates on the increasingly ambiguous complicity between the three female characters. Both Clotilde and Eduarda try to somehow resolve Tina's situation. The father in the meantime tries to sell the baby to a prostitute (Inês de Medeiros). From then on the whereabouts of the baby becomes uncertain. The film concludes when Clotilde finds the father in Eduarda's apartment. In an act of revenge she turns on the gas cooker and leaves, locking the door to the apartment.

The narrative of the film repeatedly shows the characters living at Fontainhas going into and coming out of central Lisbon. This arrangement reinforces the contrast between the two locations. The labyrinthine narrow streets of Fontainhas are constantly set against ample spaces such as the hospital and its surroundings and Lisbon's wide avenues and open squares. While temporarily occupying these spaces, the main characters are rendered as being out of place or even invisible to the city's social fabric. The house cleaning routines performed by Clotilde are devoid of any contact with its middle-class residents, who are never seen in the film. Similarly, the wanderings of the father with the baby through the city are marked by the indifference of the passers-by. Eduarda provides the only break in the invisibility of these socially excluded characters. The nurse tries to, somehow, help the young couple and their baby and eventually dares to enter their living space. Manifestations of migrant cultures are perceptible in the film, yet *Bones* portrays a far more inclusive milieu, one which represents more diverse cultural, social and economically marginalised groups (Jorge 2014: 49). *Bones* depicts the realities of characters relying on an informal economy – non-contract temporary workers, vagrants and prostitutes – who, while somehow included in the everyday routines of the city, are cast outside its social fabric. The urban characters that populate the film, as Portuguese film critic João Miguel Fernandes Jorge argues, occupy an evolving '*post*-human' topography of poverty which reshapes cultural, historical and social identities (2009: 157; italics in the original).

In this regard, *Bones* predates (briefly) other Portuguese films set in some of the derelict peripheral neighbourhoods in and around Lisbon. Albeit in different ways, Teresa Villaverde's *Os Mutantes* (*The Mutants*, 1998), Cláudia Tomaz's *Noites* (*Nights*, 2001) and, to some extent, the 1998 Portuguese box-office success *Zona J* (*Zone J*, dir. Leonel Vieira) are structured around narratives set in problematic social locations.[4] Like these films, *Bones* reflects the limitations of the 1990s Portuguese economic and social development model imposed by the European Union. It maps broader anxieties concerning economic inequality and social exclusion which transcend the country's national borders. Several European films around that time rely on the same or related topics. Examples of this are Jean-Pierre and Luc Dardenne's *La Promesse* (1996) and *Rosetta* (1999), *The Life of Jesus* (dir. Bruno Dumont, 1997), and *La Haine* (dir. Mathieu Kassovitz, 1995), to name but a few. Though in a different way, *Bones* shares with all these films a preoccupation with depicting the lives of what Thomas Elsaesser terms 'abject heroes [or] heroines' who populate the poor suburbs of European capital cities (Elsaesser 2005: 124–5).

As in *Casa de Lava*, Costa does not present any explicit political statement concerning the conditions of the characters in the film. His stance eschews both the ideological formations which characterised militant filmmaking and the models of representation that came to shape particular strands of social-realism cinema. Reflecting on this, Costa argues that film as 'a revolutionary gun does not exist. Or if it does exist, it failed completely, because the guys [. . .] who believed in it, didn't succeed' (Oumano 2010: 216; see also Corless 2009: 29). Instead, Costa seems more invested in a 'representational mode' outside the ideological formalism which animates, for example, political agendas (see Maimon 2012: 331). Inevitably, this representational mode avoids representations commonly observed in politically driven cinema traditions, preferring instead to document the living conditions of the contemporary European precariat.

This representational mode is manifested in *Bones* through an aesthetic minimalism and non-linear and fragmented narrative which serve to depict the issues around a marginalised teenage couple and their unwanted baby. Costa gives primacy to contemplative *mise en scène* compositions, with the use of long takes in which dialogues between the characters are almost nonexistent. Likewise, the characters' physical interaction and display of emotions are kept to a minimum, denying emotional clarity and obscuring the causal effects of their actions. The plot build-up is similarly sparse, sustained by lack of narrative continuity. Scenes end in a non-conclusive way or avoid showing crucial incidents. Some scenes, for instance, avoid depicting the ultimate fate of some of the film's characters by concluding with doors or windows being closed (Costa 2005; Hong 2010: 208).

Another characteristic which contributes to narrative non-linearity is the inclusion of scenes glancing at the daily life of Fontainhas. These scenes may serve as establishing shots of some sort. Yet their inclusion implies an almost documental representation of a fictionalised narrative. One of the filmic tropes used by Costa to merge the observational and the staged is the inclusion of scenes featuring secondary characters not actively participating in the main narrative. There is an inscrutable narrative proposed in the scenes featuring some of the Fontainhas residents. As Canadian photographer Jeff Wall points out, some of the 'most intriguing' moments in the film: 'show one or two characters in silence, motionless, except perhaps when smoking a cigarette, [or] looking at the camera or to [something] near it, lost in their own thoughts' (2009: 151–2; also Wall 2010). One of these intriguing characters, played by Zita Duarte, is introduced in the first scene of the film (Wall calls this character the 'watcher'). This character emerges several times during the film, being always outside the scenes where action takes place, yet seeming to observe particular narrative moments. The relationship between fiction and documentary, however, is not just limited to these potential and tangential short narrative moments but permeates the whole of the filmic universe presented in *Bones*. As Costa explains:

> Even if there's a very strong desire [to] be a documentary, [it's] because it's made with people who are not actors, who are very close to the things that they represent. The [father] is really poor, the housekeeper, she's a housekeeper, the neighbourhood, it's a real neighbourhood. We're not in a studio, but even if there's a desire to be something of a documentary, it's nevertheless fiction that carries, that saves the film. (Costa 2005)

This tension between two filmic modes reminds us, once again, of Reis's influence on the cinema of Pedro Costa. This mode of representation addresses Fontainhas as both a film set and a place in which particular thematic, narrative and stylistic qualities are present. Other influences emerge from the filmic and narrative poetics observed in *Bones*. A source of inspiration commonly pointed out when examining the film is the work of Robert Bresson, a filmmaker that Costa claims as an early influence and who was also central in the teachings of António Reis. James Quandt, for instance, appropriately identifies the 'Bressonian arsenal' deployed in *Bones*: 'lack of establishing shots'; 'inexpressive nonprofessional actors delivering uninflected line readings'; 'a precise, materialistic treatment of objects and bodies and space' (2006: 356). Jeff Wall similarly sees in the film the work of a 'closed and attentive student of Bresson', particularly of his later films (Wall 2010).[5] The nature of representational modes and filmic influences in *Bones*, however, are also informed by the arrangements taking place at the film set, as well as the production context which made such arrangements possible.

NEGOTIATING LOCATION

The production process of *Bones* was informed by different financial and logistical characteristics from those observed in the making of *Casa de Lava*. In financial terms, earlier on Paulo Branco secured financial support from the Council of Europe's fund initiative Eurimages, the Portuguese Cinema Institute, RTP and Danish film production company Zentropa. This last, founded by filmmaker Lars von Trier and producer Peter Aalbæk Jensen, was at the time actively promoting the production values imposed in the *Dogme 95* manifesto (see, for example, Hjort and MacKenzie 2003: 199–200). Analogies between the production and aesthetics of *Bones* and this manifesto can be tentatively drawn and these particularities surely helped to raise the interest of Zentropa in the project. Perhaps more pertinently, it is noted that the company already had links with Portuguese producers. Zentropa had previously participated in the co-production of *A Comédia de Deus* (*God's Comedy*, dir. João César Monteiro, 1995), produced by Joaquim Pinto. Later, with Madragoa Filmes, Zentropa would also co-produce *Tráfico* (*Traffic*, dir. João Botelho, 1998). These links between Zentropa and Portuguese producers indicate an early interest on the part of the former company in collaborating in productions originating in the context of small nations' cinema industries. Zentropa took these collaborative practices further in the early 2000s, albeit in different national contexts (see Hjort 2010: 17–18).

These co-production arrangements facilitated the choices of the technical crew and cast of *Bones*. The film crew was mostly composed of professionals who participated in *Casa de Lava*, including cinematographer Emmanuel Machuel and sound technician Henri Maïkoff.[6] Unlike *Casa de Lava*, however, the cast was prominently Portuguese – the only exception being Moscow-born professional actress Mariya Lipkina. The main roles were allotted to both professional actors, such as Isabel Ruth and Inês de Medeiros, and non-professional actors, including, among others, Nuno Vaz, Vanda Duarte and Zita Duarte. Recruited mostly from Fontainhas and the surrounding areas, these non-professional actors lived in the midst of the social issues observed in the film and had serious problems with drug dependency. The participation of these actors in the film proved to be problematic. Their personal experiences help in defining the characters, yet their routines initially interfered with (and later conditioned the pace of) the shooting process (Costa 2012; Costa et al. 2012: 42).

Further constraints were imposed by both the social and spatial specificities of Fontainhas. The shooting of *Bones* took place between November 1996 and February 1997, with the first two weeks shooting on locations in central Lisbon and the remaining six weeks at Fontainhas (da Silva 1997: 28). Beforehand, the production team sought out the support of the community centre, while simultaneously 'negotiating' with key figures connected with the local informal economies (Costa 2012; Machuel 2012). Adapting to the limits imposed by the drug trafficking routines, the film crew had to unobtrusively impose their position on the location. As cinematographer Emmanuel Machuel explains, 'we respected the somewhat tacit rules: "No filming on X day at X time." We didn't go where we weren't supposed to be' (Machuel 2012). Other constraints were imposed by spatial arrangement of the neighbourhood. The maze of narrow streets and dark alleys created numerous technical issues for the transportation of filming apparatus. As Costa comments: 'the production planning didn't match the neighbourhood, the trucks [carrying the equipment] couldn't pass [the narrow streets]' (Costa et al. 2012: 36). These spatial restrictions are clearly perceived in some of the scenes in *Bones*. Adapting to such spatial limitations, the film crew had to work around architectural elements such as windows, doorways and partitions. These elements acquire a staged presence, being metaphors for the spatial division between characters. This treatment of the filmic space, however, also suggests the difficulty in placing unwieldy shooting apparatuses in constricted spaces. These architectural elements came to be included in the framing of some of the scenes, with the film crew having to operate the camera from the streets and through windows (Figure 2.3).

As a communal living space temporarily turned into a film set, Fontainhas also impacted extensively on some aural characteristics of *Bones*. The sound team led by Henri Maïkoff, for instance, had to incorporate the constant sounds of everyday life in the neighbourhood in the soundtrack. Jeff Wall's observations are once again pertinent in this discussion since, as he notes, the nature of the soundtrack of *Bones* is shaped by the constant presence of non-diegetic sounds:

> dogs barking, other people talking, clatter of people going by, automobiles and so on, which penetrates all the little rooms and spaces of the neighbourhood where most of the action takes place. (Wall 2010)

As Wall implies, the presence of these aural elements in the film inscribes a further sense of spatial presence of the real-time events taking place in the neighbourhood. Complementing the fictionalised narrative, these sounds strengthen the documentary feel of the film. In a similar way, the cinematography of *Bones* reflects adjustments to the conditions offered by the location. For instance, Emmanuel Machuel and Pedro Costa had to change the lighting effects initially

Figure 2.3 Resolving spatial restrictions through *mise en scène*: still of *Bones* (1997) featuring Vanda Duarte, Isabel Ruth and Mariya Lipkina

planned. The imposing and intrusive brightness shed by heavy-duty lighting used at night brought complaints from some of the residents. Needing to reduce the use of lighting, Machuel developed techniques which enhanced the colours of the interiors while, simultaneously, darkening the aspect of Fontainhas' narrow streets. Likewise, and as Costa explained to me, there was a constant and persistent work of placing objects in predominant places on the set in order to create textures that would substitute for the absence of professional light sources (Costa 2012).

The making of *Bones*, and *Casa de Lava* before it, illustrates the negotiations between directorial agency and the constraints of producing a film in challenging locations – both in spatial and social terms. These successive steps in adapting to the conditions offered by Fontainhas call our attention to two central aspects that Costa would subsequently refine in his *oeuvre*. The first aspect is a filmic representation attentive to the multifaceted qualities of the location where his works are set. Costa's directorial agency takes into consideration the social realities observed *in situ*, and its different contexts become part of the filmmaking process. Secondly, these films also elucidate the increasing importance given to non-professional collaborators. It needs to be emphasised that *Casa de Lava* and *Bones* are the result of filmmaking processes tied to professional and normative frameworks. As discussed above, however, the making of both films is also shaped by mediations between formal and informal practices. These characteristics would soon be central in Costa's radical approach to filmmaking.

NOTES

1. These images were included in the scientific documentary *A Erupção do Vulcão da Ilha do Fogo* (1951). A proficient photographer, Orlando Ribeiro edited different photograms, which were enlarged and trimmed in order to compose the film (Furtado 1995: 6).
2. Both documents are part of the collection of the Portuguese Cinematheque Library archives in Lisbon. In an email I received from ICA (former IPC), it was revealed that the funding was granted to the project when it was still called *Terra a Terra*. It can be assumed that the document referred to here as *Down to Earth* is the English-language version of the same script treatment submitted by Madragoa Filmes to the IPC funding contest in 1992, probably to help gather funding internationally.
3. The four films commissioned by RTP were produced between 1992 and 1993.
This film tetralogy comprises: *O Último Mergulho* (*The Last Dive*, dir. João César Monteiro, 1992), representing 'Water'; *Das Tripas Coração* (*Twin Flames*, dir. Joaquim Pinto, 1992), representing 'Fire'; *O Dia dos Meus Anos* (*On My Birthday*, dir. João Botelho, 1992), representing 'Air'; *O Fim do Mundo* (*The End of the World*, dir. João Mário Grilo, 1993), representing 'Earth'.
4. Villaverde's *Mutants* was shot in several economically deprived urban and suburban locations in and around Lisbon; *Nights* was partially filmed in the Portuguese capital city's notorious neighbourhood of Casal Ventoso (once labelled by the British tabloid *The Sun* as the 'Junkie Capital of Europe'). As for *Zone J*, the film takes its title from the neighbourhood once situated in Lisbon's Chelas area, which in the 1990s had a similarly notorious resonance to Fontainhas in the Portuguese press.
5. These influences can also be extended to the work of Yasujirō Ozu and Kenji Mizoguchi, and to Charlie Chaplin's 1921 film *The Kid* (Costa 2005; also Sante 2010: 23).
6. Considering the filmic influences informing *Bones*, it is relevant to note that Emmanuel Machuel worked as a cinematographer on Bresson's *L'Argent* (1983).

CHAPTER 3

Digital Filmmaking at the Interstices

In March 1999, *Cahiers du Cinéma*'s editors Thierry Lounas and Emmanuel Burdeau visited Lisbon to observe Pedro Costa working on his new feature film. The article resulting from their visit expresses equal amounts of flummox and commendation at the way Costa decided to shoot the follow-up to *Bones*, the film which consolidated his critical acclaim among the French film-specialised press. Their report tells us about an unconventional film shooting in which Costa uses a mid-range digital video camera to document the realities of the secretive and 'dangerous' setting of Fontainhas (Burdeau 1999: 60). The article transmits some understandable uneasiness over stories concerning the *Cahiers*' editors meetings with some of the residents. More significantly, this article is also an early account of the making of *No Quarto da Vanda* (*In Vanda's Room*, 2000), providing clues to a new working process which came to characterise Costa's filmmaking ethos from then on.

After the completion of *Bones*, Costa went back to Fontainhas equipped only with a digital camera and other inexpensive and portable recording equipment. For a period of approximately two years, either alone or occasionally relying on a small number of film professionals, the filmmaker recorded the everyday of the neighbourhood. This setup served to resolve restrictions imposed by the technical processes and professional timescales which previously characterised the shooting of Costa's third feature film. The use of affordable digital video technology made possible working methods which neither depended on specialised technical requirements nor strictly conformed to the divisions of labour and professional hierarchies. Instead, the shooting process of *In Vanda's Room* is informed by Costa's creative partnership with a cast of non-professional actors, under a reduced budget and dispensing with professional routines and shooting schedules. Costa's detachment from the means of production which made possible his previous work was, however, only partial. Terminating his professional relationship with producer Paulo Branco, Costa came to rely instead on the Portuguese production company Contracosta Produções. The company was founded by a group of former students of the Lisbon Theatre and Film School, and centred on the producer Francisco Villa-Lobos. The production support offered by Contracosta obeyed the norms commonly observed in the European co-production model.

The in-between working process supporting *In Vanda's Room* calls attention to the relationship between artistic expression, film technology and production models adopted by Costa in the late 1990s. Central to this relationship is the notion of 'interstitial production'. This term is used by Hamid Naficy to define both working practices and a cultural positioning of a group of contemporary filmmakers occupying an in-between position in contemporary art cinema. As Naficy argues, this interstitiality is informed by low-budget ambivalent filmmaking practices which negotiate between an artisanal disposition and different production setups. 'Interstitial' filmmakers – for instance, Chantal Akerman, Amir Naderi and Elia Suleiman – seek 'additional financing from a range of public and private sources', in order to support formal and informal collaborative practices (2001: 46–8). I should stress that the term interstitial, as applied by Naficy, concerns contemporary filmmaking practices commonly placed in exilic and diasporic contexts. I argue, however, that this term is also particularly apt to accommodate a constellation of different filmmaking practices which rely on low budgets and on the use of digital video.

I offer here a context to this interstitial digital filmmaking paradigm, as well as its production and discursive relational dichotomies. By adopting this medium to shoot his films, and benefiting from the low cost of its use, Costa was able to negotiate between artisanal processes and industrial formations. The former characteristic is particularly patent in the intertwinement between production and aesthetics made possible with the use of such technology. Filmic deceleration and an observational style came to be two main characteristics in Costa's *oeuvre*. I consider, therefore, how these aesthetic tropes come to be formulated within the possibilities and constraints of digital video. This analysis of the interstitial quality of Costa's work needs also to consider the production and financing procedures supporting the making of *In Vanda's Room*. Thus questions arise as to how this film, while shot using an artisanal framework still, nonetheless participates in normative mechanisms of European art cinema.

'NOT CINEMA?': DIGITAL VIDEO AS A FILMMAKING PARADIGM

Pedro Costa claims that *In Vanda's Room* did not rely on 'methods and processes normally used in the making of a "cinema film"' (Oliveira 2000: 27; quotation marks as in the original). Such a notion put forward by Costa came to animate some of the discussions around the film at the time of its domestic release, in March 2001. Film critic João Miguel Tavares, for instance, suggested that 'Pedro Costa does not like the words "action" and "cut" anymore [but] still likes cinema' (2001: 42; quotation marks as in the original). João Bénard da Costa, on the other hand, enquired as to the impact that the use of digital video created in the film's aesthetic, understood as somehow between the observational and the fabricated (2001: 56). These observations only partially address the ambiguous contours of the production blueprint adopted by Costa. The making of this feature film is seen as a detachment from normative methods and processes usually observed in contemporary art film. Such understanding is extended to other works circulating in the art-house circuit at the time. Among others, films such as *Festen* (*The Celebration*, dir. Thomas Vinterberg, 1998), *Sud* (*South*, dir. Chantal Akerman, 1999), and *Les glaneurs et la glaneuse* (*The gleaners and I*, dir. Agnès Varda, 2000) have been framed in similar terms. These are examples of a possible filmmaking paradigm freed from technical and financial constraints. Like *In Vanda's Room*, however, these films still rely on a network of financial, production and circulation institutions shaping the European art film.

More broadly, the use of digital video in contemporary global art cinema has elicited several discussions about artistic freedom, as well as on the renewing possibilities of filmmaking placed outside industrial norms. Examples of these discussions are presented by Geoff King (2014) to address the intricate impact of this technology on contemporary American independent filmmaking. Chris Berry et al. (2010) and Luke Robinson (2013) offer a similar analysis when examining the use of digital video in contemporary underground Chinese film. May Adadol Ingawanij and Benjamin McKay (2012) discuss comparable technological inflections in different film practitioners in Southeast Asia, often at odds with their national cinema industries. These scholarly discussions look into distinct film production contexts. Nonetheless, these express similar dichotomised characteristics, negotiating between 'individual' and 'professional' agency, and between independent 'artisanal practices' and 'negotiated dependencies' (see, respectively, Robinson 2013: 21–2; Ingawanij and McKay 2012: 4). Such relational characteristics underlie an understanding of recent digital filmmaking practices deviating (to varying degrees) from mainstream production practices and normative divisions of labour. This is more the case considering that digital filmmaking relies on similar discursive formations that once animated discussions around celluloid film formats. Implicit in these discussions is a revitalisation of particular discourses concerning artistic freedom and independence from production and financial processes. As Chris Darke notes, the use of digital video by Chantal Akerman, Agnès Varda or Chris Petit – European filmmakers who like Costa made the 'transition' from film to digital video – can be understood as 'a continuation of a tradition' once observed in different configurations of 'independent and avant-garde cinema' (Darke 2001: 47).

Similar dichotomies can be observed when considering Costa's filmmaking from *In Vanda's Room* onwards. Costa maintains a professional agency sustained by pared-down and informal practices. As already mentioned, however, such filmmaking is still supported by (or dependent on) international art cinema institutions. Costa's digital filmmaking gains further nuanced qualities when considering the ambiguous production and circulation contexts of Portuguese film. As Jacques Lemière characterises it, this national cinema is sustained by the practices of 'artists-filmmakers of a small country, without a cinema industry, that resists [commercial values] while submitting to the European film production and work practices' (2006: 731). Both historically and in contemporary terms, this lack of reliable domestic infrastructures compelled film professionals to adopt an ambivalent position towards production and consumption: creative independence while dependent on national and international funding; small-scale domestic production models combined with resources offered by European co-production partnerships. This positioning is also noted in terms of film exhibition and circulation. With reduced exhibition and artistic recognition at home, Portuguese filmmakers are dependent on the international circulation offered by the film festival circuits and the cultural legitimation that comes with it (see Liz 2018a: 4–5).

In this context the expression 'artisanal' gains multifaceted meanings. The term applies to the poor infrastructural conditions of this national cinema, but also to define filmmaking practices conveying creative independence and skilful professional attitude. This attitude is more often than not at odds – professionally and in discursive terms – with industrial and commercial formations (see Graça 2016: 94). Historically, this artisanal ethos was manifested in the 'humble' work of António Reis and Margarida Cordeiro, or in the 'militant dissidence' maintained by some filmmakers commonly categorised under the so-called 'Portuguese School' (Baptista 2010: 12; Grilo 2006: 37ff.). This artisanal approach assumes a position at the interstices in which creative independence is made possible by small-scale production models relying on a co-dependence of national and international public funding. In contemporary terms, the possibilities offered by digital video give further expression to this interstitial position. As Daniel Ribas points out, digital video became part of a Portuguese film 'production paradigm' which helped to ease costs and provide access to an alternative filmic apparatus; something that, in turn, led to an increasing visibility of filmic formats such as short film and documentary (2009: 95). The adoption of digital video somehow minimises the industrial and budgetary restrictions which characterise this national cinema. Yet it also creates further awareness of the permanent infrastructural deficiencies which limit Portuguese newcomers and, in some cases, established filmmakers. These conditions were further aggravated with the disinvestment in cinema support during the economic recession of the 2010s (see Liz 2018a: 4).[1]

Costa's digital filmmaking practice reflects these domestic and international small-scale production models that mediate between independence and co-dependence. As Costa argues, however, his adoption of digital video was not tied to a lack of professional resources so much as to the need to use an alternative setup to unsatisfactory production routines and the heavy filmic apparatus that had been used for his previous films. As Costa explains:

> You don't need the big bucks and the big trucks to make a film. [. . .] Stay a bit longer in a place. Stay with the person you are filming a bit longer, and refuse the kind of military raid which cinema has transformed itself into: coming to a location, conquering it, shooting it and then running away – that's how a film crew operates nowadays. (Guarneri 2015a)

The narrative of production offered by Costa also reveals a preoccupation with establishing a more protracted relationship with his collaborators. As Costa himself has noted on several occasions, digital technology allowed him to have the 'luxury of time' (see, for example, Corless 2009: 30; Paradelo and Arias 2012). This narrative of production privileges a slow working process characterised by unscheduled and improvised location shooting. Such a protracted process is, accordingly, free from constraints in terms of the amount of material recorded. These different possibilities are reflected in Costa's film aesthetics.

A DIGITAL AESTHETIC OF SLOWNESS

The possibilities offered to Costa by the use of digital video facilitated a further exploration of aesthetic preoccupations which were already manifested in *Casa de Lava* and *Bones*. This is clear when considering the rapport between documentary and fiction. The technical and non-intrusive quality of digital video, as Darke points out, allows film practitioners to create low-budget works of a 'more personal and subjective' nature, and to explore 'new permutations' between fictionalised and documental modes (2001: 47). In aesthetic terms, the less intrusive nature of the digital video camera came to augment Costa's flexible approach to a documental filmic style initially explored in the fictionalised narratives of his previous works.

As Nicholas Rombes reminds us, digital video has enabled (hypothetically, at least) a 'one-to-one correspondence between real time and represented time' (2009: 25). It facilitates recording during lengthier periods of time (when compared with the length of film reels), while avoiding the costs inherent in the use of photochemical film stock. This is reflected in the increase of visibility of a digital art cinema in which 'duration and observation' became central stylistic tropes (de Luca and Jorge 2016: 10–11). A significant body of filmic works, such as the ones directed by Wang Bing, James Benning, Jia Zhangke, Apichatpong Weerasethakul or Lav Diaz, are characterised by the deployment of long shots, minimalism and narrative deceleration. Understandably, not all forms of aesthetic slowness in contemporary art cinema spring from recording processes made possible by the use of digital video. I argue, however, that such contemporary filmic slowness can be understood not only as an aesthetic trope but also as a mode of digital filmmaking practice.

This is particularly evident when considering the work of Pedro Costa. As Àngel Quintana suggests, the 'stylised' and 'static' aesthetic nature of Costa's cinema presents a depiction of the real onto which 'the digital [. . .] bestow[s] a new plasticity', defined by an undramatic and unflinching style which attests to the filmmaker's 'clear personal involvement' (2009: 24–5). Volker Pantenburg goes further in defining the links between digital technology, aesthetics and creative agency. According to Pantenburg, Costa's 'digital realism' can be characterised as:

> (1) explicitly bound to an intimate and collective production process that guarantees a proximity and forms of collaboration that would not be conceivable without a small camera and practically unlimited stock. [. . .] (2) [In] Costa's Fontainhas films the ontological doubt that has infested discussions about the potential manipulations of digital images does not really carry weight; it is more than compensated for by the testimonial powers of the lens and the optical apparatus. [. . .] (3) The time that [Costa's films] depict does not follow narrative concerns. The fixed shots tend to sink in and persist, not flow. [. . .] (4) [R]ealism is a temporal form of experience that needs a certain extension in time. This realism relies on duration and patient observation, on the side of the director as well as on that of the spectator. (Pantenburg 2010: 60)

Pantenburg's formulation is particularly apt to define such a cogent aesthetic informed by the intersection between the technological and collaborative practices emerging from the shooting process. It can be noted that Costa's approach to digital video relies on his previously acquired technical know-how with relation to the use of film stock. His works since the early 2000s are largely informed by the aesthetic and technical qualities of such a medium to explore the potentialities offered by the digital. Moreover, and as further discussed in the next chapter, Pantenburg's notion of 'digital realism' is not limited to practices situated in the shooting process, but it also takes shape at the level of reception.

This digital realism also takes into account the informality of the filmmaking practices used in Fontainhas. *In Vanda's Room* is not just Costa's initiation into digital video, but also his first work relying exclusively on a cast of non-professional actors. The film depicts the routines of a group of residents living at Fontainhas at the end of the 1990s, and their adaptation to the ongoing process of the neighbourhood's demolition. As the title of the film indicates, Vanda Duarte's small room (which she shares with her two sisters, one of whom was in prison during the shooting of the film) functions as the visual and thematic epicentre of the film. The film is structured mostly on Duarte's everyday life and interactions with her close family and friends, either passing through or visiting her dwellings. Numerous scenes also depict her drug consumption routines carried on in her room, either alone or with her sister, Zita Duarte.

The routines taking place in Vanda's house are intertwined with other moments depicting the neighbourhood. From these moments two main thematic groups emerge. The first one depicts the routines of a group of young men who circulate around the neighbourhood, some of whom are Duarte's childhood friends. These men occupy empty houses soon to be demolished, looking for temporary living spaces as well as privacy to shoot heroin. These scenes offer a thematic contrast with the ones taking place in Duarte's home. As Costa discloses in conversation with Cyril Neyrat, these two groups of scenes represent the almost complete division between the world of the 'girls' and the world of the 'boys' in the neighbourhood – the former more expressively 'theatrical', the latter more introspective and 'filmic' (Costa et al. 2012: 52–3). Complementing these two groups of scenes, which are mostly filmed in interior locations, another group of scenes included in *In Vanda's Room* documents the streets of Fontainhas. These scenes bring into full view the neighbourhood's daily routines: the preparation of the communal spaces, the drug addicts' incessant activities, children playing in the streets, Vanda Duarte wandering through the neighbourhood selling vegetables. All these different groups of scenes become merged through the visual and audible perception of the ongoing demolition works.

Even given the complementary nature of these different scenes, *In Vanda's Room* is largely devoid of any continuous and linear narrative. The film montage gives primacy, instead, to small episodic narratives. These episodes emerge from scenes of an observational nature, mostly composed by fixed long takes and with little movement. This observational mode prompts questions about documentary conventions. Documentary is commonly associated with authenticity. As Elizabeth Cowie argues, such quality aims to manifest a portrait of reality in a 'scientific and rational' format while, simultaneously, approaching the real 'not as knowledge but as image, as spectacle' (1999: 19). This tense relation between presentation and re-presentation emerges when attempting to define the stylised nature of Costa's cinema. Jonathan Romney, for example, characterises *In Vanda's Room* as an 'engrossing but gruellingly unadorned *semi-documentary*' (2008: 46; italics added). James Quandt, however, calls attention to the film's lack of documentary conventional factuality, pointing out that 'Costa is clearly uninterested in any kind of documentary "look" as a fake signifier of authenticity' (2006: 357; quotation marks as in the original). Suggesting a similar reading on the negotiations between filmic presentation and re-presentation in Costa's cinema, Ira Jaffe argues that 'Costa's way with light, colour, texture and composition transforms' the 'deprived and unglamorous' Fontainhas into a setting where stylistic artifice offers a rapport between 'aesthetic richness and physical decrepitude' (2014: 125). Jaffe's argument echoes Jacques Rancière's reading of the stylised ambiguity conveyed by *In Vanda's Room* and subsequent films directed by Costa. As Rancière asserts, Costa 'seems to seize every opportunity to dwell on the décor of the shanty-town undergoing demolition' (2014: 129; see also Rancière 2009b).

This stylistic tension between fiction and documentary can be further contextualised if we consider the changes operated by digital video on Costa's authorial and directorial practices. *In Vanda's Room* transmits an approach to a location and a group of collaborators differing from the production routines and filmic apparatus used in *Bones*. As Costa explains in conversation with Cyril Neyrat, his films shot in digital video do not concern 'characters'; instead his approach is more based on 'the person' in front of the camera and the 'reinterpretation' of his or her life – a process which redefines the imposed distance between him and the non-professional collaborator (Costa et al. 2012: 82). As Costa explains in another interview:

> the actors in my films are not professionals, so they move differently. I'm not saying they are closer to real life or that they are naturalistic. But I have to respect their rhythms. Some guys are slow and they speak slowly, and I tend to see if they go together and let it happen more or less. Then there's my rhythm that's constructed, and I have to think about that a lot, mainly when I'm editing the film. [. . .] I let the words come from the actors and don't impose my thing. I bring less imagination into the [shot] and let her or his imagination [give] the tone, the rhythm of the film. (Oumano 2010: 87–8)

This observational quality establishes a rapport between the informality recorded by the camera and Costa's authorial control. The artistic exchanges expressed above can surely be understood as exceptional, as these do not adhere to strict professional procedures. It is clear, however, that the digital video camera is not just a possible channel between the reality observed and the spectator. Costa's professional agency is central in organising both the shooting process and the recorded material originating from it.

The shooting of the film was dependent on Costa's process of discovery and experimentation in adapting to the potentialities and pitfalls of digital video. The camera used by Costa, a Panasonic DX100, inevitably provides specific visual qualities related to the depth of field, image density, and the brightness and saturation of colour. The 'green and blurred' colour-processing of this camera, as Costa points out to me, visually matches the green and 'tatty' colours of Fontainhas (Costa 2012). These visual characteristics significantly inform the cinematography of the film (also credited to Costa), which relies on the predominant use of key-light sourced from small windows or from domestic lights – a technical process initially explored by Costa and Emmanuel Machuel during the shooting of *Bones*. The camerawork techniques used during the shooting of the film reflect similar concerns with the constraints imposed by the equipment. One of the central stylistic tropes in the film is the extended long take, registered without any camera movement. As Costa explains during an interview with the magazine *Sight & Sound* in 2009, *In Vanda's Room* was shot with 'exactly the same gentleness and care and precision' as when filming in 35mm, and this is so even if Costa was aware of the lightness and flexibility of the digital video camera (Corless 2009: 30). Furthermore, Costa resourcefully explores the constricted possibilities of shooting in cramped spaces with no camera movement – the most perceptible example being the confined room inhabited by the Duarte sisters. The fixed shots that compose all the scenes in the film were a way of not contradicting the reality of the images depicted, leaving undisturbed the movement taking place in front of the camera. These procedures transmit the sense of aesthetic stillness whereby the actions of the residents of Fontainhas are patiently recorded. Costa often points out Yasujirō Ozu's influence in the *mise en scène* of the film, but also acknowledges that this technique was adopted because of spatial and budget constraints (Costa et al. 2012: 83).

From this working process emerge carefully crafted minimal compositions which recall the tonality and composition of a painted still life. Considering the image definition offered by digital video these prolonged and stationary shots may also allow avoiding pixellation caused by moving the camera. While privileging stillness, however, these compositions are still animated by the unstable pixel nature of digital video. This dialogue between different media once again calls our attention to Costa's professional background in film. As Thom Andersen observes, *In Vanda's Room* presents digital video as 'cinema', smoothing the once-marked differences between film and video aesthetics

(2010: 248). More than just a practice negotiating between technology and aesthetics, however, Costa's digital realism is also a result of an attentive observation of a particular setting made possible by a protracted shooting process.

RECORDING THE EVERYDAY

This dialogue between aesthetics and technology can be further extended to the ways in which Costa opted to shoot *In Vanda's Room*. The procedures used in the film deeply contrast with the professional division of labour and work routines previously used in *Bones*. As Neyrat describes it:

> [*Bones*] was a traditional production, shot in 35 mm, with tracks, floodlights, and assistants. Costa was a professional, a part of the Portuguese film industry. The shoot proceeded with everyone doing his job, following the routine of European art film. (Neyrat 2010: 11)

The shooting process of *In Vanda's Room* dispensed with such traditional logistic and technical paraphernalia. Costa explains that he used a reduced shooting setup, comprising mostly a digital camera, a tripod and a microphone (APORDOC 2002: 79–80). Moreover, the filmmaker reformulated his professional agency as a director, and aimed at working without time budgets and recording constraints. The initial shooting process of the film was largely based on a repetitious and laborious daily routine, carried on for an estimated period of almost two years. This protracted shooting process stands in stark contrast to the timescale under which Costa first filmed in this community. As explained in the previous chapter, *Bones* was shot during a period of approximately six weeks, a timescale that did not allow building any substantial personal and professional links with the local residents. As Costa confided to me, it was only after an extended stay in Fontainhas that he was able to create and gradually strengthen a prolonged and close rapport with a cast of non-professional actors who, in his words, would become his 'extended family' (2012).

Unconcerned with any professional schedules, the shooting of *In Vanda's Room* was mostly conditioned by the everyday routines of the non-professional actors who participated in the film. Costa gives an account of this shooting routine in the documentary *Tout refleurit: Pedro Costa, cinéaste* (*All Blossoms Again: Pedro Costa, Director*, dir. Aurélien Gerbault, 2006). In one scene of the documentary, shot in an open field where Vanda's house once stood, Costa explains his daily routine:

> I would take the No. 58 bus. I'd come in [through] one of the entrances to the Fontainhas neighbourhood. [. . .] In the morning there were two bars [open] [. . .]. I'd have some coffee. I'd come back through there . . .

to Vanda's house . . . Vanda and Zita would be asleep. Knock knock. No answer. I go inside. [. . .] I'd set up my things [. . .]. And if [Vanda] woke up, I'd film a bit of what took place. If she didn't wake up, I'd take the camera . . . and go out . . . [. . .] I'd go to Pango's house, who lived over there, with someone else called Paulo who had crutches. [T]hen I'd go that way . . . out in the middle [of Fontainhas]. I'd simply wait there with my camera. I'd film. Someone would come speak to me. [Later] I'd go back to the girls' house.[2]

This rapport between the residents' own rhythms and Costa's shooting routine gave rise to the different groups of scenes already discussed. In the description provided above it is also perceptible that the film was shot without any script or prior planning.

Costa was able to shoot this material mostly by himself, only occasionally relying on a small number of film professionals (Peranson 2010: 140). One of these professional collaborators was the sound engineer Philippe Morel, who would join the production team intermittently during breaks from other film productions (see Costa et al. 2012: 104). Another professional supporting Costa at Fontainhas was filmmaker Cláudia Tomaz. At the time, Tomaz was researching the possibilities of digital video, which she soon after used in her first feature film, *Nights* (2001). As Tomaz recalls in a personal communication, Costa would spend most of the time inside Vanda Duarte's room or household; however, and 'depending on what was happening in people's lives or in the neighbourhood' elsewhere, other activities would be incorporated into this daily shooting routine: 'a demolition, men playing cards, someone making lunch or someone waiting for an ambulance . . . ' (Tomaz 2013). These events can be categorised under the rubric of the everyday actions. Yet these events took place within the context of harsh lifestyles and the numerous issues faced by the non-professional participants. As Tomaz elaborates:

> the conditions were physically and humanly difficult, it was cold, people lived in extreme poverty, some people were becoming homeless and displaced, there was the drugs routine . . . [. . .] We had to keep up with it all and try to film it on a daily basis the best we could, sometimes it was challenging to be just an observer/filmmaker. (Tomaz 2013)

These observations provide evidence regarding the overlapping between professional and personal involvement taking place during the shooting of the film. This calls our attention, once again, to the ambiguous mixture between observational and stylistic artifice conveyed in *In Vanda's Room*. Costa's digital realism accounts for an observation placed at the interstices of professional and personal relationships. The non-intrusive nature of the digital video camera used is patent in the film. Yet, and as Thom Andersen argues, there is also a perceivable 'close mutual respect and friendship between Costa and the people he filmed' (2010: 247).

While seemingly observational, however, the film's intimate quality transcends the mere observation of spontaneous moments. As Costa explained to me, his directorial supervision also consisted in insistently re-enacting particular scenes and, occasionally, adding small props in the *mise en scène* to enhance the episodic narratives depicted in the film (2012). Some of the scenes shot in Duarte's room, for instance, were not simply recorded by the camera as they happened. On some occasions, the actors staged them to recreate particular occurrences, either witnessed by Costa or told to him. An example of these recreated scenes depicts Vanda and Zita Duarte speaking about their childhood memories of Fontainhas, offering a bittersweet recollection of the environment before drug-trafficking activities overtook the neighbourhood. Another instance of such re-enactment of memories is the evocative scene in which Vanda Duarte and Pedro Lanban share reminiscences of a deceased friend. Costa explains in a conversation with Cyril Neyrat that this scene was recreated several times, spanning an interval of six months between the first and the last take (Costa et al. 2012: 65–7). The staging of these fragmented memories gives an interstitial tone to *In Vanda's Room*. Though informed by stylistic artifice, the film nonetheless manages to capture the realities dormant in these members of a community which, in itself, was also increasingly interstitial. At the time, the inhabitants of Fontainhas were placed between the gradual demolition of the neighbourhood and their relocation to new estates outside Lisbon's periphery.

PRODUCING AT THE INTERSTICES

The above discussion makes clear that the shooting of *In Vanda's Room* had artisanal contours, proficiently supported by a digital video and by an intertwinement between individual and collective creative agency. As Emmanuel Burdeau contends, the use of digital video under such conditions enables an aesthetic 'desacralisation' of cinema (1999: 62). This desacralisation, I should point out, also concerns professional and financial processes. As Costa remarks, *In Vanda's Room* 'is a film that started with zero and ended with everything paid', including both its production and post-production processes (2012). It is not clear in Burdeau's article for *Cahiers du Cinéma*, however, how the results of this filmmaking practice are reflected in the post-shooting of *In Vanda's Room*. Similarly, the qualities of Costa's digital realism that are cogently argued by Volker Pantenburg seem to preclude any financial aspects of such practice.

The non-professional characteristics which supported the shooting of the film reveal economically unaccounted informal practices that illustrate 'below the waterline' transactions in capitalist production (see, for example, Gibson-Graham 2006: 69–71). The film results also, however, from practices which are still tied to European art cinema financial, production and post-production processes. As the producer of the film, Francisco Villa-Lobos, pointed out to me, Costa's discourse on self-sufficiency and non-professional collaborative practices should be taken into consideration. Yet, as Villa-Lobos also notes, *In Vanda's Room* relied on 'paid professionals' and depended heavily on normative financial and post-production processes that could not have been 'sustained by personal relations alone' (2013). While Costa enjoyed a generous creative leeway, the production of the film was still dependent on particular professional procedures. The producer pointed out to me that, for instance, Costa elaborated an initial script treatment. This document was never used during the shooting but was important for sparking interest in the project among Portuguese and international financiers (Villa-Lobos 2013; see also Robert 2001: 90). Villa-Lobos, moreover, asserts that the shooting process of the film was only made possible after receiving initial funding support (2013).

These procedures illustrate the interstitial production qualities of *In Vanda's Room*. The film mediates between informal shooting routines and production formalities. The making of the film reflects the arrangements of late 1990s and early 2000s European art cinema co-production models. This model is sustained by the 'convergent' interests of a complex network of 'variegated film industries' constituted by small-scale production units and by pan-European, national and regional public institutions and funding initiatives (Jäckel 2003: 25). This network operates under what Thomas Elsaesser designates as a 'European post-Fordism': 'small-scale production units, cooperating with television as well as commercial partners, and made up of creative teams around a producer and a director' (2005: 69). The production of *In Vanda's Room* relies on these convergent financial and production formations. The funding process of the film took into consideration particular technical tasks, negotiated individually by the film producer with the different European funding partners. This support then allocated resources to particular production and post-production processes.

As with Costa's previous works, *In Vanda's Room* was financially supported by the ICAM (the Portuguese institution which succeeded the IPC in 1997) as well as by different institutions and producers from Germany, Switzerland and Italy. The initial funding was provided by ICAM in 1997, via a funding programme dedicated exclusively to documentary productions. Once again, Villa-Lobos's explanations shed light on the financial process of the film. As the producer points out, this initial amount would be topped up later with more funding from the same institution, making the equivalent of approximately €50,000 (2013). With this funding covering part of the shooting process, Villa-Lobos negotiated other sources of financing that could support further stages of production. Later funding was provided in 1998 by the German television channel ZDF, under the financing scheme of the programme *Das Kleine Fernsehspiel* (DKF, henceforth).³ According to ZDF producer Jörg Schneider, the low-budget characteristics of the project were in accordance with the ethos of the programme. DKF contributed 100,000 DM (approximately €50,000). This amount was, according to Schneider, the 'usual budget for international co-productions', and in exchange ZDF retained exhibition rights on the film for eight years (2013).

The convergent interests of these different financial partners in the project are also reflected in the image and sound post-production stages of *In Vanda's Room*. The post-production team had to solve some of the deficiencies of the digital video image and sound. As the film editor, Patrícia Saramago, explained to me, the post-production process highlighted the careful filmic artistry which characterises Costa's work by enhancing 'the formal image and sound' aspect of the film and minimising the deficiencies inherent in the technology used during its shooting (2013). Details of the intricacies of this process are provided by Costa in conversation with Jean-Pierre Gorin (included in the audio commentary in the 2010 Criterion Collection DVD edition of the film). During this conversation, Costa provides details on how sound deficiencies were resolved, explaining the post-synchronisation of particular scenes made by Vanda and Zita Duarte; he also describes the role of sound editor Waldir Xavier, whose personal sound archive was used to enhance the aural perception of the ongoing demolition process (Costa and Gorin 2010). In this conversation Costa also offers details on the cataloguing and editing of the abundant material recorded. According to the filmmaker, this material totalled approximately 140 hours. (Patrícia Saramago thought differently and indicated to me that the material looked at comprised approximately 200 hours.)

These activities resulted in a labour-intensive process of post-production, which had to be covered in both financial and technical terms. This process was partially financed by arrangements between Contracosta and producer Karl Baumgartner (Pandora Films). Baumgartner initially provided the Avid editing system, used to edit *In Vanda's Room* in Lisbon. Subsequently, Pandora Films also supported the sound editing and mixing of the film. This stage of the post-production was completed at the Konken Studios (Hamburg) and supported with German regional funding made available to Baumgartner (Villa-Lobos 2013). In a similar way, the colour correction and conversion to 35mm film exhibition format of the film was financed by the Swiss/Italian production company Ventura Film SA, and produced by the Zurich-based company Swiss Effects. Convergent interests, once again, were key in these post-production processes. As Villa-Lobos disclosed to me, some of these arrangements had the direct endorsement of Marco Müller – at the time artistic director of the Locarno International Film Festival, where *In Vanda's Room* was about to premiere – something which further stimulated the participation of these different financial and technical collaborators (2013).

These intricacies of the post-production technical and financial processes of *In Vanda's Room* provide further clues to the nature of low-budget digital video filmmaking practices. It can be observed, for example, that there is an emphasis on technical, financial and time-allocation tasks to cover different stages of post-production. This process took approximately nine months – a period which, as Saramago notes, was substantially longer than the '2 or 3 months' commonly allocated to other film productions (2013). Moreover, Costa's digital filmmaking came to be supported by more variegated funding sources. This is particularly so when comparing *In Vanda's Room* with Costa's previous films produced by Paulo Branco, *Casa de Lava* and *Bones*. The partnerships supporting these different stages of the production and post-production of the film illustrate the financial dynamics shaping contemporary art cinema during the 2000s. As Villa-Lobos explains:

> participating with small amounts of money in a film [was] many times more interesting than [investing] large amounts. It's less risky and, at the time, it was particularly easy to find that money. [The amount invested by Karl Baumgartner in *In Vanda's Room*] for example was a very small portion of what he had available for the whole of his projects. (Villa-Lobos 2013)

These funding dynamics also reflect the transnational framework of different public and private institutions which support Portuguese cinema. At the time of *In Vanda's Room* domestic release Villa-Lobos stated to Portuguese journalists that, from a budget of approximately €450,000, only 25 per cent came from Portuguese institutions and partners (Martins 2001: 9). Villa-Lobos's statement clearly expresses the lack of financial support faced by this national cinema. It also may constitute a retort to the constant derision expressed by Portuguese right-wing intellectuals, who insistently accused filmmakers – Costa in particular – of wasting public funds on films which are 'unappealing' to domestic audiences and that 'ruin the country's image abroad' (Baptista 2010: 16–17). More relevant to the discussion here, these financial dynamics also account for the way in which Costa's digital filmmaking practices managed to adapt to the variegated nature of the European co-production model. The interstitial production of *In Vanda's Room* fits the financial options offer by different public and private sector producers operating under a constellation of pan-European, national and regional initiatives. The different stages in the making of the film show how artistic practices and industrial formations are intertwined within a low-budget economic model made possible by the use of digital video.

It can be suggested that Costa's digital filmmaking does not only rely on aesthetic formulations but is also the result of interactions between modes of production and the available technology. The depiction of Fontainhas and its inhabitants in the film was achieved through a laborious and protracted shooting, and made possible by the re-formulation of professional roles under personal and collaborative practices. Digital video allowed the freedom to maintain this artisanal shooting process. But the constraints of this technology also become apparent when looking into the post-production processes of *In Vanda's Room*. The emphasis placed on different post-production tasks, as well as on its international financial backing, reveals a filmmaking which increasingly relies on back-end technological procedures. These different technical and financial aspects in Costa's digital filmmaking tend to be obfuscated by a narrative of production around his films. Notions of artistic freedom and non-compliance with formal aspects of filmmaking are commonly transmitted in film-specialised literature and conveyed in numerous interviews by Costa himself. Public knowledge about Costa's filmmaking practices is predominantly tied to discourses of artistic authenticity and stoical filmmaking. These notions are surely pertinent. More than informative, however, these notions also serve as a symbolic currency that informs the reception of his films.

NOTES

1. A first-hand reflection on the situation lived by Portuguese filmmakers in this period is offered in *Ó Marquês, anda cá abaixo outra vez!* (*The 'M' of Portuguese Cinema*, dir. João Viana, 2012). In this documentary, twenty Portuguese filmmakers pertinently question the disinvestment in Portuguese film production incentives at a time when this national cinema had a considerable increase in international exposure and critical acclaim.
2. This citation uses the English subtitles of the documentary, which were included in the extras of the 2010 Criterion boxset *Letters from Fontainhas*.
3. Since its creation in 1963, *Das Kleine Fernsehspiel* ('the little teleplay') has been a successful development workshop supporting low-budget fictional and documentary works. The programme has supported directors such as Rainer Werner Fassbinder, Jim Jarmusch, Theo Angelopoulos and Agnès Varda. More recently it supported the initial works of internationally critically acclaimed German filmmakers including Christian Petzold, Fatih Akin and Angela Schanelec, among others. Concerning the role of the DKF in European art cinema, see Grieb and Lehman (2007: 84).

CHAPTER 4

Critical Reception and the International Film Festival

The response to *Juventude em Marcha* (*Colossal Youth*, 2006) at the 59th Cannes Film Festival is indicative of the divided reception the films directed by Pedro Costa have received over the years. Included in the festival's main competition section, the premiere of the film was marked by a steady stream of film critics leaving the screening room and was followed by some derisive accounts (see, for example, Ebert 2006). Such reactions, however, also drew passionate praise from Costa's burgeoning fan-base, whose vocal defence of the film helped to convert contempt into valued cultural currency. These walkouts, Kieron Corless asserts, were 'not dissimilar' to the reception accorded four decades earlier by Cannes audiences to Michelangelo Antonioni's now critically canonised *L'avventura* (1960); this was taken as a sign of potential 'masterpiece' status for *Colossal Youth* by Costa's fans, the film critic suggests (2008: 12).

This contentious critical reception illustrates how different forms of value are discussed within sanctioned film institutions such as the film festival circuit. The presence of Costa's cinema in this international arena allows the possibility of its exhibition and subsequent distribution. Participation in this circuit provides a 'global exposure' that, while no substitute for theatrical 'distribution', nonetheless provides a 'value-added aspect of flow' that cannot be ignored by film professionals outside international mainstream distribution (Iordanova 2009: 24–5). This participation, moreover, also creates conditions for Costa's inclusion in 'world film knowledge', which potentiates artistic recognition and consecration (Wong 2011: 14–15). The discussion of these different forms of value, as argued here, is dependent on the interactions between different agents who inhabit the film festival – film professionals, programmers, audience members, film critics, representatives of diverse cultural industries, film scholars (see, for example, de Valck 2007: 32–3). While only some of these agents may serve as direct gatekeepers to potential economic transactions, most of them participate, in subtle ways, in the discussion of nonmonetary value which sustains discursive formations around prestige and taste.

Accordingly, this nonmonetary value is the main currency of the 'economy of prestige', to borrow a Bourdieu-informed term coined by James F. English. Film festivals function as economies of prestige, being circuits that accommodate broad notions of value 'to include systems of nonmonetary, cultural, and symbolic transaction' (English 2005: 4). Costa's work prompts a range of responses from the specialised press and scholarly contexts which, inevitably, trade on different forms of value. These responses reflect the values at stake when considering the economy of prestige around contemporary art cinema. As already hinted, Costa's reception is not uniform and, therefore, is subjected to dynamic and ambiguous transactions of symbolic value. Central to these negotiations are the ways in which critical reception deploys forms of categorisation to define and discuss such a body of work. This is particularly evident when analysing the feature film *Colossal Youth*, but also the documentary *Danièle Huillet/Jean-Marie Straub: Où gît votre sourire enfoui?* (*Where Does Your Hidden Smile Lie?*, 2001). The reception of these two works directed by Costa reveals how subsumption into particular stylistic categories and taste formations is mobilised by different agents to generate and condition attribution of symbolic value.

Different *strata* can be considered when explaining the attribution of symbolic value to these two works. The first is the critical reception of Costa's cinema taking shape at the film festival. The reception of *Colossal Youth* in this setting reveals forms of symbolic value that, while contested, nonetheless offer a form of classification. Such classification can be addressed in more detail by, secondly, considering how discursive formations position Costa's cinema under particular filmic taxonomies. Both film critics and scholars commonly draw on relational readings to either approximate Costa's work to film lineages such as the modernist 'difficult art film', or to include it under contemporary descriptors such as 'Slow Cinema'. The inclusion in such taxonomies organises critical responses which reflect taste formations informing contemporary art cinema.

This inclusion, however, only partially addresses the different forms of capital transacted at the international film festival. A look at the relationships between the roles of filmmakers, producers and distribution networks operating in this field of cultural production brings forward readings that are distinct from those resulting from the enclosed discourses in film criticism and academia. Here I also examine, therefore, intertwinements between nonmonetary and monetary currencies informing Costa's cinema. This ambivalence between different currencies is particularly noted when considering the participation of the Portuguese filmmaker in the Jeonju Digital Project, a funding and programming initiative organised by the South Korean Jeonju International Film Festival. The cinema of Pedro Costa, and the currency it comes to embody, illustrates some of the mechanisms operated by the prestige-based economy of contemporary art cinema.

VALUE FORMATION AT THE FILM FESTIVAL

The film festival circuit has provided Costa with an incremental form of international exposure, both in terms of exhibition and circulation and in his artistic recognition. Costa has maintained a constant presence on what Marijke de Valck calls a two-tier circuit, with his works being premiered at major festivals and subsequently circulating through a 'series of medium- and smaller-sized' festivals (2007: 106). Costa's work can be understood as native to this exhibition and circulation arena; *Blood* and *Bones* premiered at Venice in 1989 and 1997, *Casa de Lava* and *Colossal Youth* at Cannes in 1994 and 2006, and *In Vanda's Room* and *Horse Money* at Locarno in 2000 and 2014 respectively. All these films subsequently circulated through the festival network during a period of about a year, providing exposure which substantially complements, albeit without resolving, their limited international commercial release.

More than just assuring international circulation, however, this steady inclusion in the film festival also signals Costa's active participation in the economics maintained by this all-year-round network. Understandably, inclusion of particular films in the film festival is dependent on decisions at an institutional level. This is clearly exemplified by a myriad of programming choices that respond to the dynamics of a highly competitive circuit operating through economic and noneconomic value transactions (see, for example, Elsaesser 2005: 72; Stringer 2001: 134). Inclusion in this circuit grants Costa some form of relevance, potentiating a value conferred through the critical scrutiny of his films. This scrutiny reveals itself through operations such as discussion, comparison and subsumption into (existing or new) stylistic, thematic and geographic lineages. These operations are contingent to the agency of the different participants, equipped to award artistic consecration and establish the formation of taste through their professional and personal capabilities. This agency is dependent on the 'will to transform or conserve' practices of classification, as well as on the agents' 'capacity to produce classifiable practices and works, and the capacity to differentiate and appreciate these practices and products' (Bourdieu 2010: 165–6; see also Bourdieu 1980: 278). As literary critic Barbara Herrnstein Smith argues, however, cultural arenas are communities in which 'the tastes and preferences of subjects will sometimes be conspicuously divergent or indeed idiosyncratic'

(1991: 39). Negotiations of prestige taking place at the film festival acquire a complicated expression. The variegated discursive formations operated within this cultural arena result in a dynamic dialogue between divergence and convergence which, in turn, potentiates forms of symbolic capital.

The reception of *Colossal Youth* at the 2006 Cannes International Film Festival illustrates this dynamism. The walkouts from the screening of the film indicate that Costa's work, as film critic Dennis Lim understands it, is not 'uniformly loved by world-cinema tastemakers' (Lim 2007). James Quandt points out a similarly divisive quality among critical responses to the film, by observing that 'Cannes is increasingly inimical' to films such as *Colossal Youth*; this is so even when, as the critic suggests, 'much else at the festival was pandering and blandishment' (2006: 356). This unfavourable reception of Costa's film is not just confined to film critics and audiences, but was also extended to the festival's jury, chaired in that year by filmmaker Wong Kar-Wai. According to *LA Weekly* film critic Scott Foundas, *Colossal Youth* 'bitterly' divided the jury, which eventually decided not to grant any award to the film (2006).

It was not the first time that a film festival jury exhibited such an intense response to Costa's work. These disagreements between members of the Cannes jury echo similar reactions at the 2000 Locarno International Film Festival, in which *In Vanda's Room* was included in the main competition. In my 2013 interview with Francisco Villa-Lobos, the producer recalls that the film was received as

> something never seen before. The production process [of the film] was strange, [its] filmic style was new. [. . .] I know that there were discussions and controversies among the jury [members], and there was the potential for the film to win an award, something that didn't happen in the end. (Villa-Lobos 2013)

Recalling the same event, Costa points out that 'there were four members of the jury that threatened to leave if [*In Vanda's Room*] received any award [laughs]' (2012). Ultimately, the film only received the festival's Youth Jury Award that year. It is relevant to note, however, that since then Locarno became far more receptive to Costa's cinema, as the Best Direction Award bestowed in 2014 on *Horse Money* seems to attest. As regards *Colossal Youth*, while the film did not receive one of the main tokens of prestige awarded by the film festival circuit, it did nonetheless amass (as *In Vanda's Room* six years before) a form of distinction through the public disclosure of such dissonance among jury members, as somehow implicit in the aforementioned accounts provided by Lim and Quandt.

The non-consensual appraisal of Costa's work offers a form of classificatory process, one in which critical disputes provide a 'nuanced' form of symbolic currency. Walkouts and other unfavourable forms of critical display such as catcalls are not uncommon at film festivals like Cannes (see, for example, Hagman 2007). Yet both the Lim and Quandt quotes above disclose, to a degree, how these adverse reactions to Costa's films convey some form of artistic distinction and exclusiveness. These qualities are particularly valued, even favoured, by some cinephiles receptive to certain filmic trends. The symbolic value gained through contention responds to the aspirations of some audiences in engaging passionately with such distinct cultural artefacts. Adrian Martin, for example, proposes that *Colossal Youth* attained a status of cult film through its critically divisive and potentially audience-alienating qualities. As he points out:

> [*Colossal Youth*] has offered a bracing example of a hard-line *arte povera* in the Straub-Huillet tradition that is not easily recuperated – and, not surprisingly, a rallying point for cinephiles who want to keep their severe passion from attaining an easy-to-afford market price. (Martin 2008: 42)

Costa's fans seem concerned with keeping a status confined to the fringes of a cinephilia populated with filmmakers seemingly invested with artistic visions too arcane for wider audiences; in essence this is the epitome of a cult filmmaker. Martin's argument expresses, moreover, the different forms of capital enclosed in *Colossal Youth*. Firstly, Martin's quote points out an approximation to a particularly filmic lineage included in aesthetically difficult art-house cinema trends (more of which later); secondly, it provides a characterisation of the role of cinephiles in expressing an active and passionate agency towards the film, which can be read as an expression of investment in a selective taste culture; and the third characteristic, to some extent generated by the previous two, is the recognition of a position of exclusiveness and prestige provided by the potentially restricted market value of the film – economically, but also in terms of its symbolic value.

The mediation of this expression of value transpires in numerous press articles which aim to contextualise Costa's cinema to international audiences. *The Guardian*'s film critic Peter Bradshaw, for example, labels Costa the 'Samuel Beckett of cinema', drawing comparisons between his films and the bleak existentialism and minimal style commonly attributed to the works of the Irish author. As Bradshaw understands it, Costa is categorised by fans and detractors alike as 'a cult-master, a figure who is widely considered on the festival circuit to be for hardcore auteur followers only' (2009). Particularly indicative the potential of the divisive reception of Costa in amassing a selective and non-consensual prestige is Lim's already cited article for the *New York Times*. Lim points out that the stringent criticism of Costa's detractors, as well as the 'ferocious rhetoric' of his 'pretty vociferous fan club', provides the filmmaker a 'forbidding air of a high-art Spartan' among festival audiences (2007). Perhaps one of the most visible acts of such vocal fans at the film festival circuit was the 'Vote for Pedro' campaign carried on by the Canadian magazine *Cinema Scope* and spearheaded by its editor and publisher, Mark Peranson. The magazine produced T-shirts containing the message 'Vote for Pedro (Pedro Costa, that is)' – a parody of similar apparel that featured in Jared Hess's 2004 directorial feature film debut *Napoleon Dynamite*. Peranson and others among Costa's fans used the T-shirts during the 2006 Toronto Film Festival, where *Colossal Youth* was screened.

Both factual and anecdotal, these different accounts reveal how polarised reception and (prestigious or notorious) characterisation frames Costa's cinema as belonging to a contemporary fringe film culture rooted in forms of cultural distinction around particular 'difficult' filmmakers. Again, as Martin suggests in the abovementioned article, Costa shares with Philippe Garrel a divisive critical reception which gives their films a cult status among particular cinephiles (2008: 42). Tentatively defining this cinephile fringe, Quandt points out that some film festival participants express derision towards the 'glum cultists, po-faced devotees of a particular brand of Lusitanian pornomiseria'; this devoted reception is extended to works of other contemporary 'pan-European band of miserabilists', such as Bela Tarr, Fred Kelemen, and Sharunas Bartas (Quandt 2006: 356). This cult status is further encouraged by the endorsement given to Costa's works by an older generation of filmmakers also commonly placed in the niches of art cinema, albeit already canonised. Among others, we can mention Jacques Rivette and Jean-Marie Straub and Danièle Huillet (see Bonnaud 2001; Lim 2007). These endorsements call our attention to Costa's inclusion in possible stylistic lineages which are deployed to critically assess and, subsequently, to include contemporary art film works in already-established canonical formations circulating at the film festival.

TRACING STYLISTIC LINEAGES

Other forms of symbolic capital emerge when considering that Pedro Costa is included in classificatory formations. These classifications approximate his films to both film traditions which have acquired a canonical status through culturally sanctioned formations, and to contemporary film trends still gaining expression at the film festival. Concerning the former, Costa's public disclosure of his cinephilic preferences and artistic influences helps to articulate a critical discourse which approximates his works to past stylistic lineages that are already legitimised through critical and scholarly discussions. As Mark Peranson points out, Costa's films shot at Fontainhas can be understood as 'post-Ozu', and 'post-Bressonian' (Peranson 2010: 127). This characterisation simultaneously helps to situate these films aesthetically and in production terms. It also reveals a critical discourse which awards to Costa the role of inheritor of particular filmic traditions.

In contemporary terms, and as Argentinian film critic and programmer Quintín argues, 'keeping alive' the filmic 'tradition' invoked by Costa 'requires relentless explanations, in contrast to the old masters' practice of disregarding film criticism and refusing to talk about their work' (2009: 31). The discursive nature of Costa's narrative of production is key here, as it offers mediation between his films and their audiences. Costa seems particularly aware of the necessity to provide detailed accounts of the collaborative and uncompromising production practices which make his films possible, as well as of possible aesthetic affiliations which inform his authorial process. This knowledge is articulated thorough numerous interviews with international specialised and popular press, and by being included in different ancillary materials (for example, commentaries and extras included on DVD editions of his films). This information provides context for Costa's films. Yet it is also filtered through discursive practices situated at reception which, as mentioned above, help us to discuss artistic credibility and aesthetic significance, and to create links with established art film traditions.

Costa's association with Jean-Marie Straub and Danièle Huillet particularly illustrates this latter characteristic. Costa's exposure to the work of Straub and Huillet (as the two filmmakers are usually referred to) happened earlier in his formative years. In terms of international reception, however, such a link is mostly the result of the documentary *Where Does Your Hidden Smile Lie?*, directed by Costa (with the assistance of Thierry Lounas) for the TV series *Cinéma, de notre temps* (1964–). The documentary, directed while Costa was still engaged on the later stages of production of *In Vanda's Room*, provides a close account of Straub and Huillet's working methods. It depicts the painstaking montage process of the third version of their feature film *Sicilia!* (*Sicily!*, 1999) undertaken by the two filmmakers at an editing suite of Le Fresnoy, Studio national des arts contemporains, in Tourcoing (north-northeast of Lille).

The discreet shooting setup developed by Costa during *In Vanda's Room* matched the restrictive requirements imposed by the French filmmakers, who did not want to be disturbed by an intrusive filmic apparatus when editing the film. As Portuguese filmmaker Miguel Gomes humorously notes, *Where Does Your Hidden Smile Lie?* could be called 'In the Straubs' Room' (2009). Indeed, the stylistic similarities between *Where Does Your Hidden Smile Lie?* and *In Vanda's Room* result from the same process of intimate observation in which the small digital video apparatus manages to capture a reality confined to a small space with reduced lighting. Equally restrictive were the conditions imposed by the producers of ARTE, who commissioned the episode, and who initially wanted to abide by the length format of the other episodes in the series. Costa wanted to do a 'longer version of the documentary', and this was later made possible with an agreement between Costa and ARTE, and with the financial support of Portuguese and French public institutions (Villa-Lobos 2013). The extended version of the documentary, approximately 30 minutes longer than the version initially broadcast, was premiered at the Venice Film Festival in 2001. Costa would also use some of the material not included on *Where Does Your Hidden Smile Lie?* to compose six short vignettes about Straub and Huillet, presented as a short film titled *6 Bagatelas* (2001).

Where Does Your Hidden Smile Lie? constitutes a direct link to an already canonical filmmaking tradition recognised among film critics and cinephiles. The filmmaking duo and Costa share austere film aesthetics and uncompromising production values, as is manifest in the documentary. As Patrick Tarrant observes, by depicting the rigorous montage routine of Straub and Huillet 'Costa is able to foreground the time that filmmaking takes and, by extension, to put us in mind of the duration of his own enterprise' (2013: 3). The documentary noticeably transmits Costa's admiration for the French filmmakers. It reinvents, as Jean-Pierre Gorin argues, the notion of 'portrait' or 'homage' while avoiding being a 'sentimental hagiography' (2009: 255). More than just creating awareness of Costa's reverence for Straub and Huillet – and corresponding praise from the two filmmakers – the documentary also generates a symbolic kudos which links younger and older generations of filmmakers with equally austere filmic aesthetics and obstinate production values. Since this documentary, and as Costa himself recognised in an interview with me, there has been a connection between his and Straub and Huillet's intransigent authorial images, as being considered 'rebel types unwilling to deal with [film] producers and the media' (2013). This filial connection tentatively acquires meaning in one of the photos used to promote *Where Does Your Hidden Smile Lie?*, taken by Richard Dumas during a photographic session for the French newspaper *Libération* (Figure 4.1). This complicity is mostly noted in aesthetic terms, and the approximation to Straub and Huillet's filmic style is evident from *Colossal Youth* onwards. The (apparent) minimal simplicity of Costa's cinema reclaims a narrative and visual asceticism that is commonly attributed to that of the French filmmakers. Straub and Huillet's filmic style has been characterised as post-Bressonian functional austerity, with monotonous delivery by actors and stillness in camera style (see Kovács 2007: 148; Walsh 1981: 45–6). *Colossal Youth* attunes its minimalistic visual and decelerated narrative tropes to a similar austerity to that observed in some of Straub and Huillet's works.

Colossal Youth continues the collaboration between Costa and some of the Fontainhas residents. This film, however, pays closer attention to the neighbourhood's older generation, and the film is centred on the non-professional actor Ventura. According to Costa, Ventura was 'one of the pioneers, who

Figure 4.1 'Family photo': Jean-Marie Straub, Pedro Costa and Danièle Huillet in 2001. Photo by Richard Dumas. Reproduced with kind permission of its author

built the first shacks' at Fontainhas, and soon after 'was involved in a terrible accident at work', which left him disabled 'when still very young' (Corless 2008: 12; also Ferreira 2006:14). Making a thematic link to *Casa de Lava*, the narrative of *Colossal Youth* is centred on the personal story of this retired builder, who came from Cape Verde in the early 1970s to work on Lisbon's construction sites and whose life was dramatically affected by the 1974 Revolution and its aftermath. *Colossal Youth* is composed of a series of filmic *tableaux vivants* structured around narrative reiteration. The film is predominantly marked by a visual stillness, provided by the long take and minimal camera movement. Indeed, the film's cinemetrical measures reveal that in the 110 shots which compose the two and a half hours of the film, only five scenes use any camera movement. This filmic stillness is further perceived by the use of long shots, some extending to more than ten minutes. These characteristics enhance Costa's careful and rigorous compositions and *mise en scène*, and the stoical stillness of the actors' delivery. Such stillness becomes further enhanced by the cinematography of the film (credited to Costa and Leonardo Simões), as it recalls the tonality, dramatic lighting, and composition values of the still-life painting tradition (Quandt 2006: 359; Romney 2008: 46; also Rancière 2014: 129).

This austere filmic stillness suits the idiosyncratic presence of Ventura. The film follows the character wandering between what is left of Fontainhas (at the time of shooting the process of demolition of the neighbourhood was almost concluded), and the recently-built Casal da Boba social housing estate (to which some of the former residents of Fontainhas were relocated). Throughout the film, Ventura visits several of his 'children', many of them characters or participants who also populated *In Vanda's Room* (Vanda Duarte, António Semedo, Paulo Nunes and others). Moving between these two locations, Ventura claims to be making a final effort to gather all his 'sons and daughters' so they can join him in a new apartment at Casal da Boba. These visits make apparent that the offspring are not Ventura's biological kin but the whole of the Fontainhas 'family', a community dispersed because of the neighbourhood's demolition.

Ventura's wanderings are not just confined to the physical space of these two neighbourhoods. As Costa points out during an interview with Portuguese film critic Francisco Ferreira, 'there are two parts in this film, a past and a present at Fontainhas, [two parts that] coincide with the before and after the 25th of April [Revolution]' (2006: 16). The biographical details of Ventura's life are blended with historical facts, composing a narrative with flashbacks alternating between a past located sometime around 1974 and a present, giving expression to his traumatic memories. The incorporation of these flashbacks is not stylistically signalled, providing the narrative of the film with a fragmented nature which merges the (possibly) factual with the spectral. These subjective representations of Ventura's memories span the time from his and his friend Lento's (played by Alberto Barros) arrival in Lisbon and the immediate aftermath of the 1974 Revolution. Throughout the film we are presented with reports of the ordeals and problems lived by Ventura and Lento in adapting to the city, as well as the hard toil and back-breaking work they undertook on numerous building sites. Towards the end of the film the commotion caused by the events following the 1974 Revolution is also made apparent, even if unclearly manifested in narrative terms. These flashbacks show the two characters barricaded in the shack they occupy, fearing the potential violence that could be inflicted on the immigrant population of Lisbon.

Colossal Youth indicates a further refinement of Costa's tightly manufactured *docufiction* format, fusing representation and presentation in a visually stylised minimalism and decelerated and fragmented narrative. This filmic style approximates Costa's aesthetic preoccupations to those revealed in Straub and Huillet's cinema, particularly in terms of rigid acting and austere narrative. It needs to be noted, however, that this approximation is more inspirational than formal. As Tag Gallagher rightly argues, these filmmakers have different approaches to direction of actors, montage and the use of diegetic and non-diegetic sound (2007). Costa's aesthetics are, moreover, inevitably intertwined with a *sui generis* thematic universe centred in the harsh realities lived by characters placed at the fringes of Portuguese society. While inspired by the French filmmakers, aesthetically and politically, Costa's filmic universe is presented through a mode which favours a detached and contemplative standpoint towards the characters populating his films. This standpoint differs from the radical Marxist position that informs Straub and Huillet's *oeuvre* (see Rancière 2009b).

Even considering these differences, Costa's approximation to Straub and Huillet accounts for the former's inclusion in the canon of the 'difficult' art film epitomised by the latter filmmakers. Costa's filmic style is commonly understood as a re-articulation of aesthetic tropes of the modernist art film canon, branding him not just 'post-Ozu' and 'post-Bressonian' but also a post-Straub and Huillet filmmaker. In this regard, several contemporary filmmakers share a filmic sensibility that is a sort of revival of the European modernist cinema. As Darren Hughes asserts, Costa's films reflect 'the same nostalgia for Modernism that characterizes so much of today's art cinema' (2008: 161). As Hughes makes clear, this is so even when considering that Costa's cinema reveals different stylistic and ethical preoccupations to those offered by other contemporary filmmakers.

Mark Betz similarly points out that the works of a number of contemporary filmmakers, Costa included, offer a stylistic resumption of Modernist art cinema's most 'difficult' trends (2010: 31). Betz draws upon David Bordwell's notion of 'parametric narration'. This term is used by Bordwell to define one of the different narrative trends emerging during the mid-twentieth-century Modernist art cinema. Bordwell associates this filmic style with filmmakers such as Alain Resnais, Robert Bresson and Yasujirō Ozu, all of whom share a set of similar aesthetic parameters. These parameters include, among others, narrative redundancy and the insistence on the long take and minimal montage (1985: 284–5). These parameters, Betz argues, re-emerge as filmic style tropes in the works of a number of international filmmakers whose works gained visibility in the film festival circuit after the 2000s. Among others, this 'contemporary parametric' aesthetic is observed in the work of European filmmakers such as Costa, Garrel and Tarr, but also work from others further afield, such as Lisandro Alonso, Carlos Reygadas, Jia Zhangke, Hou Hsiao-hsien and Apichatpong Weerasethakul (see Betz 2010: 39–40). The contemporary 'parametric' art film (and its links to already canonised filmic traditions) raises interest also among some film critics. In a *Guardian* article from 2000, Jonathan Romney called attention to the 'reinvention' in global terms of a former 'dissident' and 'slow' cinematic style in the work of Costa, Tarr and Kelemen, as well as Aleksandr Sokurov and Bruno Dumont (2000). Particularly relevant in this article about such a possible filmic trend is the mobilisation of taste hierarchies to critically assess the work of these filmmakers.

Non-academic debates concerning the term 'slow' are also a vehicle for the expression of symbolic value and thus significant in understanding the reception of Costa's work in general terms and *Colossal Youth* in particular.

SLOW CINEMA AND THE EXPRESSION OF (SUBCULTURAL) TASTE

Discussions around the term 'Slow Cinema', which emerged in British and US film criticism parlance in the early 2000s, are particularly centred on taste formations. This is so even if, later, this term potentiated other far more diverse scholarly discussions (see, for example, Çağlayan 2018; de Luca and Jorge 2016; Jaffe 2014; Flanagan 2008). As discussed elsewhere, Slow Cinema has been incorporated in cultural discourses conveying resistance or alternatives to both mass-market industrial processes and endemic accelerated lifestyles taking shape at the turn of the millennium (de Luca and Jorge 2016: 3; see also Lim 2014: 2–5; Rothermel 2009: 265–6). The prefix 'slow' comes to define social and consumption practices, as well as lifestyle options which, loosely, take their cues from the 'Slow Food' movement. Terms sharing this prefix – 'Slow Fashion', 'Slow Money', 'Slow Travel', 'Slow Media' or even 'Slow Academia' – have been incorporated into the early twenty-first-century cultural lexicon. This prefix can be expanded to accommodate other variegated contemporary cultural practices: the unhurried lifestyle advocated by Tom Hodgkinson, the writer of the UK bestseller *How To Be Idle* (2005) and editor of the magazine *The Idler*, the emphatically slow-paced experimental musical sub-genres such as Drone Metal (also known as Slow Metal), and deliberately lengthy and natural-paced Slow Television programmes broadcast by northern European TV channels.

Either structured around social commitment or just as a form and expression of cultural fruition, these different practices share similar taste discourses deemed to be oppositional to mainstream corporate culture and consumer tastes. Slow Cinema became a signifier for taste hierarchies that feed on binary oppositions as a form of distinction. As Thomas Elsaesser argues:

> the 'cinema of slow' sees itself as a reaction to 'accelerated continuity', where slowness – however expressed or represented – becomes an act of organized resistance: just as 'slow food' is a reaction to both the convenience and uniformity of fast food, appealing to locally grown ingredients, traditional modes of manufacture and community values. No longer along the lines of 'art versus commerce', or 'realism versus illusionism', slow cinema [. . .] counters the blockbuster's over-investment in physical action, spectacle and violence with long takes, quiet

observation, an attention to detail, to inner stirrings rather than to outward restlessness, highlighting the deliberate or hesitant gesture, rather than the protagonist's drive or determination – reminding one, however remotely, of the 'go-slow' of industrial protest, but also the 'organic' pace of the vegetal realm. (Elsaesser 2011: 117)

It is clear that Slow Cinema offers a vehement contrast with the Hollywood 'blockbuster' filmic formulas, shaped by an 'intensified continuity' which privileges fast editing and visual stress (Bordwell 2002b: 24). Contrasting with accelerated filmic formulas, contemporary slow films deploy '(often extremely) long takes, de-centred and understated modes of storytelling, and a pronounced emphasis on quietude and the everyday' (Flanagan 2008).

Slow Cinema comes to be contextualised as a sensorial experience which responds to the tastes of cinephiles looking for both filmic authenticity and cultural distinction. In the February 2010 edition of *Sight & Sound*, Jonathan Romney once again enthusiastically praises the virtues of slow films, pointing out that films such as *Colossal Youth*, *Stellet Licht* (*Silent Light*, dir. Carlos Reygadas, 2007), *El cant dels ocells* (*Birdsong*, dir. Albert Serra, 2008) or the works of Lisandro Alonso, participate in the

> increasing demand among cinephiles for films that are slow, poetic, contemplative – cinema that downplays event in favour of mood, evocativeness and an intensified sense of temporality. Such films highlight the viewing process itself as a real-time experience in which, ideally, [audiences] become acutely aware of every minute, every second spent watching. (Romney 2010: 43)

The demand among cinephiles for filmic (as well as sensorial) authenticity denotes a form of cultural consumption which, as already pointed out, positions itself in clear contrast with taste formations receptive to mainstream entertainment. This positioning reflects an enduring 'polarized film culture' which classifies filmic works in aesthetic terms, but also through its locus in polarised exhibition and circulation arenas (Bordwell and Thompson 2011). Furthermore, this distinction is extended to other binary oppositions taking place at the film festival. Indeed, the 'difficult' and slow art film translates an affirmation of difference which contrasts with some contemporary world cinema with 'light' narrative formulas, commonly circulating in this international circuit (Elsaesser 2005: 509).

This oppositional stance given to Slow Cinema and the taste formations associated with it is not just set as antagonistic to both mainstream tastes and particular film festival trends, but has also become contextualised – as have other cultural expressions encompassed by the 'slow' prefix – as an alternative to the increasingly fast pace of neoliberal capitalism. It bears repeating that both academics and film critics commonly point out the links between contemporary decelerated filmic narratives and modernism. Slow Cinema is commonly framed as a sort of 'retro-art-cinema' which, as Emre Çağlayan sees it, 'appears both out of date and *à la mode*' (2018: xiv). Yet the contemporary slow film can also be understood as a reflection of far more contemporary anxieties. As Romney argues:

> Slow Cinema might be seen as a response to a bruisingly pragmatic decade in which, post-9/11, the oppressive everyday awareness of life as overwhelmingly political, economic and ecological would seem to preclude (in the West, at least) any spiritual dimension in art. (Romney 2010: 44)

Such understanding may lessen (while not resolving) accusations of a belated, nostalgic or even anachronistic filmic style. The contextualisation of a slow filmic style as a contemporary artistic force with spiritual contours offering a genuine alternative to, or an escape from, overpowering actual realities is surely pertinent. The works of the filmmakers listed in Romney's article are indubitably an expression of artistic preoccupations that resist the oppressive speed and cynical superficiality of early twenty-first-century neoliberal capitalism. Yet it also hints, once again, at ongoing taste formations aiming at being at the fringes of contemporary culture. The character of distinction offered by the works of filmmakers commonly placed under Slow Cinema illustrates the dynamics of a cultural consumption based on alternative tastes and that often transpires to other cultural formations.

One of the signs of the potential subcultural capital of slow films is their inclusion in a group of contemporary artistic practices centred on an aesthetic of slowness. A particularly illustrative example of this is the 2012 edition of the AV Festival – the British festival of art, technology, music and film – which took place in several venues located across the northeast of England. The festival's curatorial choices gathered different non-mainstream artistic practices under the collective title of 'As Slow as Possible'. Taking place in March, the festival was presented as a run-up and alternative to the accelerated mainstream entertainment that would soon be offered by the London 2012 Summer Olympics (whose motto was 'Faster, Higher, Stronger'). It included a screening of *Colossal Youth*, alongside films directed by Tarr, Alonso, Weerasethakul, James Benning and Lav Diaz among others, as well as several exhibitions, symposia and experimental music concerts. All these different events shared their slow-pace and contemplative credentials with the final event of the festival, a *Slowalk* led by British artist Hamish Fulton.

While understood as a possible manifestation of a contemporary slow movement, this positioning of Slow Cinema in the myriad practices evoked by the slow prefix is ambiguous and vague. Contrary to many of the cultural practices listed above, Slow Cinema does not reveal manifesto-driven articulated intentions and it is mostly confined to film criticism, cinephilia and academic discourses. Moreover, this term is ignored or dismissed by film practitioners commonly associated with it. Pedro Costa, for example, is particularly disapproving of the term, associating it with 1970s European art film:

> I prefer the word 'fast'. [. . .] [Slowness] reflects the formal preoccupations of filmmakers like [Andrei] Tarkovsky or [Theo] Angelopoulos . . . those are preoccupations that I don't have and will never have . . . [. . .] Slow cinema was the nightmare I had to endure during film school. The *auteur* cinema at that time was dreadful . . . the long shot, contemplation . . . there are lots of misconceptions about that. Not many people talk about Jean Rouch [films], a fast cinema. He solved quite a lot of [formal] problems, the [representation of] myths and folklore, how to move to the other side of the camera, how the film crew becomes part of the film [narrative] . . . all that is by far more interesting [to me]. (Costa 2013)

Costa does not recognise the importance of such a descriptor for the aesthetic of his films, preferring instead to place potential aesthetic preoccupations as part of the routines of his filmmaking practice.[1] As discussed in the previous chapter, the slowness in Costa's films is largely the result of a digital filmmaking with protracted and observational qualities. Costa offers further context to his decelerated filmmaking practice in an interview which took place during the 2005 Vienna International Film Festival:

> The film is rolling like the earth is rolling. You should be in the same speed. [. . .] I don't have ideas to make films, I just follow the movement. So I followed this community I'm with, Vanda and her family and another family; all these people in the neighbourhood. (Berlakovich 2005)

According to Costa, the narrative deceleration sensed in *In Vanda's Room* and *Colossal Youth* is a consequence of his observation of the lives of the Fontainhas residents. This proximity to the Fontainhas community, moreover, reveals a discourse that organises film production, collaborative practices and decelerated film aesthetics under a professional and personal agency. This understanding of Costa's authorial agency becomes less discernible under generic forms of classification which are operated at the reception stage. The filmic works commonly classified with terms such as Slow Cinema are the result of a constellation of different production and cultural contexts. Moreover, films categorised as 'slow' are often directed by filmmakers who may have dissimilar, even opposing, aesthetic preoccupations. Such filmmaking plurality, nonetheless, becomes conditioned under classificatory categories generated by critical scrutiny.

Forms of classification generated in film criticism, moreover, often denounce their binary taste formations. This is made particularly evident in the numerous debates around Slow Cinema carried on by film critics. Two particular articles illustrate how this term, at least in reception terms, serves foremost as a categorisation for taste formations in contemporary film culture. The first is Nick James's April 2010 *Sight & Sound* editorial. In it the film critic questions contemporary 'slow' films' aesthetic and political relevance by claiming that the 'passive-aggressive' qualities of many of these films serve only to provoke boredom and guilty feelings of cultural philistinism (2010: 5). The second article, written a year later by Dan Kois for the *New York Times*, similarly questions the assumptions made about the artistic merit of films categorised under such label. Kois admits his 'cultural fatigue' and lack of interest – both as a critic and spectator – in 'eating cultural vegetables' such as *Meek's Cutoff* (dir. Kelly Reichardt, 2010), *Le Quattro Volte* (dir. Michelangelo Frammartino, 2010), and in digesting art-house classics such as *Solaris*, directed in 1972 by Andrei Tarkovsky (Kois 2011).

Even if articulated differently, the articles penned by James and Kois challenge taste assumptions permeating contemporary film culture. The positioning of both film critics makes clear how affirmations of difference are central to the workings of cultural taste (see Bourdieu 2010: 49). Accordingly, the subsequent rebuttal of, or support for, both articles sheds light on how discussions of symbolic value are shaped by oppositional taste discourses. Cinephiles such as Harry Tuttle, the curator of *Unspoken Cinema* (a blog dedicated to 'contemplative contemporary cinema') accuses James of expressing a customary 'anti-intellectual, pro-entertainment inclination' that affects contemporary film culture (2010). Cultural critic Steven Shaviro sees Slow Cinema differently, as a signifier of '"serious art cinema" [but] without having to display any sort of originality or insight' as previously observed in the work of Antonioni or Tarkovsky (to name a few of the canonical filmmakers pointed out in his blog post); this lack of originality, Shaviro contends, renders contemporary slow films 'profoundly nostalgic and regressive' (2010). The article by Kois similarly draws comparably polarised views. An example of such a response was provided by colleagues of Kois at the *New York Times*, Manohla Dargis and A. O. Scott, who matched his fatigue with the lethargic consumption of 'boring' and 'repetitive' contemporary Hollywood sequels (2011). This latter article prompted online discussions among professional and non-professional film fans. Such discussions were clearly animated by binary views which came to shape the reception of Slow Cinema – boring versus transcendent, original versus outmoded, intellectually enhanced versus artistically pretentious (see, for example, Scott et al. 2011; Bordwell and Thompson 2011; Emerson 2011).

BETWEEN MONETARY AND NONMONETARY VALUES

Both James's 'passive-aggressive' and Kois's 'cultural vegetables' articles, as well as their subsequent responses, draw on categories supported by differing taste discourses and the potential symbolic value expressed in them. Discussions concerning Slow Cinema come also to question the monetary aspects of the economy of prestige promoted by the film festival. The criticism offered by James, for instance, extends to the role of taste-making agents such as film critics and festival programmers in maintaining what he calls the 'critical orthodoxy' around slow films. As he speculates,

> some [slow films] offer an easy life for critics and programmers. After all, the festivals themselves commission many of these productions and such films are easy to remember and discuss in detail because details are few. (James 2010: 5)

James does not explicitly name any particular film festival, although it is understood that he is referring to production initiatives such as Berlin Film Festival's World Cinema Fund or Rotterdam's Hubert Bals Fund (HBF). The latter initiative is recognised by its support to filmmakers commonly placed under Slow Cinema such as Reygadas, Diaz, Alonso, Weerasethakul, already mentioned, but also Amat Escalante and Nuri Bilge Ceylan among others (see de Luca and Jorge 2016: 11).

Such scrutiny of the role of these production initiatives in contemporary art cinema extends to scholarly discussions. In his analysis of the contemporary parametric film, Mark Betz raises comparable questions to those expressed by James. As Betz points out, these initiatives 'potentially [bind filmmakers] to a marketplace that cannot but have an effect on the stylistic choices that they make' (2010: 32). Miriam Ross offers a similar critique on how these funding initiatives shape filmic trends circulating in the festival circuit. Filmmakers geographically situated outside Europe supported by the HBF initiative may become conditioned to respond to festivals' expectations in support and exhibit works conveying filmic and thematic authenticity. As Ross argues, this is something which often motivates accusations of encouraging the circulation of 'poverty porn' for the enjoyment of art-house audiences (2011: 262). Implicit in these discussions is the argument, pertinent and problematical in equal terms, that these film festival-driven practices help in creating and sustaining particular filmic trends.

In the past, Pedro Costa also benefited from similar film festival initiatives. Soon after the completion of *Colossal Youth*, Costa was commissioned by the Jeonju Digital Project (JDP) to direct a short film to be premiered at the 2007 Jeonju International Film Festival (JIFF). The remits of this initiative concern film practices exclusively supported by the use of digital video and operating under a low budget. Created in 2000, the JDP supports the production of short films by filmmakers who have been defined by film critics and scholars as partaking in a contemporary expression of filmic slowness. It has awarded funding to filmmakers including Jia Zhangke and Tsai Ming-liang (in its 2001 edition), Weerasethakul (in 2005), Diaz and Naomi Kawase (in 2009) and James Benning in 2010. The participation of these filmmakers in the JDP may raise similar suspicions to those mentioned above on how festival initiatives may condition the production and circulation of particular aesthetic trends. The remits of the JDP, however, give primacy to specific technological and production practices rather than particular filmic aesthetics. These remits are ample enough to support the production of short films by, for instance, Japanese filmmakers Shinya Tsukamoto and Sogo Ishii, or British video practitioner John Akomfrah. The works of these film practitioners contrast significantly with the aesthetic qualities commonly subsumed under Slow Cinema.

Aiming at expanding their remit outside the Asian region, the 2007 edition of the JDP was focused exclusively on filmmakers based in Europe. These commissions included short films directed by Costa, Harun Farocki and Eugène Green, grouping these filmmakers' works under the title *Memories*. Costa's contribution to this anthology was the short film *A Caça ao Coelho com Pau* (*The Rabbit Hunters*, 2007). The inclusion of this short film in the group of works previously supported financially by the JDP suggests the interest of the film festival in supporting, as well as being associated with, a filmmaker whose international reputation is informed by a professional practice which matches the remits of such funding initiative. As already examined, the production contexts of *In Vanda's Room* and *Colossal Youth* acquire particular importance in Costa's authorial discourse and are, subsequently, incorporated into the critical discussion of his films. Costa's short film commissioned by JIFF shares with these abovementioned feature films a production framework developed by the filmmaker and his collaborators inhabiting Fontainhas and Casal da Boba. Moreover, *The Rabbit Hunters* is also tied to *Colossal Youth* in thematic and narrative terms, being a result of Costa's collaboration with Ventura (as further discussed in the next chapter). The short film is structured around Ventura's memories, serving, to some extent, as a continuation of the narrative observed in *Colossal Youth*.

A short text written by Costa and included in the press release of *Colossal Youth* shed light on the textual and production contexts of this feature film which, subsequently, would also inform *The Rabbit Hunters*. In it Costa explains the way in which *Colossal Youth* evolved around Ventura's memories, making clear that the authorial process shaping the film was essentially a collaborative effort. It is interesting to note that this document circumvents explanations about film aesthetics by preferring instead to concentrate on details about shooting technicalities:

> As time is precious, we tried to overcome obstacles without resorting to the classical tools of filmmaking. We had no lighting, no cables, no makeup, no [electricity] generators, no catering. [. . .] We often filmed in locations without any electricity. We used only eight or nine mirrors, some [light] reflectors, polystyrene sheets, everything that could help increase use of available light. [. . .]
>
> I used a digital camera, DAT for sound, one or two microphones and some tripods. That's all. All in all, I shot 320 one-hour DVCam cassettes. The shoot lasted 15 months, six days per week, practically all day long, shooting sometimes 20 or 30 takes per scene. (Costa 2006: np)

Costa's first-hand report provides a detailed context for the production environment of *Colossal Youth*, which would later inform most of his subsequent feature and short films, and video installations. It also expresses, I argue, a narrative of production which emphasises a stoic film practice privileging material aspects. This public stance on film production increases the prestige awarded to Costa and his films, shaping an authorial image that is dependent both on aesthetic categorisation and on an individual creative agency.

Costa's participation in the JDP initiative illustrates the interlinked monetary and nonmonetary transactions operated through the film festivals' economy of prestige. *The Rabbit Hunters* can be contextualised as an example of the mediation of symbolic and monetary values operating within this circuit. Costa received financial support but also further international exposure through the inclusion of this short film in a festival with increasing visibility in Asia. On the other hand, this inclusion allowed JIFF to become associated with filmmakers outside its initial regional geographic context, making it able to discuss an image of a festival with global remits. Stylistic qualities are surely pertinent in the discussion of this co-dependent relationship. The inclusion of Costa's film, as well as those of other international filmmakers, allows JIFF to participate in international filmic trends gaining visibility on the film festival circuit. Yet, the remits of this festival's initiative come to discuss far more inclusive filmic categories in which film aesthetics are intertwined with low-budget production values and the use of digital video technology.

Costa's involvement in the JDP initiative, moreover, illustrates the significance given to a filmmaker whose attitude towards the production and funding of his films increments, but also transcends, the potential symbolic value acquired through the subsumption into particular film trends. In this regard, Costa's authorial image also contributes to the transactions operated under an economy of prestige. As argued by the producer of *Colossal Youth*, choices in film festival programming rely on direct dealings between programmers, producers and directors, and on relationships based on individual kudos. Commenting on the possible preference given to 'slow' films by film festival programmers, Francisco Villa-Lobos is adamant in pointing out:

> people are not so fixated on styles such as 'slow cinema'. That's a myth . . . the name is more important than the label connected to that same name . . . festivals work that way! There is a level of interest which has to do with the film itself, and another level formed by the names of people [directors or producers] who get their films in the festivals. (Villa-Lobos 2013)

Villa-Lobos's observation challenges debates on the importance given to stylistic trends in programming choices. More than contradictory, however, these different understandings are informative of the inherent ambiguities in the relation between nonmonetary and monetary values operated by the film festival. This debate allows understanding that stylistic descriptors and taxonomies are surely important to establish symbolic value. However, these classification mechanisms only exist on a sliding scale, which is conditioned by the idiosyncrasies of particular authorial practices and the direct participation of filmmakers. Filmic formulae and possible stylistic lineages are, as seen, important mechanisms of symbolic value and taste formations. Yet the roles performed by the different participants in this economy of prestige also assume significance when discussing its different forms of currency.

The layered understanding of critical dialogues and taste formations around Costa's cinema reveal the ambiguous and intricate working of an economy of prestige. Reception mechanisms, such as classification under particular film aesthetics, the inclusion in stylistic lineages and debates around artistic credibility, help to situate but also to condition the symbolic value given to films such as *Colossal Youth*. Costa's contested capital is one of the most visible results of the working of these mechanisms. The polarised reception of *Colossal Youth* serves as a vehicle to enclose it under mediations of taste (which are always inherently divisive), as well as activating its artistic recognition and consecration. As evident across this chapter, such divided reception confers on both Costa and his films a form of symbolic capital structured around exclusivity, helping sustain particular critical discourses. *Colossal Youth* resists some forms of critical and economic assimilation, yet its inclusion in debates around particular filmic trends highlights forms of critical reception and consumption that have generated some symbolic currency. This currency, as we have already seen, is complicated when looking at the monetary aspects of the prestige economy maintained by the film festival. The symbolic capital provided to Costa is also formed by expectations of the agents connected with the circulation and consumption of art cinema. Costa's filmmaking, as well as the discourses it engenders, becomes a vehicle for different forms of value which, as discussed in the following chapter, transcend art cinema circuits.

NOTE

1. Costa makes similar comments about Slow Cinema, as well as about the use of long stationary shots in contemporary art cinema, in *Finding the Criminal* (dir. Craig Keller, 2010), a conversation with Craig Keller and Andy Rector included as an extra feature in the DVD edition of *Colossal Youth* released by Eureka!/Masters of Cinema in 2011.

CHAPTER 5

Between the Black Box and the White Cube

In 2014 Pedro Costa's two-screen video installation *Filhas do Fogo* (*Daughters of Fire*, 2013) was exhibited at the São Roque Church in Lisbon. This work depicted static shots of the faces of Cape Verdean women against a barren Cape Verde backdrop, images which were originally included in *Casa de Lava*. Costa's video installation was one of the artefacts of the exhibition *Visitação: O Arquivo Como Memória e Promessa*, held by the Museum of São Roque. The museum is located adjacent to the São Roque Church and to the headquarters of its presiding institution, the Portuguese charity organisation Santa Casa da Misericórdia.[1] The main exhibition was accessed through the church, which explains the *sui generis* location of Costa's video installation. Included in the exhibition yet placed outside the white-walled space housing the other works displayed, *Daughters of Fire* came to share its attention with the rich religious sculpture and liturgical objects permanently displayed in the church's interior setting (Figures 5.1 and 5.2).

The inclusion of a work by Pedro Costa in this site is an example, albeit *sui generis*, of the increasing interest by art galleries and museums in integrating cinema into their cultural remits. The practices of many contemporary artists have responded to such interest, expressed in the current merging between art and cinema's aesthetics and modes of production. Similarly, the last two decades have seen the expansion of the curatorial tenets of the art gallery to accommodate video installations created by filmmakers. Either sporadically or more persistently, video installations by filmmakers such as Apichatpong Weerasethakul, Abbas Kiarostami, Chantal Akerman, Atom Egoyan, Aleksandr Sokurov, Víctor Erice, Raúl Ruiz and Jean-Luc Godard (to name but a few) have been exhibited in such context. These filmmakers' works circulate through a complex and dynamic network of disparate venues and events

Figures 5.1 and 5.2 Pedro Costa's two-screen video installation *Daughters of Fire* (2013), displayed at the São Roque Church. Photos by the author

integrated into the international art gallery circuit. This increasing visibility of a 'cinematic' trend in the contemporary art gallery raises pertinent questions about the current role of cinema in contemporary culture. Indeed, and as curator and art historian Chris Dercon argues, this inclusion of cinema in the art circuit reframes previous inquiries such as André Bazin's archetypal interrogation ('what is cinema?') to ask instead, and perhaps more pertinently, 'where is cinema?' (Dercon 2002).

The inclusion of *Daughters of Fire* in the above-mentioned exhibition is just one of the several examples of how Costa's work is currently being resituated in exhibition but also in production terms. Since the early 2000s, Costa has been producing video works to be presented at art galleries and museums. Inclusion in this cultural arena further expanded the possibilities of exhibition and circulation offered by international film festival and art-house circuits. At the outset, Costa's works for the art gallery may be understood as exceptions to a filmmaking activity privileging the feature film format. Similarly, most of these video installations are subjected to a different presentation mode – the 'white cube' of the art gallery – a different environment for an *oeuvre* that was initially confined to the 'black box' in which theatrical exhibition takes place.

As I argue here, however, the inclusion of Costa's work in the art gallery presents more nuanced and complex characteristics. This body of work relies on aesthetic, authorial and financial characteristics which bond it to the one exclusively produced for the black box. With some exceptions, Costa's work for the art gallery presents a continuation of the same stylistic, narrative and thematic universe depicted in his works for theatrical exhibition. These works translate filmic narratives to the presentation syntax of this exhibition space by re-assembling or recuperating material initially included or originated during the shooting of his feature films. Moreover, similar authorial and financial processes came to inform both Costa's video installations and the numerous commissioned short films directed between the mid-2000s and early 2010s.

The discussion offered here considers how curatorial, technological and aesthetic aspects inform a dialogue between film and artistic practices carried on by Pedro Costa from the early 2000s onwards. Contemporary artists commonly 'recycle' and 'translate' film-related material and aesthetic into their works for the art gallery (Balsom 2013: 118–19). Similar creative and authorial strategies are also observed in Costa's video installations. These same strategies, moreover, are not confined to his works for the white cube but can also be observed in the authorial process of his short films *Tarrafal* and *The Rabbit Hunters* (both 2007), *O Nosso Homem* (*Our Man*, 2010) and *Lamento da Vida Jovem* (*Sweet Exorcism*, 2012). I direct attention to filmic aesthetics and authorial practices in order to examine these dialogues between the white cube and the black box. Overall, I discuss how Costa's narrative of production – in both practical and discursive terms – matches emerging trends in the circulation of contemporary art cinema outside theatrical circulation, and responds to the cultural and financial dynamisms presented by the international art circuit.

THE 'CINEMATIC' AT THE ART GALLERY

Pedro Costa's initial inclusion at the art gallery was facilitated by an invitation made by art curator Catherine David, who was responsible for the 2001 Biennale d'Art Contemporain at Lyon. As the filmmaker explained to me, 'David watched *In Vanda's Room* [. . .] and asked me if I wanted to show material not included [in the film]' (Costa 2013). This invitation caused Costa to re-evaluate the profuse material available. Eventually, he decided to show material already included in the feature film, if presented in its uncut and extended length. The result of this selection process was an untitled video installation (also known as *In Vanda's Room*, 2001), which uses approximately two hours of material initially shot for, and incorporated into, the feature film. This video installation was subsequently included in the exhibition *[based upon] TRUE STORIES*. Also curated by David, the exhibition took place between January and March 2003 at the Witte de With Center for Contemporary Art (Rotterdam), as part of the special programme of the International Film Festival Rotterdam. This same exhibition was also shown at São Paulo's Paço das Artes during April and June of the same year, under the title *a respeito de Situações Reais*.

Costa consolidated this initial presence on the international art gallery circuit through subsequent collaborations with already established artists, such as Portuguese sculptor Rui Chafes. The initial results of the collaboration between Costa and Chafes were shown at the exhibition *Fora!/Out!* held at the Serralves Foundation (Porto) between October 2005 and January 2006, curated by David and João Fernandes. For this exhibition Costa created four video installations with material sourced from *In Vanda's Room* and *Colossal Youth*: *Minino macho, minino fêmea* (*Little Boy Male, Little Girl Female*, henceforth *Little Boy Male*), *Benfica, Colina do Sol e Pontinha, Casal da Boba* and *Fontainhas*. These four installations were displayed in dialogue with Chafes's recognisable black iron sculptures. This collaboration with the Portuguese artist was subsequently continued in the exhibition *MU* at the Hara Museum of Contemporary Art in Tokyo (between December 2012 and March 2013). Later, Costa and Chafes also collaborated in the exhibition *Família*, held at the Roman underground gallery located under the Machado de Castro National Museum in Coimbra (Portugal) between November 2015 and January 2016.

When considering a broader context, Costa's presence in the international art gallery circuit illustrates an increasing interest on the part of art curators to include film in dialogue with visual arts, as a way of expanding the understanding of the ongoing mutations informing contemporary artistic practices. Catherine David's role in this inclusion of cinema in the art gallery needs once again to be acknowledged. With extensive curatorial experience and with a vested interest in the multidisciplinary dialogues between cinema and contemporary visual arts, David curated, among many other international art events, Documenta X in 1997. This edition of the quinquennial exhibition included video installations by (among others) filmmakers Jean-Luc Godard, Chantal Akerman and Sally Potter alongside works by a significant number of different multidisciplinary contemporary artists. Documenta X inspired the tenets of a curatorial tendency eager to understand cinema as yet another discipline to be exhibited in the white cube. This large-scale international art event offered an exhibition and curatorial blueprint to different events that, in the last two decades, has carried further this juxtaposition between cinema and contemporary arts.

This tendency looks back to aesthetic, technical and exhibition characteristics shared by cinema and the visual arts. Clear examples of this cinema museumification are exhibitions such as *Into the Light: The Projected Image in American Art 1964–1977* (Whitney Museum, New York, 2001) and *Le Mouvement des Images* (Centre Pompidou, Paris, 2006). The curatorial tenets of these exhibitions draw on possible historical links that tie early and mid-twentieth-century art and photography to different experimental cinema and avant-garde traditions. More pertinent to the discussion offered here, on the other hand, this approximation between cinema and the arts is also triggered by contemporary 'cinematic' practices that position or reposition cinema's stylistic and technological frameworks into the gallery space. The term 'cinematic' deserves some explanation. I argue that this artistic trend is expressed through artistic practices shared between contemporary fine artists and filmmakers. Accordingly, the cinematic is not just informed by similar aesthetics and production processes but also juxtaposes two different cultural sites – the museum and the cinema theatre (see Pantenburg 2008: 4; Uroskie 2014: 5–6). These practitioners, although with different artistic and professional paths, nonetheless come to share the same presentational space and institutional formation offered by the international art circuit.

Technology acquires an important role in this trend. The aesthetics, production and exhibition shaping the cinematic at the art gallery are intertwined with the evolution of cinema's modes of exhibition, and become further enhanced by the technological possibilities offered by digital video (see Bellour 2012: 29). Digital cameras and computers are tools shared between filmmakers and artists, allowing the adoption of technical procedures and professional practices that are similarly deployed by different moving image practitioners.[2] As far as contemporary cinema is concerned, the use of digital video supports filmmaking practices less constricted by technological, production and financial terms, as exemplified by Costa's filmmaking blueprint in use since the late 1990s (see Chapter 3). Thus the use of digital video created possibilities for a technological and industrial back-to-basics in filmmaking, while also enabling further post-production processes and data storage. In addition, digital technologies facilitate exhibition and circulation. Examples of this are digital supports such as the Digital Cinema Package (DCP), now widely adopted in cinema exhibition circuits. Similar characteristics are also observed in creative practices situated in the art gallery. As Chris Meigh-Andrews remind us, the advent of digital technology brought with it 'reliable inexpensive production equipment, the availability of DVD playback, high-resolution projection'; these technical capabilities decisively impacted on 'artistic expression', as well as becoming a standard 'gallery display format' (2006: 277). Artist and filmmakers currently share the same technical operations provided by digital technologies (for example, computer editing, special effects or audiovisual data storing), as well as display formats. As regards this convergence taking place in the art gallery, the latter accommodate the projection of works by both visual artists and filmmakers, populating this once exclusively white-walled exhibition space with multiscreen viewing experiences placed in darkened areas.

Digital technological apparatus has helped to blur the boundaries between cinema and artistic practices situated in the white cube. It enhanced aesthetic and production practices of contemporary artists, while also allowing filmmakers to cross over between film's aesthetics and practices of production and art installation. The attention devoted to cinema by contemporary artists primarily concerns forms of recycling and repurposing different visual references and codes, under an encompassing cross-disciplinary mode of addressing the moving image. The contemporary cinematic tendency is, to some extent, distinct from the ample historical synergies between art and cinema that took shape under early and mid-twentieth-century artistic avant-garde practices (Iles 2001: 35–9; Dercon 2002). Instead, the contemporary cinematic expression within the gallery space positions its attention on the role of cinema as an entertainment industry, and on its production contexts. As Catherine Elwes argues, contemporary artists' fascination with the cinematic can be contextualised as a 'fetishisation of Hollywood', transmitting popular cinema's broad impact in contemporary global culture (2004: 169–71). Similarly, Ursula Frohne points out the predominance of an 'aesthetic of the remake' in the practices of many contemporary artists. This aesthetic is articulated through the deployment of commercial cinema's techniques that have 'become cultural constants' to contemporary spectators (2008: 359).

Elaborating on these possible differences between historical and contemporary synergies between film and art, Dercon argues that the works of many contemporary visual artists 'show a radical difference from what has gone before':

> [f]ilm or video pieces by young artists such as Pierre Huyghe, Douglas Gordon, Sharon Lockhart, Pierre Bismuth, Mark Lewis, Georgina Starr, Matthew Barney, Stan Douglas or Sam Taylor-Wood are primarily imitations of the cinema or of its mode of production. [. . .] They imitate a wide range of western visual expression, avant-garde techniques and, inevitably, the cinema. They look for disciplines which are readily available to anyone, anywhere. Of all the arts, it is the cinema which functions as a really global medium. That cinema which is globally popular did not and does not seem to be bound by different cultural characteristics and art was looking for that. (Dercon 2002)

This understanding of the contemporary cinematic in the art gallery positions cinema as a global cultural *lingua franca*, used in artistic practices which question the current hybridity of the moving image. This is so even when noting that Dercon's analysis offers a challenging understanding of this trend, as one of rupture with historical synergies between art and cinema.

The cinematic remake in contemporary art is more nuanced and multifaceted than perceived in the analysis offered above. As Frohne also points out, the cinematic in the art gallery reveals different tendencies. One of these tendencies concerns an 'iconophilic impulse', 'responding affirmatively' to the illusory and affective principles of mainstream cinema by mimicking its techniques (as manifested in works created by Pipilotti Rist, for example); differently, other conceptual approaches to the cinematic offer instead an 'iconoclastic' tendency, by deconstructing cinema's aesthetic and narrative tropes in order to expose its constructed spectacle (Frohne 2008: 359–60). This latter tendency relies significantly on stylistic tropes such as structural repetition, the use of decelerated movement and extended filmic duration. These tropes offer a clear link with both past artistic and filmic traditions. In historical terms, tropes such as filmic duration and narrative deceleration were central to Andy Warhol's film works of the early 1960s and in filmic practices commonly included under Structural/Materialist film. Such characteristics re-emerge in works by contemporary artists such as Douglas Gordon, Sharon Lockhart and Steve McQueen (see Campany 2008: 37–9).

Pertinently, these same aesthetic characteristics have also become central in discussions of contemporary art film. Similar tropes are commonly pointed out in film criticism and scholarly discussions to contextualise contemporary filmic descriptors such as Slow Cinema. As examined in the previous chapter, debates around contemporary filmic slowness have been marked by accusations of overinvestment in stylistic formalism, and of inducing boredom among some film audiences. Contrasting with this critical response, contemporary cinematic slowness experiences a form of artistic rehabilitation within the white cube. This is manifested in art curators' current interest in commissioning new works, or including revisions of existing ones, directed by filmmakers who question cinema's visual and narrative nature through the stylistic tropes commonly associated with filmic deceleration. As Jihoon Kim argues, when discussing the work of filmmaker Apichatpong Weerasethakul, many contemporary art filmmakers are invited to 'translate' their filmic works into art installations, or to conceive 'new works only accessible in the darkened space of the gallery, while continuing to produce films for traditional theatrical release' (2010: 125–6). This ambivalent presence in both the black box and the white cube, enjoyed by Weerasethakul's as well as Costa's works (and extending to works of other filmmakers already mentioned here), presupposes the re-articulation of a filmic aesthetic which is able to respond to the different forms of artistic consumption taking place under these two presentational modes.

RECYCLING AND TRANSLATING THE PERSONAL ARCHIVE

When addressing the inclusion of Costa's works in the art gallery space, it is relevant to scrutinise how the aesthetic characteristics of his films respond to the expectations of the gallery circuit and, similarly, how authorial processes are negotiated in this arena. During a round table discussion hosted at the Jan van Eyck Academie (Maastricht) in May 2007, in which Catherine David also participated, Costa observed:

> I happen to belong to that group of filmmakers who are invited to enter the game of contemporary art. Such filmmakers are considered to be more 'pictorial' or more 'plastic' or whatever [. . .] I only allow myself to enter this game because I have this manner of making films. I have already constituted, if you like, my own archive, my own little museum. (David et al. 2007)

The idea of a personal archive, as suggested above, is particularly apt to define a collection of material generated by Costa and his collaborators which was made possible through protracted shooting processes supported by use of digital video. The use of this archival material, moreover, is not exclusive to feature films but is repositioned throughout different filmic projects for both the black box and the white cube.

It is noteworthy to discuss here how Costa's authorial process compares with artistic practices informing cinematic works at art galleries. Offering a discussion on disparate fine artists' practices concerning the cinematic, Erika Balsom argues that forms of appropriation and remaking of cinema came to be defined through different creative 'operations'. Two of these operations offer a closer relation between filmmaking processes and artistic practices. The first concerns the 'recycling' of existing film footage. As Balsom argues, this operation extends the tradition of the 'found object' through a revitalisation made possible by the use of digital technologies (2013: 118–19). When considered as an artistic practice, this operation assumes a form of appropriation which decontextualises existing filmic material that is not produced by the artist, and that is subsequently incorporated in new artworks. A similar process of recycling is observed in Costa's video installations. These works use material originated from a personal archive, initially shot to be included in his feature films. Examples of this operation are observed in the two installations already mentioned, *Daughters of Fire*, which recycles footage from *Casa de Lava*, and the installation initially presented at the Biennale d'Art Contemporain at Lyon in 2001, which reuses material taken from *In Vanda's Room*.

Even more applicable to Costa's video installations is an operation of 'translation'. When carried by artists, Balsom points out, this operation subjects a pre-existing filmic work 'to a cross-medium process'; it decontextualises textual or aesthetic particularities of a film and reworks it as a new artefact placed in a different presentational format (Balsom 2013: 119–20). This operation is, similarly, observed in Costa's works for the white cube, even when considering the nuanced differences between filmmaking and artistic practices. Three main points deserve to be emphasised when examining the translation of Costa's work to the white cube. Firstly, in technical terms, the filmmaker's video installations repurpose (or recycle, as already discussed) existing material which is, therefore, subjected to new editorial and montage processes (or as in the case of *Daughters of Fire*, to a transference from its initial film stock support to digital video). Such technical translation highlights the importance digital video acquired in Costa's filmmaking in terms of both production and post-production. This technical aspect connects his video installations to his work for the black box.

Secondly, this translation process also concerns the resituating of textual and narrative characteristics that were initially present in Costa's feature films into a different presentational context. An example of this is *Little Boy Male*, mentioned earlier, which combines material initially shot for *In Vanda's Room* and *Colossal Youth*. This double-screen installation provides a rapport with the two films: one screen shows scenes shot in the streets of Fontainhas; the other, sequences shot in interior spaces that were initially featured in both films, for example Vanda and Zita Duarte's room and the shack occupied by Ventura and

Figure 5.3 Double-screen narrative compositions of *Little Boy Male, Little Girl Female* (2005)

Lento. As Costa explained to me, this arrangement aims to present Fontainhas as a space in which 'the exteriors and interiors confound each other', while opening ways to reinterpret a location which, at the time, had already been demolished (Costa 2013). Moreover, and still according to Costa, *Little Boy Male* is an alternative version of the filmic narrative which allows 'the public to make their own editing . . . audiences can look at both screens and come up with a story' (2013). Thus, while structured differently to its initial editing for the black box, the material included in *Little Boy Male* nonetheless discusses an alternative narrative iteration connected to the thematic and aesthetic universe present in Costa's feature films (Figure 5.3).

Directly related to its textual and narrative translation, the third aspect of the operation concerns how these same characteristics are exhibited in the presentational mode of the gallery. The white cube offers a favourable setting for a contemporary art cinema that shares with the visual arts an aesthetic sense of filmic temporality. The image stillness transmitted by the use of long takes and narrative fragmentation, as observed in Costa's cinema, finds here a favourable stage for exhibition. The translation of this aesthetic to the art exhibition space, however, raises several questions. As André Parente and Victa de Carvalho point out:

> [t]he fixed duration imposed on the spectator by regular movie theatres, for example, no longer applies in cinema of exhibition. Its conditions of reception imply an elasticity of time, allowing viewers to follow their own trajectory, to participate in an experience unique to them only. Instead of a definite sequence, it offers different modalities of perception, editing and temporality. (Parente and de Carvalho 2008: 50)

The differences between the black box and the white cube presuppose a duality between a spectator's passive or (potentially) active reception. These different exhibition models are ruled not just by spatial dissimilarities but also by different viewing models. When positioned in the black box, filmic works negotiate pre-conceived modes of consumption within the theatrical setting. In other words, a dark room in which audiences sit in order to watch a film with a pre-determined length. The (darkened) space of the gallery differs from these preconceived notions of the cinema setting, as the visitors' reception is shaped by the possibility of movement and by a different time scale (see Nisa 2007: 74–5).

Implicit in Parente and de Carvalho's argument, therefore, is the notion of time economy. Video installations come to engage the visitor's attention, which is conditioned by the time allocated to each of the different works of art in the exhibition. An example of this tension between film aesthetics and time economy on the part of the visitor is presented by Costa's eight-hour installation *Casal da Boba* (2005), initially included in *Fora!/Out!*. This single screen video installation uses material shot in Vanda Duarte's new room at the Casal da Boba estate – material that would later be reused in *Colossal Youth*. The installation was designed to run during the whole period of the Serralves Museum's opening hours, inviting the public to watch it for any amount of time or, instead, to circulate around its surrounding darkened space or even out of it (Nisa 2009: 310). This viewing practice surely offers a personal and unique experience, as Parente and de Carvalho argue. As Thomas Elsaesser contends, however, the extended duration of many of these filmic works is affected by the visitor's regulated attention, something which 'creates its own aesthetics', while limiting the narrative potential initially intended (2011: 111). These works aim to iterate narrative qualities of material initially recorded for the black box, even if their extended duration presents a clear problematic factor in terms of consumption.

The works for the white cube analysed above transmit an intertextual process that connects them to the feature films directed by Costa. Only one of Costa's video installations, *The End of a Love Affair* (2003), presents an exception to such a coherent thematic and narrative universe. This eight minute video installation was developed in collaboration with Portuguese choreographer João Fiadeiro and actor and artist Gustavo Sumpta. This single screen work was initially created for the 2003 edition of *Festival Temps d'Images*. It is composed of a single shot depicting a man (Sumpta) standing near the window of a bedroom (the space's minimal decoration and lack of personal objects suggests that this is a hotel room), looking out of the window while also observing the curtains moving with the breeze (Figure 5.4). The moment depicted concerns the aftermath of a love affair, as suggested by the inclusion in the soundtrack of the song with the same title, sung by Billie Holiday. *The End of a Love Affair* is a singular work in Costa's *oeuvre*, as it neither uses material sourced from the shooting of his

Figure 5.4 An exception in Costa's coherent filmic universe: still from *The End of a Love Affair* (2003), featuring Gustavo Sumpta

feature films, nor reflects the narrative and thematic universe originated in his collaboration with the Fontainhas and Casal da Boba residents.

Returning to Balsom's operations, I argue that recycling and translation are not just confined to Costa's video installations, but are also extended to his short films. In 2007 Costa directed *Tarrafal*, commissioned by the Calouste Gulbenkian Foundation. The short was in the omnibus film *O Estado do Mundo* (*The State of the World*), which also included short films by Apichatpong Weerasethakul, Vicente Ferraz, Ayisha Abraham, Chantal Akerman and Wang Bing. During the same year, Costa also directed *The Rabbit Hunters*, which was included in the JDP initiative promoted by the Jeonju International Film Festival (see previous chapter). These short films reveal a similar relation with Costa's notion of archive by reusing the same material in different filmic objects while simultaneously reformulating its narrative potential. Establishing possible connections with the storyline of *Colossal Youth*, both these short films expand the wanderings of Ventura in and around Casal da Boba. This time Ventura meets and interacts with other characters not initially included in the narrative of the feature film. Among the moments depicted, both short films show Ventura listening to the memories of Alfredo (played by Alfredo Mendes), a ghostly character who recalls personal stories marked by unemployment, deprivation and police brutality.

Parallel to the scenes featuring the two men, Costa includes other narrative moments in *Tarrafal* and *The Rabbit Hunters*. In these scenes two new characters are introduced. The initial scene of *Tarrafal* depicts the dialogue between Zé Alberto and his mother (played by José Alberto Silva and Lucinda Cardoso respectively). In it she recalls Cape Verde, and tells her son about a supernatural entity which chooses its victims by slipping cursed letters into their pockets. This dialogue elicits comparisons with the plot of Jacques Tourneur's *Night of the Demon* (1957, also known as *Curse of the Demon*). This suggests yet another adaptation by Costa (if via a distant reference) of a work coming out of RKO's B-movie horror unit. Tourneur's film plot concerns a demonic figure which is guided to its victims through parchments with runic writings, which have been previously passed to them. A later scene in *Tarrafal* makes a correlation with this by showing a deportation notice delivered to Zé Alberto by immigration officials. This document invokes a similar curse to those preceding the demise of the demon's victims in the 1957 horror classic (Figure 5.5).

As with the scenes depicting Ventura and Alfredo Mendes's dialogues on both short films, these same narrative compositions around Zé Alberto and his

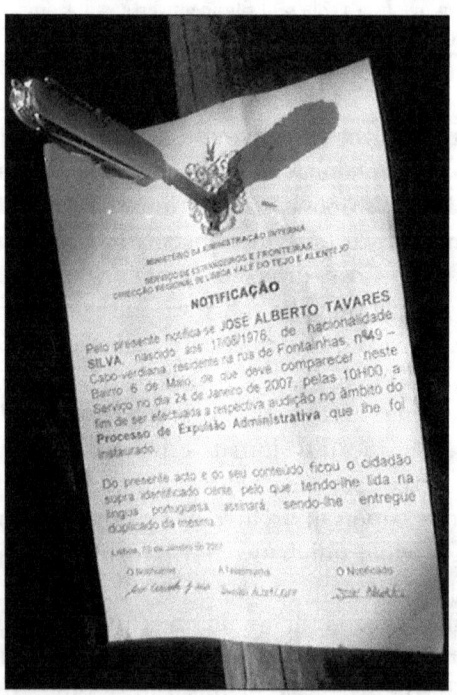

Figure 5.5 Still from *Tarrafal* (2007): Zé Alberto's deportation notice as a 'cursed document' similar to the ones used in Tourneur's *Night of the Demon* (1957)

mother are also revisited in *The Rabbit Hunters*, though structured differently. As film critic Bernard Eisenschitz notes, *Tarrafal* and *The Rabbit Hunters* are structured around these two narrative 'episodes', while presenting different takes of the same scenes, which are depicted in either shortened or extended versions (2009: 238). *Tarrafal* depicts the narrative around Zé Alberto while including a shorter version of the dialogues maintained by Ventura and Alfredo. *The Rabbit Hunters*, on the other hand, can be understood as an iteration of *Tarrafal*, with Costa inverting the narrative structure to give prevalence to the recollections of the two men. Alfredo's unsuccessful hunting efforts, suggested in the short film's title, serve as a pretext to overlap further these two narrative episodes initially structuring *Tarrafal*. For instance, in *The Rabbit Hunters* it is revealed that Alfredo is Zé Alberto's father (something omitted altogether in *Tarrafal*). Costa would later go back to these same two narrative episodes, re-editing the material included in both *Tarrafal* and *The Rabbit Hunters* to create the narrative structure of *Our Man*. This 2010 short film add yet another nuanced iteration to the reminiscences of Ventura and Alfredo.

The re-editing work of *Tarrafal*, *The Rabbit Hunters* and *Our Man* illustrates how the operations of recycling and translation, which inform Costa's video installations, are also extended to works produced for the black cube. These three short films reutilise material depicting the same two narrative episodes. Even if translated differently, these episodes have their origin in a broader textual and narrative 'archive' created and maintained by Costa. All these different works for the white cube and black box are informed by the attention given by Costa to montage. The different iterations observed in short films and video installations are still ruled by the similar narrative constructions which organise his feature films. As Costa argues: 'I'm not a video artist, I am a filmmaker and a film is a construction. [. . .] You may find me a bit reactionary but I think cinema can never forget its narrative foundations' (David et al. 2007). This preoccupation with narrative structure reminds us of the influence of Straub and Huillet in Costa's work. This is so particularly when considering the close attention given to film *découpage* – the choice and arrangement of shots – shared by the filmmakers. Appropriately, such preoccupation is also perceived in the work within the work depicted in *Where Does Your Hidden Smile Lie?*. While recording the meticulous montage process carried out by Straub and Huillet, Costa's documentary also calls our attention to the possibility of different narrative iterations comprised in it: the work being edited by the French filmmakers (the third editing of the feature film *Sicily!*); the possible alternative stories emerging when observing their montage methods; and the account of their activities, shot and later edited by Costa.

These processes of recycling and narrative permutation are also used in *Sweet Exorcism*. This short film was a commission by Guimarães 2012 European Capital of Culture to be included in *Centro Histórico*, an omnibus film that also contained shorts directed by Manoel de Oliveira, Aki Kaurismäki and Víctor Erice. This work can be understood as a narrative and thematic continuation of *Colossal Youth* and subsequent short films. It is also a narrative prelude to Costa's following feature film, *Cavalo Dinheiro* (*Horse Money*, 2014). *Sweet Exorcism* is structured around three main narrative moments. The first scene, taking place at night, depicts the efforts of several characters to find Ventura in a rocky woodland similar to the one used as a backdrop in some scenes of the *Rabbit Hunters*. These characters are positioned in what seems a group of *tableaux vivants* and played by, among others, Costa's regular collaborators Alberto Barros, António Semedo and Isabel Cardoso. The second narrative moment, the lengthiest of the three, depicts Ventura trapped in an elevator with a soldier figure covered in bronze paint (António Santos), resembling a statue or a human-size toy soldier. The allegorical figure of the soldier provokes Ventura to relive his memories of the period around the 1974 April Revolution, previously alluded to in *Colossal Youth*. Such a process of recalling memories serves both as a lament (as indicated on the Portuguese title, translated as 'lament for a lost youth') and as an attempt to exorcise Ventura's painful memories around a particular incident. The narrative of *Sweet Exorcism* closes with a day scene, positioning Ventura in the same location featured at the beginning of the film, making clear that the nightmarish moments lived in the elevator are now, somehow, resolved.

Costa would later re-edit *Sweet Exorcism* and include its first two narrative moments in *Horse Money*. Comparing the two works, it is clear that some short scenes of the first narrative moment in *Sweet Exorcism* were not included in *Horse Money*. In the second narrative moment of the short film Costa maintained most of the structure of these scenes. In *Horse Money*, however, the non-diegetic soundtrack of these scenes is slightly different; also some of the scenes were cut short, and the last scene initially included in the short film was omitted. This transposition of material from *Sweet Exorcism* to *Horse Money* suggests both continuation and permutation of a thematic and narrative universe centred in Ventura's memories, which spans several feature and short films and video installations. The recycling and translation operations informing these works contribute to a cogent authorial process which bridges different filmic formats. This is so even if considering that these aesthetic, textual and thematic qualities are positioned in different presentational modes.

AN ARTISTS' ECONOMY?

More than just confined to authorial choices – and the archive that sustains them – these operations also call our attention to a production framework which responds to the particular tenets of the international art gallery circuit.

Pedro Costa's video installations and short films are not just connected by similar creative intertextual qualities that recycle and translate previous material. The different works are also tied to similar financial and production processes. With the exception of *Our Man*, Costa's short films and video installations suit exhibition and financial tenets of different cultural institutions. These works are financially supported by disparate organisations participating in the international film festival (as in the case of the Jeonju International Film Festival), the art circuit (the Serralves Foundation or the Lyon Biennale), as well as by institutions with variegated cultural remits, such as the Calouste Gulbenkian Foundation or the European Capital of Culture initiatives. These film commissions exemplify how Costa's filmmaking practice is able to adapt to the diverse remits ruling these different cultural formations.

This ambivalence in successfully negotiating a presence on both cinema and art circuits is the result of a production blueprint alleviating budgetary and time restrictions. Understandably, this production blueprint also factors in a successful inclusion in the art circuit financial models. As Costa argued during a debate with Rui Chafes that took place at the Portuguese Cinematheque in January 2015:

> cinema lives from an excessive amount of money. [. . .] Jean-Marie Straub, quoting Luis Buñuel, used to say that every new film made has to be more expensive than the previous one, or else you won't be [considered] a filmmaker. Nowadays, that is clearer than ever before. [. . .] I think filmmakers need to be closer to the economy of a painter, a photographer . . . closer not to their art, but to their economy, meaning [. . .] not just the money but how time is deployed. Personally, I feel more affinity with the economy of artists. (Costa and Chafes 2015)[3]

This potential approximation to the economy of artists expresses Costa's well-known attitude towards contemporary filmmaking practices. His production blueprint allows an ambivalent approximation to different financial and exhibition circuits, as well as potentiating several collaborations with artists. Examples of these collaborations are the video installation made with João Fiadeiro, already discussed, and his continued collaboration with Rui Chafes.

While ambivalent, this inclusion in the art gallery circuit is bound to economic aspects which need to be further contextualised. Particularly considering the differences between cinema and the art world, Elsaesser reminds us that these cultural institutions are shaped by different 'actor-agents, different power-relations and policy agendas, different competences, egos and sensibilities' (Elsaesser 2011: 109). Indeed, these differing dynamisms come to reinforce the different presentational modes and curatorial aims ruling these institutions.

These differences become somehow less acute, however, when we consider that these institutions operate within a similar economy of prestige. As discussed in the previous chapter, the international film festival is a stage on which are discussed nonmonetary and monetary values. These values can be attributed through the circulation and exposure of filmic works but also, in some cases, through financial support. Costa's inclusion in the art gallery circuit expands on such value discussion to other cultural settings. The art institution dispenses similar nonmonetary and monetary currency, offering exhibition and circulation venues to Costa's works, as well as financially supporting some of his filmmaking activities.

Such inclusion is ruled by circulation and production dynamisms of the art gallery, which are informed by discursive and institutional framings that bring together the disparate artistic practices associated with it (see Balsom 2013: 40). It is clear that the white cube is not just an exhibition setting, but also an institutional network shaped by cultural discourses, competitive practices, and geographical and economic interests. These dynamics are disparate yet, again, somehow alike to those observed in the international film festival circuit. The circulation of filmmakers' works in the art gallery is concomitant with the development of a complex network of international art events. The nodes included in this network, though varied in scale, nonetheless mimic curatorial and exhibition models offered by mega-events such as Documenta, Manifesta and Venice biennales (see Filipovic 2005: 68; O'Neill 2012: 69). As Elena Filipovic argues, this international art network is shaped by a multitude of political, cultural and geographical contexts, with 'an explicit ambition [. . .] to display a decidedly international panorama of contemporary production, an ambition that influences the scale and general circumstance attached to [these events]' (Filipovic 2005: 65). These events seem particularly invested in mapping new geographies in the art world, and in including the latest multidisciplinary artistic and curatorial trends.

The presence of filmmakers like Costa in this 'global white cube' arena, as Filipovic terms it, does not substitute for the flow offered by the film festival circuit. Yet it potentially offers analogous forms of prestige, translated in an overlapping between the role of 'filmmaker' and 'artist'. Particularly revealing of this equivalence is the invitation issued to Costa in 2008 by the Portuguese Secretary of State for Culture to represent the country at the Venice Biennale, which took place in the following year. As Costa explained to me, the short deadline imposed on him to complete the work made him 'decline the invitation' (2013). As some Portuguese newspapers suggested at the time, this offer followed several rumours that controversial visual artist Joana Vasconcelos was the favourite to represent the country at this event (Rato 2008). We may speculate as to whether this fact hints at particular preferences or curatorial aims among the Portuguese organisers. More significantly, this episode reveals how the filmmaker's accrued prestige at global cultural arenas allowed him to be offered a presence at an art event with considerable international scope. While declining to participate in this event, Costa would eventually participate in the Venice Biennale in 2013, by having video installations included in the Cuban Pavilion alongside works by Rui Chafes and several Cuban and international artists.

More than just negotiating forms of prestige, Costa's participation in the global white cube calls our attention to the financing possibilities offered by such milieus. The economic dynamism of the international art gallery circuit is sustained by regional or national public funding bodies and private sponsorship, supporting initiatives which 'produce, promote and reconfigure the concept of "contemporary" artist practice through new commissions' (O'Neill 2012: 53). This is a commission-based financial model centred on international art curators, who serve as gatekeepers for both nonmonetary and monetary value. Such a model is highly flexible in supporting and shaping disparate multidisciplinary artistic practices, including filmmaking. It does, however, abide by different remits to the model offered by the variegated financial institutions supporting contemporary art cinema. During the round table discussion hosted at the Jan van Eyck Academie, Catherine David expressed this argument clearly by calling attention to how particular filmmakers are able to adapt to the art world's financial model:

> The issue is simply where to get the money and where and how to distribute. [. . .] So in the case of Pedro [Costa] and others who are not working with a big budget the question – as I see it – is, 'Is your conceptual and production structure coherent?' [. . .] [I] don't think of the museum as an alternative. It is one more space of exhibition. It's one more source of financing – but not for any project. (David et al. 2007)

As suggested by David, Costa's adaptation to an economy previously understood as exclusive to contemporary fine artists is operated under conceptual and production characteristics that, while included within a broad filmmaking practice, nonetheless need to respond to the particular tenets of the art world. Costa explained at the same event how his works are integrated in the white cube:

> It's more or less accepted now, this separation between commercial, mainstream filmmakers whose work is shown in multiplexes around the world, and the 'artistic' filmmakers who are judged as 'almost painters,' closer to the beaux-arts. [. . .] [It] also had to do with the cliché that we have a more distant, detached relation to money. In fact, it's about the absolute opposite, we must think about it all the time because of the simple fact that we don't have it. (David et al. 2007)

As Costa's observations suggests, while aesthetic characteristics of his films surely arouse the attention of art curators, his approximation to the art circuit reflects the necessity of constantly being aware of potential funding opportunities complementing those offered by film institutions. Costa was able to negotiate an interstitial position operating under contemporary art cinema's nonmonetary and monetary activities. This position is ambivalent enough to correspond to curatorial expectations and to adapt to the art gallery's financial model.

This understanding of an ambivalent filmmaking practice, framed discursively by Costa as close to an economy maintained by artists, alludes to a Bourdieusian understanding of cultural production. Even if operating within different practices of production and consumption, contemporary art cinema and the art world nonetheless are bound to a 'disavowal condition' shaping the economy of prestige (see Bourdieu 1980: 261–2). Giving primacy to forms of symbolic value, the economy of prestige maintained by both these institutions reflects, nonetheless, different production and financial aspects. Costa's small-scale and low-budget filmmaking practice propitiates an adaptation to the convergent financial and production *modus operandi* of contemporary art cinema. These same characteristics play an important role in adapting to similar dynamisms shaping the international art gallery institution. This assumed approximation to the artists' economy helps the Portuguese filmmaker to carry on an ambivalent professional practice which, to some extent, enables an authorial presence transcending cinema institutions. Filmmaking activities remain at the core of Costa's authorial practice. Yet his collaborative practices with art curators such as Catherine David and artists such as Rui Chafes expand an authorial practice once confined to the feature film format. One of the most recent examples of such interest in maintaining different extra-filmic projects is Costa's collaboration in 2016 with the Portuguese music ensemble *Os Filhos do Tejo*, creating images projected during the show *Cinema e Música*, which took place at the Calouste Gulbenkian Foundation in Lisbon.

This attitude towards an ambivalent filmmaking practice is, however, dependent on different contextual characteristics that facilitated the inclusion of contemporary art filmmakers in the art gallery. Costa's filmic aesthetics arouse the interest of art curators as these are in dialogue with contemporary artistic trends that interrogate the pictorial and narrative natures of the moving image. These same aesthetic characteristics extend the exhibition potential of such works within the space of the art gallery. Costa's attitude towards the financial and production factors within this cultural circuit brings forth productive and complex discussions concerning how authorial agency affects exhibition and distribution processes outside theatrical consumption of film. The narrative of production supporting the production of both his works for the black box and the white cube adapts to both symbolic value aspirations and financial remits of the art gallery, a circuit that seeks in contemporary art cinema a creative source to sustain its interdisciplinary exhibition operations.

NOTES

1. The exhibition comprised archival material and works of art included in the museum collection of the Santa Casa da Misericórdia charity. These works were exhibited alongside Costa's video installation and works created by Portuguese photographer Daniel Blaufuks.
2. My argument here does not disregard previous technological overlapping between cinema and visual arts. Indeed, this approximation was previously facilitated by the use of moving image technologies such Super 8 film and analogue video, as well as by 16mm film stock. The latter was, for several decades, a staple format for low-budget cinema, documentary and moving image artistic practices, and negotiating its presence in both the black box and the white cube. This approximation between cinema and visual arts through these technologies (once considered obsolete) is still visible in contemporary terms as these are still used by some contemporary filmmakers and visual artists.
3. This session was part of the programme 'Pedro Costa: Realizador Convidado', hosted by the Portuguese Cinematheque in January 2015. Spanning a period of three weeks, this programme included the screening of Costa's feature and short films, as well as works by Tourneur, Warhol, Rivette, Straub and Huillet, Renoir and Chaplin (among others). These film sessions were complemented by conversations with guests invited by Costa. They included the architect José Neves, artists João Queiroz and Rui Chafes, photographer Paulo Nozolino and Costa's collaborators Leonardo Simões (cinematographer) and Olivier Blanc (sound director).

CHAPTER 6

Renegotiating Circulation: Retrospectives and DVD Releases

The years 2009 and 2010 were particularly prolific in terms of the international exposure of Pedro Costa's cinema. The filmmaker's new feature-length project, the music documentary *Ne Change Rien* (*Change Nothing*, 2009), had its theatrical release in Portugal, France, Spain and Japan, while also circulating in a considerable number of international film festivals in Europe and in North and South America. Costa's directorial debut, *Blood*, also enjoyed new theatrical distribution in the Portuguese market during the second half of 2009. This was soon followed by its release on DVD, made by British film distributors Second Run and by Portuguese Midas Filmes. Around this same period, Costa's other works also enjoyed renewed attention. His *oeuvre* benefited from a complete retrospective at London's Tate Modern between September and October 2009. Soon after, in March 2010, *Bones*, *In Vanda's Room* and *Colossal Youth* were included in a DVD boxed set titled *Letters from Fontainhas*, released by prestigious New York-based home video distribution company The Criterion Collection. These coinciding exhibition and circulation activities made possible the recuperation of a body of work previously restricted to the geographical boundaries of the film festival and art-house circuits, and confined to special screenings and video releases that were mostly unavailable. Moreover, these initiatives helped renew the interest in Costa's cinema among an already resilient fan base, while also responding to the demand of the broader cinephile communities for an *oeuvre* which, at the time, was amassing increasing attention among international film critics and scholars.

These different initiatives were informed, to a considerable degree, by Costa's effort to search for further opportunities to distribute his works. The filmmaker actively engaged in collaborations with several cultural institutions receptive to holding exhibition activities such as special screenings and retrospectives. He also became directly involved in processes of re-mastering and release of his films on DVD and, in some cases, on Blu-ray. In a broader sense, this effort constitutes a form of disintermediation, in which the role of producers becomes increasingly subdued. As Dina Iordanova points out, disintermediation comes to 'undermine' the traditional roles of the producer and distributor, making possible a direct interaction between filmmakers and audiences (2012: 4–5). Iordanova contextualises disintermediation processes as one of the facets of the technology supporting the contemporary global digital economy. These processes, however, also result from a professional agency that aims at renegotiating forms of ownership. As Iordanova further explains, many artists 'opt to keep the copyright to their works and engage in dissemination strategies over which they have direct control', allowing the 'content creator to handle both production and dissemination' (2012: 12).

Costa's professional ethos has impacted on the ways the works he directs are shot and produced. Over the years, this helped the filmmaker to retain control over production and financial processes which inform the different stages of the making of his films. This professional agency also extends to activities around consumption. Authorial processes and collaborative practices which took shape in the mid- to late 2000s significantly inform these disintermediation characteristics. This period corresponds to the end of an increasingly problematic professional relationship with producer Francisco Villa-Lobos, and the beginning of a partnership with the production company Sociedade Óptica Técnica/OPTEC Filmes (OPTEC Filmes henceforth). Central to this change was Costa's effort to impose further authority on both production and distribution practices. This change in production companies came also to impact on dissemination practices engaged in by Costa. His professional agency came to preclude some of the tasks commonly undertaken by producers and sales agents. This suggests a form of authorial control which is manifested in practical but also in discursive terms. As Catherine Grant reminds us, notions of authorial and creative control are commonly translated in forms of 'auteurist awareness', which

> comprises a complex series of interrelated film production, marketing, and reception practices and discourses which are all underpinned by a shared belief in the specific capability of an individual agent – the director – to marshal and synthesize the multiple, and usually collective, elements of filmmaking for the purposes of individual expression, or to convey in some way a personal or, at least, 'personalized' vision. (Grant 2008: 101)

For Pedro Costa, this authorial presence (or 'awareness') has been incrementally built on production and dissemination practices resulting from disintermediation. As examined here, these practices may reflect forms of (individual) authorial control; yet they are greatly sustained by the interactions of different agents with variegated professional and personal interests. As Grant makes clear, moreover, this awareness also relies on discursive formations. Thus here I also take into account the discursive contours of Costa's authorial presence, as revealed by activities around film retrospectives and DVD releases.

TOWARDS DISINTERMEDIATION

The end of the professional relationship with Paulo Branco in the late 1990s signals a shift from Costa's professional role as a film director, working under financial and schedule strictures imposed by the producer, to a filmmaker aiming to secure control of production practices. This effort was sustained by Costa's subsequent partnership with Contracosta. As explained in previous chapters, Contracosta produced the feature films *In Vanda's Room* and *Colossal Youth* and the documentary *Where Does Your Hidden Smile Lie?*. Another work initially produced by Contracosta was the 2005 short film *Change Nothing*. The music documentary was initially a twelve-minute film produced by Francisco Villa-Lobos, later reworked as a feature length film with the support of OPTEC Filmes in 2009. Through this production company Costa was able to assume control on a protracted and small-scale shooting process of all these works, while depending on the support provided by different European companies and public institutions.[1]

This period of prolific collaboration with Contracosta also sees Costa's interest in gaining decision-making power over both production and distribution deals. This effort put a considerable strain on his relationship with Francisco Villa-Lobos, and would precipitate the end of their professional partnership soon after the post-production of *Colossal Youth*. Central to their disagreement was Costa's attitude towards both the production and distribution of the film. As Villa-Lobos explained to me:

> Pedro didn't agree [with the international distribution of *Colossal Youth*] ... decided to start doing it himself, contacting people at universities and critics he knew. Already at that time Pedro had the idea of making something alternative, concerning the museum and university circuits, the [art] galleries ... Pedro had already started, since *In Vanda's Room*, [video] installations with the material that we've filmed and that was edited by technicians [contracted by Contracosta]. He was aware that he could get out of a normal situation and do other things, even in financial terms. (Villa-Lobos 2013)

According to the producer, Costa started to boycott ongoing distribution negotiations, making unviable a potential agreement for the international distribution of *Colossal Youth*. Costa also complicated the negotiations with the distribution company Équation, responsible for the theatrical release and subsequent DVD edition of the film to the French market (Villa-Lobos 2013). By way of a retort to Villa-Lobos's arguments, Costa explained to me that this partnership with Contracosta was an 'intermediate stage' in his filmmaking activities; while initially different, this relationship increasingly became 'like the work relations with Paulo Branco, [. . .] the routines became too similar' (Costa 2013). The end of this increasingly tense partnership triggered Costa's approach to the Portuguese production company OPTEC Filmes.

While established as a film and television production company since 2001, OPTEC Filmes has its origins in Bazar do Video, a business founded in the mid-1980s that specialised in selling and renting middle-range and high-end film and video equipment to cinema and television professionals. Costa acquired the digital camera used in *In Vanda's Room* in the shop, and came to rely on the technical support and expertise provided by the company's founder and director Abel Ribeiro Chaves. The producer provides context to the professional relationship between OPTEC Filmes and Costa:

> Pedro was a regular visitor at the [Bazar do Video's] shop [. . .]. I cannot pinpoint a starting point in our work relationship. [. . .] But before the first film produced by [OPTEC Filmes] I was already following and helping Pedro in different projects. We can say that the beginning of my relationship with Pedro was when he stopped [using] film stock and adopted digital [video] in *In Vanda's Room*, for which I was a sort of technical adviser. So our work relationship started in 2006 but goes way back. (Chaves 2018)

OPTEC Filmes made possible a production framework which responds to the significant importance given by Costa to technical aspects of his filmmaking. As Costa explained to me: 'instead of having a producer [. . .] contacting [different financiers], to me it's more important to have the technology and equipment because, personally, money was always secondary and now even more so' (Costa 2013). The discursive disavowal of the financial side of filmmaking in Costa's observation is clear. It also, however, succinctly defines a framework which was increasingly able to support him in technical terms.

This framework becomes particularly evident when examining the two different iterations of *Change Nothing*. As Costa explained in an interview with Portuguese journalist Francisco Ferreira, this collaborative project between himself and the actress and singer Jeanne Balibar was developed over 'a period of five years, with intervals lasting several months, between each stage' (Ferreira 2010: 158). This corresponds to a period in which Costa was working on different projects, including *Colossal Youth* and several video installations.

Costa and a small number of professionals would sporadically accompany and record Balibar's band's musical activities, as well as the actress's voice coach sessions. A small amount of the material recorded was used to edit the 2005 version of *Change Nothing*. The short film is structured around three moments. The first is a sequence of Balibar and her band backstage, preparing for a concert. This moment is followed by a stage performance of the song that gives its title to the short film (an original song written by Balibar and French musician Yves Dormoy). The film closes with a rendition of the song 'Torture', initially recorded in the early 1960s by one-hit wonder American singer Kris Jensen. This initial cut of *Change Nothing* would later be revisited in 2009. Using material previously omitted, Costa and film editor Patrícia Saramago re-edited and expanded the film to approximately 100 minutes.

In the broader context of Costa's *oeuvre*, both iterations of *Change Nothing* reveal nuanced textual and production qualities. In textual terms, these films depict a different thematic and narrative universe to those tying Costa's films and video installations. The music documentary offers a clear narrative intermission from the works shot at Fontainhas and Casal da Boba. Lasting approximately twelve minutes, the initial version of the film reminds us of a music video, a format which Costa would later revisit in *Horse Money* (2014). The extended version of the film, similarly, is close to a music documentary format. It depicts stage performances, rehearsals and recording sessions, giving emphasis to the repertoire included in Balibar's band's two albums, *Paramour* (2003) and *Slalom Dame* (2006).

Although a music documentary, the feature film does not rely on a linear narrative and circumvents any possible contextualisation of Balibar's musical activities. As Chris Fujiwara observes, *Change Nothing* 'does not pretend to offer a simulated or reconstructed experience, some surrogate closeness or wholeness, something visual and active for the viewer to participate in' (2010: 315). Instead of these qualities commonly observed in the music documentary format, the fixed long shots in *Change Nothing* document the activities of Balibar and her collaborators in a non-intrusive and detached manner. While distinct thematically, *Change Nothing* nonetheless conveys an aesthetic approximation to other works included in Costa's *oeuvre*. Inevitably, the film's studied compositions and shadowy and saturated black and white cinematography – also credited to Costa – invite comparisons with the monochrome ambience created in *Blood*. It also seems to allude to the intimate chiaroscuro portrait of Vanda Duarte in *In Vanda's Room*. Perhaps more pertinently, *Change Nothing* reveals Costa's fascination with processes of artistic creation. The documentary offers a discreet examination of artists at work that is thematically and in structural terms similar to that depicted in *Where Does Your Hidden Smile Lie?*

The two iterations of *Change Nothing* also illustrate Costa's increasing control over production decisions, as well as his problematic work relationship with Contracosta's producer. When asked about the production process of *Change Nothing*, Villa-Lobos is adamant in pointing out:

> [*Change Nothing*] was a 'satellite' production of JeM [*Colossal Youth*], in the sense that it used the technical means and technicians paid to work in [it], and it was possible to pay for initial expenses [of *Change Nothing*] by using just the cash flow [. . .] coming from the financial process of JeM. (Villa-Lobos 2018)

Still according to the producer, in 2008 Costa acquired all of the initially recorded camera and sound masters and used that material in the extended version of the project, while already working with OPTEC Filmes (Villa-Lobos 2018). Understandably, this came to aggravate further the producer's discontent with the way Costa conducted the project.

The financial arrangements supporting the extended version of *Change Nothing* similarly reflect the small-scale co-production model that made possible Costa's previous feature films shot in digital video. According to Costa, the 2009 version of the film 'cost a hundred thousand euros' (Ferreira 2010: 163). OPTEC Filmes worked in collaboration with Tokyo-based distribution company Cinematrix (which covered the costs of the shooting of Balibar's band's performance in Japan) and with the French production company Red Star Cinéma, which supported post-production. It needs to be acknowledged that, regarding production, *Change Nothing* is a transitional project. The production of both the short and feature length documentaries are still dependent on the international co-production model. The ample technical support provided by OPTEC Filmes, however, greatly eases shooting and post-production costs. The subsequent films directed by Costa become increasingly removed from the necessity of international co-production agreements. This mode of production surely responds to an effort towards depending less on the financial side of production and more on the technical logistics of filmmaking.

These changes in production elucidate Costa's increasing autonomy from the role of producers, which in turn impacted on both authorship and ownership. While to some extent successful, such an attitude towards production and circulation is still dependent on negotiations about the copyright status of his films. Having been one of Trópico Filmes's partners, Costa retained the copyright of his first feature film, *Blood*. Similarly, current arrangements between Costa and OPTEC Filmes give the filmmaker access to all the works produced by this company. Costa was also able to negotiate the use of *In Vanda's Room* and *Colossal Youth*. In late 2000s, Villa-Lobos 'decided to sell the rights' of the films produced by Contracosta to the Portuguese Ministry of Culture, in order to end the troublesome work relationship with Costa (Villa-Lobos 2013). Although the details of this transaction are not publicly documented, this change of ownership allowed Costa to negotiate exhibition and distribution rights for these films directly with this public institution, both for theatrical exhibition and home viewing releases.

The exception to this situation which is favourable to Costa is the copyright status of the films produced by Paulo Branco. The ownership of *Casa de Lava* and *Bones* is currently held by the Portuguese media and communications conglomerate NOS (formerly ZON Lusomundo). In 2005, the cinema distribution company Lusomundo acquired (via PT Multimédia, currently also part of the NOS conglomerate) several assets of Paulo Branco's production and distribution companies, soon after their financial insolvency. These assets comprised the copyright and the distribution rights of approximately ninety films previously held by Madragoa Filmes, Atalanta Filmes and Medeia Filmes. Included in these assets are the two works directed by Costa, as well as several films by Portuguese filmmakers João César Monteiro and Manoel de Oliveira. Pedro Borges, the founder and director of distribution company Midas Filmes (the current distributor of Costa's films in Portugal) explains the problematic access to the rights of these films: 'since [. . .] 2005 these films are in the hands of the companies that succeeded PT/Lusomundo; companies that do nothing to [distribute] these films, unless when forced to do so' (2014). The disintermediation efforts undertaken by Costa are still tied to such ownership technicalities. This elucidates the multifaceted nature of an activity which, while relying on a discourse of independence, is still dependent on normative professional processes. As Costa himself explained to me, over the years he had to 'insistently' persuade Lusomundo representatives to agree to the release of his films by different international DVD distributors (Costa 2012). Though bounded by some constraints, such efforts clearly reflect a proactive stance aimed at establishing a professional framework less dependent on intermediaries, something which would help the dissemination of his works from the mid-2000s onwards.

ON TOUR: FILM RETROSPECTIVES AND SPECIAL EVENTS

Costa actively engages in different practices of dissemination maintained through a network of flow comprising cinematheques, film archives, art galleries and university-related venues. The exhibition practices taking place at these cultural institutions offer Costa a propitious stage on which to further show his films and promote his filmmaking practice. Moreover, these dissemination initiatives help increase the recognition of his work among niche audiences, as well as generating social practices of consumption around his presence. The prevalent format adopted by these venues is the complete or partial film retrospective. Retrospectives give Costa the opportunity to show his earlier films, rarely seen after their usual run in the film festival circuit and theatrical release. Many of these events also allow Costa to participate directly in consumption activities such as post-screening debates and master classes.

Early examples of these dissemination events were the complete retrospective of Costa's films held at the Sendai Mediatheque in 2005 and the intensive course in filmmaking delivered by the filmmaker at the Tokyo Film School a year earlier. This form of dissemination was soon extended to numerous other initiatives, such as retrospectives in 2009, held at the *Filmoteca Española* (included in PhotoEspaña, Madrid's International Photography Festival) and the retrospective at Tate Modern already mentioned. Costa also received the attention of the Cinémathèque Française, hosting a complete retrospective of his *oeuvre* in January 2010. Other initiatives acquired a more long-term form of circulation. An example of this is the itinerant retrospective *Still Lives: The Films of Pedro Costa*, organised by Portuguese film curator Ricardo Matos Cabo. This touring event circulated between late 2007 and early 2008 in eleven cities in Canada and the United States.[2] This same format would also be adopted in an initiative promoted by the Centro Cultural Banco do Brasil, under the title *O Cinema de Pedro Costa*. The retrospective toured the Brazilian cities of São Paulo, Brasilia, Rio de Janeiro and Belo Horizonte in 2010. More recently, the theatrical release and film festival circulation of *Horse Money* was accompanied by several retrospectives, such as *Let Us Now Praise Famous Men: The Films of Pedro Costa*, held at the Film Society of Lincoln Center (New York) in July 2015.

These events came to complement the exhibition and circulation offered by the art-house and film festivals. It is disingenuous, however, to minimise the importance of these circuits in the dissemination of Costa's work. As discussed in Chapter 4, the filmmaker enjoys a consistent exposure, circulation and artistic legitimation provided by international film festivals. Costa's films produced by Paulo Branco and Francisco Villa-Lobos similarly benefited in the past from the flow sustained through deals with distributors and public institutions. This is particularly the case in continental Europe, where these deals created conditions for regular theatrical distribution and occasional television broadcast of Costa's cinema, particularly in countries such as Portugal, Germany, France and the Netherlands. Moreover, cultural sites such as museums and academic institutions are also, traditionally, venues integrated into the circuit supporting the consumption of international art cinema. These sites complement the circulation offered by the film festival and art-house arenas by similarly assigning artistic legitimation and cultural importance to disparate cinema traditions and practices (see, for example, Pantenburg 2008: 4; Wasson 2005: 16).

Film retrospectives are, equally, a format commonly integrated in the activities organised by the film festival. Costa's film retrospectives taking place in cultural settings are complemented with others held at film festivals. Among other examples, his works enjoyed the exposure offered by retrospectives at the International Film Festival of Marseille and the Hong Kong Film Festival in 2007, at the Jeonju International Film Festival in 2010, and a retrospective dedicated to Portuguese Cinema promoted by the Taipei Film Festival between June and July 2015. These numerous retrospectives taking place at different sites of cultural consumption illustrate the ambivalent circulation that Costa's works have undergone since the mid-2000s, with the filmmaker being a regular presence at the international film festival, cinematheques, art venues and academic-related circuits. The support of cultural venues such as museums and university-related venues is not a substitute for the film festival or the theatrical exhibition of the art-house circuits. Costa's presence in these venues reflects, instead, the activities of an exhibition network particularly receptive to his effort to increase authority in exhibition and circulation.

The engagement with these venues seems as much a choice as a necessity. As Portuguese film critic Luís Miguel Oliveira remarks, it was Tate Modern that held the 2009 UK retrospective of Costa's *oeuvre*, while cinema-related venues such as the British Film Institute seemed more invested in captivating broader audiences by hosting 'a Penélope Cruz retrospective' (Oliveira 2009: 9). This aside may reveal a possible lack of interest in Costa's work by some cinema institutions. However, it also alludes to the receptivity of cultural venues to accommodate the needs of a film culture commonly congregated around Costa and other filmmakers often placed at the fringes of the art-house circuit. Film critics tend to characterise fans of Pedro Costa as committed cinephiles eager to maintain the cult status normally conferred on his films (see Chapter 4). Adding to the commitment shown by this cinephile community, Costa's works receive international attention from art curators, museum patrons and artists, and generate interest among Film, Arts and Humanities scholars. The network of art and academic venues devoting increasing attention to his films, as well as the activities taking place around them, present a favourable environment for the social interaction maintained by these overlapping constituencies.

Costa reciprocates in this social interaction as his approach to these cultural venues indicates a similar effort to establish a direct dialogue with fans and potential audiences. He is particularly vocal in his disenchantment with the film festival as a setting once favourable to the active participation of cinephile communities but which is currently less equipped to integrate and maintain such direct interaction. As Costa asserts:

> film festivals changed a lot [. . .] the critics, other colleagues . . . the ones who I appreciated in the past, I have no idea where they are now. [. . .] The people who replaced them don't have the same stature. [. . .] Before

there were more opportunities to discuss cinema, in the cine-clubs and [such spaces], and the festivals were fewer . . . The festivals became too burdensome; the films are less seen, there are more films than previously. (Costa 2013)

The critique offered by Costa, while conveying nostalgic undertones, clearly addresses what the filmmaker sees as a problematic lack of tangible direct access to a film culture willing not just to watch but also to discuss his work. Conversely, initiatives such as retrospectives and related events seem to offer Costa a contrasting response to this lack of interaction. More than serving exclusively to screen his films, these events accommodate disparate activities that overlap film exhibition with informal and academic activities. Such events also comprise post-screening Q&A sessions and parallel sessions with debates, university lectures and conferences, as well as occasional master classes.

These activities promote forms of social interaction between the filmmaker and audience members, in which the latter acquire contextual and extra-textual knowledge of his films. Audiences participate in events which have a mark of distinction, being unique experiences that set them apart from conventional theatrical exhibition. These consumption activities are customarily accompanied by promotional materials, which provide further contextualisation for the aesthetic, authorial and production practices informing Costa's films. Moreover, these events capitalise on the presence of the filmmaker, with audiences enjoying a privileged immediacy that is normally only given to professional film critics. Costa's presence at many of these activities provides a first-hand account of the making of his films, while also enabling informative and discursive knowledge. On the one hand, these sessions provide an understanding as to how cinephile influences, professional collaborations and production practices impact on the filmic universe of the works he directs. On the other hand, these interactions give Costa latitude to explain his aesthetic and political preoccupations, as well as to express his attitude towards filmmaking. Inevitably, the textual, contextual and authorial-related knowledge brought together in these events foregrounds Costa's presence as a pivotal point in shaping evaluative and discursive reception practices.

Film retrospectives and related events, moreover, allow theatrical exhibition outside restrictions – financial, geographical, and programming – imposed by the art-house circuit, and increase the circulation and exposure offered by the international film festival. The *Still Lives* tour and the Tate Modern retrospective, for instance, made Costa's work visible to North American and UK cinephiles. Before 2009, these constituencies had no or very limited access to some of the films screened. These initiatives are also important to the circulation of Costa's *oeuvre* in East Asia, particularly in

South Korea, Hong Kong and Taiwan. It is relevant to note that this region, either within film festivals or through special events such as retrospectives, brings a nuanced characterisation to the social profile commonly ascribed to his international fans. The cinema of Pedro Costa seems to cater, broadly, to male adult western cinephile constituencies. Jared Rapfogel, however, offers a distinctive outlook on Costa's fandom when reporting on the retrospective programmes dedicated by the 2010 Jeonju International Film Festival (JIFF) to his own and James Benning's works:

> though [the festival] programming would seem to place it in the category of festivals that appeal primarily to the hard-core festival crowd (to career critics, editors, film programmers, and the like), the routinely sold-out screenings are dominated by locals. And a shocking percentage of these festivalgoers seem to be high-school-age students, leading to the bizarre, incongruous site [sic] of hordes of teenagers avidly pouring into screenings of films by Benning or Costa, and then dominating the postprojection Q&As. Indeed, one of the many pleasures afforded by the [JIFF] is the opportunity to imagine, even to find yourself inhabiting, however briefly, a strange but wonderful world in which James Benning and Pedro Costa are teen idols. (Rapfogel 2010)

Still considering this region, retrospectives and similar events also impacted on the awareness of Costa's cinema among Japanese cinephiles. These initiatives paved the way for his regular presence on this country's art-house theatrical circuit and home video market. Costa's relationship with Japan is particularly telling with regard to the overlapping nature of different exhibition and circulation initiatives maintained by both cinema and cultural circuits, as well as their incremental and complementary nature. Initially, Costa gained the attention of Japanese cinephiles in 2001, when *In Vanda's Room* was included in the international competition section of the Yamagata International Documentary Film Festival (YIDFF). The film was awarded the festival's FIPRESCI Prize. Later, in 2004, *In Vanda's Room* was released theatrically in art-house venues in Tokyo and Osaka. The theatrical release of the film was complemented with a retrospective held at Tokyo's Athénée Français Cultural Center. These initiatives were soon followed by the 2005 retrospective in Sendai (already mentioned), and by the theatrical and DVD releases of Costa's subsequent feature films.[3]

Significantly, these different initiatives are the work of Costa's fan Kazuyuki Yano. Yano is the programmer of the YIDFF and director of the film company Cinematrix, which distributes Costa's films in Japan. In an email communication, Yano described to me the YIDFF and Cinematrix regular co-organised events:

when [Cinematrix] releases [Costa's films], we always held [a] retrospective [. . .]. In 2004, we held the [video] installation of *In Vanda's Room*, [in 2010] the installation [*Little Boy Male, Little Girl Female*]. In 2012 we held the carte blanche of [films selected by] Pedro Costa and Rui Chafes, when the Hara Museum held their exhibition. (Yano 2014)

The different events undertaken by Cinematrix, in collaboration with different cultural agents, shed light on the intersection between conventional theatrical release and special events around retrospectives. Generating complementary forms of exhibition and direct access to the filmmaker, such initiatives transcend film exhibition. As understood above, these events are normally programmed to coincide with the theatrical and DVD releases of Costa's films, as well as with exhibitions in art galleries. Moreover, and as Yano also explained to me, Cinematrix collaborated with other companies to organise a concert by Jeanne Balibar's band in Tokyo. This event coincided with the 2010 theatrical release of *Change Nothing* and yet another retrospective of Costa's works (Yano 2014).

These dissemination activities reflect the local specificities of an art cinema *milieu* which equally responds to and generates an enthusiastic fandom around the filmmaker. Japanese film director Nobuhiro Suwa, cited in the Portuguese daily *Público*, points out that Costa's 'charisma' captivates local cinephiles, and that his films are considered as 'very *cool*' (Crespo 2012, italics in original). The article penned by Luís Miguel Oliveira, already cited, provides further clues to the anecdotal aspects of Costa's fandom by describing how some of his Japanese fans occasionally visit the Portuguese Cinematheque in Lisbon to 'ask how to get to Fontainhas' (Oliveira 2009). It is clear that these two Portuguese articles adopt a laudatory tone when describing Costa's reception in Japan, which is generally similar to other accounts concerning the international responses to his films (see Chapter 4). Yet these articles also provide us with clues about Costa's international cult figure and the taste formations in which he is commonly included.

More relevant here, these articles also allude to social dynamics of these events. The retrospectives and special events maintained by Costa, in partnership with Yano and other Japanese cultural agents, reflect both professional and personal forms of agency. Two main aspects are central to understanding the cinephilia network currently sustaining the circulation of Costa's works. The first aspect concerns its nature, animated by economic and professional links but also sustained by informal ties. Costa's fans, working directly with the filmmaker, assume an active role in taking up practices of dissemination. These collaborations, secondly, respond to fans' needs. Retrospectives and special events, as nonsequential dissemination practices centred on the presence of a filmmaker, also contribute to ease the lack of access to Costa's work internationally.

In the examples of the North American and Japanese markets examined above, the access to Costa's work is made available via theatrical release, either in an extended exhibition format or as a one-off screening. Newly released films are shown simultaneously with previous works – the latter already outside its initial commercial theatrical circulation.

AUTHORSHIP AS COMMODITY: HOME VIDEO RELEASES

International access to Costa's cinema has been consolidated with releases for the home video market. The release of several of his films on DVD and Blu-ray has partially resolved the problem of lack of access to Costa's works among international fans. The home video releases of Costa's films have come to re-affirm forms of authorial presence taking shape in screening events discussed above. This presence is manifested in the variegated information that accompanies such commodities, helping to create awareness of Costa's filmmaking ethos among international cinephile communities.

While trying to move away from the producers and sales agents, Pedro Costa has nonetheless been receptive to his work's international release for the home viewing market, privileging opportunities in which he could have direct intervention. In large part, these opportunities coincide with partnerships with different producers, already described but which need further contextualisation. Until the end of the 2000s, the circulation of Costa's films on DVD was mostly confined to releases for the Japanese and French markets. For the latter market, Paulo Branco's Gemini Films released *Casa de Lava* and *Bones* (in 2005 and 2008, respectively). Capricci Films released a boxed set of *In Vanda's Room*, accompanied by a book with an extensive interview with Costa by Cyril Neyrat in 2008. Complementing these editions, Équation's subsidiary Swift Productions released *Colossal Youth* in 2009. These DVD editions for the French market are, initially, the result of the distribution practices carried out by Branco, later complemented with the negotiations carried on between Villa-Lobos, Équation and Capprici. The period between the end of the 2000s and early 2010 saw an increase of DVD editions of Costa's work for the European market. Intermedio released a DVD boxed set for the Spanish market in 2011 which included *In Vanda's Room*, *Colossal Youth* and *Where Does Your Hidden Smile Lie?*.[4] *Change Nothing* had DVD editions in Spain and France, released by Cameo in 2011 and by Shellac in 2012, respectively. This latter period corresponds to Costa's increasing participation in distribution deals for the home view market. This participation is particularly evident in Portugal where Costa maintains a prolific partnership with the distribution company Midas Filmes. This company is responsible for both his works' theatrical exhibition and DVD editions. Midas Filmes released *Blood* and *Where Does Your Hidden Smile Lie?* on DVD in 2009. This was followed by the DVD releases of *Change Nothing* (in 2011), *In Vanda's Room* (in 2013) and, in 2016, *Horse Money*.

While available for purchase online, the different DVD editions listed above tend to cover only particular domestic territories. Costa's work acquired a more consistent and wide dissemination with successive DVD releases for the English-speaking market. To this end, from the end of the 2000s onwards, Costa started a professional partnership with the UK distribution company Second Run. The company released *Blood* on DVD in 2009, a release timed to coincide with the retrospective at Tate Modern. Later, in 2012, this company also released *Casa de Lava*, and was responsible for the UK theatrical release of *Horse Money* in 2015 and its subsequent DVD and Blu-ray releases in 2016. Costa also responded positively to the interest demonstrated by US Criterion Collection and UK Eureka! in releasing his films shot at Fontainhas. The former company released the boxed set comprising the three feature films in 2010; Eureka! released *Colossal Youth* in 2011, in its Masters of Cinema series. More recently, *Horse Money* and *Casa de Lava* were also released on both DVD and Blu-ray by the New York based companies Cinema Guild and Grasshopper Film (in 2016 and 2017, respectively).

These different DVD and Blu-ray editions responded to increasing access requirements of Costa's films among Anglophone cinephiles. As Second Run's manager Chris Barwick argues:

> Pedro already had a great reputation amongst critics, and yet no-one (at the time we released *Blood* [in 2009]) had released any of his films in the UK (*Colossal Youth* had a small festival run at the ICA [Institute of Contemporary Arts, in London]) so our releases certainly brought him to the attention of more writers, critics and a wider viewing audience. (Barwick 2014)

Second Run's DVD editions, like those released by Eureka! and Criterion, acquired a wider global availability, made possible by its use of an international *lingua franca* enabling worldwide circulation. As Barwick also pointed out to me, the attention generated by Second Run's DVDs is not confined to British cinephiles and professional film critics. As he asserts:

> Our releases were very well received both in the UK and abroad by both writers and customers. [. . .] Our titles always sell well abroad – not just in the US and Canada – and we have a lot of US-based critics who regularly review our releases. (Barwick 2014)

This worldwide visibility is augmented by the considerable prestige enjoyed by the Criterion Collection and the Masters of Cinema series, as well as the increasing importance that Second Run's catalogue has acquired among global cinephiles. The inclusion of Costa's films in the catalogues of these three distributors places his films among a constellation of past and contemporary works directed by canonical world filmmakers. Reflecting on the inclusion of *Colossal Youth* in the Masters of Cinema catalogue, Craig Keller, one of the collection's producers, enthusiastically contends that:

> [*Colossal Youth* is] one of the greatest and most important films we've released. However, [. . .] its reputation hasn't yet percolated to the level occupied by those 'canonical classics' that seem to take at least 50 years to be accepted by wider margins as a Great and Essential Film. (Keller 2014)

Sales of the DVD editions released by Second Run and Masters of Cinema reflect this limited yet potentially increasing visibility. Both Keller and Barwick eschew disclosing information on sale numbers. Yet both distributors are happy to reveal their satisfaction with the number of copies sold. Barwick, for instance, points out that both *Blood* and *Casa de Lava* DVDs 'have sold well, if not in unusually huge numbers' (2014). Keller gives a similar, still more laconic, account of the sales of *Colossal Youth*: 'Yes, [it] was a success' (2014).

What transpires in my correspondence with spokespersons for both Second Run and the Masters of Cinema collection is the intertwinement of professional and personal interests informing the production of these DVDs. On the one hand, both Barwick and Keller are responding to a lack of distribution of Costa's films by adding to their catalogues works not yet widely released internationally. On the other hand, these agents display a personal commitment to this activity, openly assuming their fan-driven interest in Costa. This leads to further discussion on the network of dissemination around Costa's work. As in the case of Kazuyuki Yano, both Barwick and Keller assume an active part in a broad cinephile community populating the international film festival and related cultural sites. These sites are not just stages for film exhibition but are also efficient 'systems of flow' (Iordanova 2009: 24). This flow concerns filmic texts as much as the participants in such systems, as these provide a favourable setting for formal and informal exchanges between film professionals, distributors and fans. Kazuyuki Yano, who first saw *In Vanda's Room* at the international documentary film festival Cinéma du Réel in 2001, acknowledges the potential of the film festival network. Yano had the opportunity, later that same year, to 'meet and [talk] to' Costa when the filmmaker attended the Yamagata International Documentary Film Festival (Yano 2014). Similarly, Craig Keller points to the importance of the screening of *Colossal Youth* at the 2005 Cannes

Film Festival, as well as its divided reception, as the event which propelled his interest in releasing the film on DVD (Keller 2014). The process culminating in the DVD editions released by Second Run and the Masters of Cinema collection is tied to the exchange of contacts made possible through these cinephile systems of flow. While already aware of Costa's work, Barwick recalls that it was Apichatpong Weerasethakul who facilitated the contact between Costa and the company, and 'who recommended to [Costa] that he let us release some of his films' (Barwick 2014).[5] Likewise, Craig Keller explained to me that he met Costa in New York via a mutual friend, the film critic and programmer Andy Rector (Keller 2014).

The flow of this network is not just expressed in distribution deals and DVD editions, but also extends to the various extra features included in these releases. The meeting between Costa and Keller mentioned above, for instance, would result in an extensive filmed conversation, in which Rector also participated. This recorded conversation would be later released as *Finding the Criminal* (2010), which was included as an extra feature in the Masters of Cinema's DVD edition of *Colossal Youth*. This interview is only one of the numerous examples of the materials produced by the different agents comprising the cinephile network around Costa. Indeed, the DVD editions discussed above include a significant number of extra features – essays, filmed interviews, audio commentaries – in which different film critics and scholars, filmmakers and artists give expression to their appreciation of Costa's cinema. These different materials provide audiences with forms of knowledge which allow the sustaining of the filmmaker's public figure as the main authorial force in the making of his films. When included in DVD editions, these extra features serve to explain Costa's aesthetic and thematic characteristics, as well as providing awareness of his authorial and production processes. Ambiguously, these materials enhance but also condition the consumption experience of his films. These extras come to grant further cultural value to commodities which already transmit some sort of prestigious exclusivity, due to their inclusion in a film boutique market.

The symbolic value of these DVD editions is further enhanced by Costa's direct involvement in their production. As the filmmaker explained to me, his working routines often include dealing with the workflow around the release and exhibition of his previous films:

> it's necessary to have the [film master] copies, to examine, watch them, to package, to send them [to distributors]. It's a substantial amount of office work that I do alone, but which is easy to do. [. . .] Dealing with past films is part of my routine. (Costa 2013)

This workflow also encompasses direct participation in technical aspects of these releases. Second Run's DVDs of *Blood* and *Casa de Lava*, for instance, enjoy new masters directly supervised by Costa. Unhappy with the existing materials, Costa supervised the new master of *Blood* at the Portuguese Tobis in Lisbon (a master which was also used in the Portuguese DVD release). In a similar way *Casa de Lava* was subjected to a lengthy process of re-mastering. As Chris Barwick explained to me, Costa 'was very unhappy with the existing materials, so he was determined that we should not release [the DVD] until we had a new master he was happy with' (2014). This decision delayed the DVD of the film for approximately two years. These activities undertaken by Costa reflect the necessary practicalities of an ongoing disintermediation process. Moreover, information about these routines is also incorporated in the material made available by distribution companies, adding further value to these DVD editions. The packaging of the DVD editions for the UK and US markets, for instance, make clear Costa's close supervision of the re-mastering process of the copies used in these different releases. Complementing the variegated extra-feature materials, such information provides forms of knowledge about the production of the films they include and also about the production process of these commodities, generating further authorial awareness. They make cinephiles aware that they are acquiring a product approved by, worked on and, in many cases, provided by Costa himself.

These DVD releases, like the numerous retrospectives and special screenings dedicated to Costa's films, provide an overlapping of different possibilities of consumption. In this sense, different dissemination initiatives have facilitated a return to the exhibition of works previously less consistently shown within international circuits. Film retrospectives, special screenings and related events become central to the international consumption of Costa's work. The regularity of these activities, undertaken by Costa in partnership with several institutions and agents, presupposes a dissemination framework in which the release of each of his films is accompanied by concurrent DVD editions and social activities around previous works. As a whole, these different but complementary dissemination practices respond to the necessities of contemporary cinephiles who aim at an immersion in the world of particular films and filmmakers. This engagement is made possible by a continuum which traverses individual consumption and collective practices (Hagener and de Valck 2008: 23). Through these activities and practices, different films come to be integrated as part of a coherent collection, offering audiences opportunities for aesthetic assessment and comparison. This cinephile immersion enables forms of consumption which make sense of a possible interconnected authorial universe that transcends different films. In the cinema of Pedro Costa, thematic and narrative elements become intertwined in an ever-increasing filmic universe. This universe acquires, inevitably, further meaning through these different consumption practices.

NOTES

1. For production details of *In Vanda's Room* and *Where Does Your Hidden Smile Lie?* see Chapter 3 and Chapter 4, respectively. *Colossal Youth* was produced by Contracosta and the French companies Unlimited and Les Films de l'Etranger (the latter co-founded in 2003 by Villa-Lobos and Philippe Avril, Unlimited's CEO), and Ventura Film SA (Switzerland) in collaboration with Franco-German television network Arte. The film's financial support came from the ICAM (formerly IPC) and RTP (Portugal), and CNC (France).
2. *Still Lives* started at Toronto's Cinematheque Ontario (currently TIFF Cinematheque), followed by screenings at the Vancouver International Film Center, Manhattan's Anthology Film Archives, the REDCAT arts centre in Los Angeles, the Harvard Film Archive, the Cleveland Museum of Art, Chicago's Gene Siskel Film Center, Seattle's Northwest Film Forum, Rochester's George Eastman House and the Wexner Center for the Arts in Columbus, Ohio. This touring retrospective concluded at Berkeley's BAMPFA, the Pacific Film Archive of the University of California.
3. As Kazuyuki Yano indicated to me, *In Vanda's Room* was released on DVD in 2004; *Colossal Youth* had its theatrical release in 2008 and subsequent DVD edition in 2009; *Change Nothing* was released in Japanese film theatres in 2010, with a subsequent edition on DVD in 2011. *Blood*, *Casa de Lava* and *Bones* had Japanese DVD editions in 2008. According to information available at the YIDFF website, *Horse Money* was released in Japanese cinemas in 2016, with its premiere attended by Costa, and coinciding with a theatrical re-run of *In Vanda's Room* and *Colossal Youth*. Available at <http://www.yidff.jp/news/16/ex160609-e.html> (accessed 7 September 2018).
4. This boxed set also included the book *Un mirlo dorado, un ramo de flores y una cuchara de plata*, a translated version of the interview in book format initially released by Capricci Films in France. The special DVD edition of *In Vanda's Room*, released by Midas Filmes in 2013, also includes a Portuguese translated version of this book.
5. At the time, Apichatpong Weerasethakul's films *Blissfully Yours* (2002) and *Tropical Malady* (2004) had already been distributed in the UK by Second Run, in 2006 and 2008, respectively.

CHAPTER 7

A 'Document of Documents': Authorship, Intertextuality and Politics in *Horse Money* (2014)

Between October 2018 and January 2019 the Serralves Museum of Contemporary Art in Porto hosted *Companhia* (*Company*), an exhibition dedicated to the creative dialogues between the cinema of Pedro Costa and works by several other artists. This initiative presented some of the results of numerous collaborations maintained by the filmmaker over the years with Rui Chafes, Straub and Huillet and the non-professional actor Ventura. More patently, the exhibition was structured around numerous sources which, in diverse ways, exert a direct influence on Costa's authorial practice. The filmic heritages of Robert Bresson, John Ford, Fritz Lang, António Reis and Margarida Cordeiro, Charlie Chaplin and Jacques Tourneur gained central importance in this exhibition. Other media influences also gained visibility. Among others, *Company* included works by poet Robert Desnos and photographers Jacob Riis, Walker Evans and Jeff Wall, and by artists such as Pablo Picasso and Maria Capelo. This assemblage of different works – film stills, painting, sculpture, video installations, poems, photographs – illustrates an authorial process which, firstly, reflects prolonged collaborative practices and which, secondly, is organised through the entanglement of different intertextual and intermedial influences. Indeed, the sentence used to contextualise *Company* to the public encapsulates these two characteristics animating Costa's creative practice: 'each film is a letter written by a thousand hands'.

The collaborations and documental confluences organising *Company* are also particularly visible in *Cavalo Dinheiro* (*Horse Money*, 2014). This feature film reflects an evolving and prolonged collaborative process. As in previous works directed by Costa, *Horse Money* relies on a group of non-professional collaborators who contributed with their personal stories and who imprinted their lived experiences onto the film. The long-term creative collaboration between

Costa and Ventura was crucial to the making of the film. The authorial process of the film also relied on a new collaborator, Vitalina Varela, a non-professional actor whom Costa met during the shooting process. It bears repeating that Costa's cinema reflects a creative process of an intertextual nature. This intertextuality is manifested in several allusions and adaptations of a constellation of disparate filmic works which, since *Blood*, give expression to a creative practice with strong cinephile contours. *Horse Money* is a vehicle for such creative expression informed by cinephilia. Costa commonly cites works which, at least potentially, contributed to the creative process of the film: Tourneur's *Stars in My Crown* (1950), Mark Robson's *The Seventh Victim* (1943) and *Bedlam* (1946) (see Peranson 2014; Bahadur 2015). Adding to these films, Costa also points out to Mark Peranson, in an interview for *Cinema Scope* in 2014, that Straub and Huillet's *Nicht versöhnt* (*Not Reconciled*, 1965) was a central influence on the narrative devices structuring *Horse Money* (Peranson 2014).

The contours of this intertextuality can be extended to include other media sources. *Horse Money* is the feature film in which the deployment of pictorial and sound references and documental sources gain noted assertiveness. Examples of these sources are the photographs by Jacob Riis which open the film. The depiction of these photographs is followed by a scene showing Théodore Géricault's painting *Portrait of a Negro*. Other sources emerge during the film: Vitalina Varela's personal documents, which she reads in several scenes; the musical interlude halfway through the film featuring the song 'Alto Cutelo' by the Cape Verdean group Os Tubarões. The intertextuality offered by such different artefacts and sources, moreover, is augmented by narrative and visual references to previous films directed by Costa. These different materials are organised through the recreation of Ventura's memories. The actor's personal accounts of historical and political contexts serve as pivotal points, as similarly observed in *Colossal Youth*, as well as in the short films *Tarrafal* and *Rabbit Hunters* (2007), *Our Man* (2010) and *Sweet Exorcism* (2012). The confluence of these different sources turns *Horse Money* into a palimpsest of possible documentable but also subjective realities. Either brought in to the creative process by Costa or sourced among the personal belongings and memories of his collaborators, these items attest to factual veracity but also serve as props to enhance the narrative and visual artifice of the film.

The reference to Straub and Huillet's work is worth taking further, as it suggests a possible way to interrogate the complex intertextual nature animating *Horse Money*. As Gilberto Perez argues, every Straub and Huillet film may be described as 'a document of documents', by juxtaposing 'concrete pieces of evidence' concerning particular historical contexts, which are then 'compared with one another in the present' (Perez quoted in Brady 2016: 75). The entanglement of different documental sources deployed by the French filmmakers to structure films such as *Chronik der Anna Magdalena Bach* (*The Chronicle of Anna Magdalena Bach*, 1968) or *Geschichtsunterricht* (*History Lessons*, 1972) offers layered textual meaning. This authorial approach imprints thematic, narrative and stylistic connections between these films and other works. As I discuss here, this notion of a document of documents is also particularly apt to define both the authorial practices and the intertextual qualities of *Horse Money*. The authoring of the film is as much indebted to Costa's creative authority as it is to his interactions with Ventura and Varela. Personal recollection and historical setting are merged to represent the issues experienced by both actors: immigration, social displacement and isolation, and lack of basic living conditions. These contexts are expressed through the use of particular aesthetic tropes, which offer mediation between the personal accounts of the actors and the film's political dimension.

The historical and political dimensions alluded to in *Horse Money*, moreover, call our attention to the tense dialogue between film aesthetics and politics transmitted in Costa's cinema. Over the years, Costa refined a representational mode that alludes to the political context lived by non-professional actors in his films. While serving to transmit coherency to the narrative universe transcending several films, however, this representational mode does not convey a clear articulation of political message or meaning (see Chapter 2). I address here this confluence of authorial practices and intertextual dialogues in the making of *Horse Money*. The tense relation between aesthetics and politics transpires in professional critical discourses around Costa's cinema. I also give attention, therefore, to how possible political expression in Costa's authorial practice is negotiated via critical discourses. My aim is to reflect how these confluences and negotiations shed light on creative practices informing the cinema of Pedro Costa, as well as to question practical and discursive facets of authorship.

COLLABORATIVE AUTHORSHIP AND STYLISTIC DEVICES

The making of *Horse Money* reflects the production framework and prolonged collaborative practices informing previous works directed by Costa. The film consolidates the filmmaker's current partnership with OPTEC Filmes. The production of the film relied on financial and technical support exclusively from Portuguese institutions. With the exception of his directorial debut, *Horse Money* is the only one of Costa's feature films not supported by an international co-production framework. The project received financial backing from the Portuguese Film and Audiovisual Institute (ICA, the public institution which succeeded the IPC and ICAM) and from Lisbon Municipal Council, in total approximately €120,000. As the film producer Abel Ribeiro Chaves stresses, however, the film 'cost a lot more' than this financial support would cover (Chaves 2018). The producer's remarks suggest that the technical and logistic support given to the film falls into the provision of OPTEC Filmes, instead of being outsourced to other international companies covering particular production and post-production processes. This framework still reflects a form of interstitial production that informs Costa's previous filmic projects. However, it also presents an alternative to the intricate financial arrangements and complex network of producers and financial gatekeepers which comprise the international coproduction model.[1]

The authorial process of *Horse Money* also reveals connections, albeit nuanced, with Costa's previous works. Again, the importance of Ventura in the project needs to be emphasised. The actor provided Costa with access to a personal universe which is reflected in the themes and narrative structuring the film. As Costa maintains during several interviews, however, the initial ideas around the project were planned as a collaboration between himself and Ventura, but also with the American poet and musician Gil Scott-Heron. As Costa explains at length during an interview with Neil Bahadur published in *Film Comment*:

> One day I was in New York and I asked a friend who knew [Scott-Heron], and I said: 'It would be great to have them talk!' Because Ventura doesn't speak any English, and Gil couldn't speak Portuguese. So I showed him my films, and he called me and said: 'I like this. Let's meet.' He was playing in Lisbon so I went to meet him, and I proposed [my idea], and he said yes.
>
> He was supposed to write what you see today in [*Horse Money*] – probably the montage with the people in the neighborhood, this voyage through the night. That first version was supposed to be written by him, with music by him, and shot perhaps in the same place . . . Or perhaps not.
>
> [. . .] I thought of something like that – that the film could be a long rap, and Scott-Heron could do that. I thought we could get him, and Ventura would sing and Scott-Heron would say poems. Because Ventura likes to sing, and in *Colossal Youth* there's not really that chance. (Bahadur 2015)

This potential collaboration, however, was brought to an end by Scott-Heron's death in May 2011. Consequently, the project was at a creative standstill for several months. Costa also provides details of this impasse and its resolution in interviews conducted at the time of the theatrical release of *Horse Money*. As he explained to the Portuguese daily *Público*: 'I was six months without knowing what to do, but then Ventura told me a story haunting him [. . .], of a soldier who tried to kill him' (Carmo 2014). Ventura's traumatic story, which took place in the aftermath of the 1974 April Revolution, was the starting point for a narrative moment that began to be worked on in early 2012. The result of this initial work was the scene sequence set inside an elevator. These scenes were used first in the short film *Sweet Exorcism*, and would later be included as the narrative denouement of *Horse Money*.

As discussed in Chapter 5, this scene sequence positions Ventura sharing the confined space of an elevator with a soldier (António Santos), a statue-like figure completely covered in bronze paint. Particularly as concerns the soundtrack, this sequence presents a clear contrast with the sensorial quietness transmitted in the rest of the film. Ventura maintains a dialogue with the mostly motionless soldier, whose lips we never see move. The tension transmitted in these scenes increases when several disembodied voices, which we understand to be Ventura's friends and wife, are added to the dialogue maintained between the main character of the film and the soldier. These voices give further expression and emotional density to Ventura's inner fears. The intricately layered non-diegetic sound used in these scenes reflects some of the initial ideas discussed with Scott-Heron. As Costa pointed out to film critic Jonathan Romney, their discussion concerned the creation of 'an oratorio', that the two envisioned as being a long musical and filmic piece created without resorting to musical instruments (Romney 2015b).

Adding to this narrative moment, Costa worked closely with Ventura to structure the plot of *Horse Money*. As he describes in an interview with Aaron Cutler, this process consisted in '[mapping] out the past with questions as though we were making a chart on a table' (2015). This work around Ventura's memories came to compose a narrative in which different understandings of time – chronological and subjective, lived or imagined – bond individual stories to particular historical moments and political contexts. In this sense, and as already mentioned, *Horse Money* can be understood as a development of a personal narrative initiated in *Colossal Youth*. As in the feature film produced in 2006, the narrative of *Horse Money* is structured around Ventura's personal stories, re-enacted as conforming neither to a linear structure nor to the verisimilitude of chronological time. This artifice is solidly imprinted in the film, even considering that it is partially set around specific historical occurrences.

The short synopsis of *Horse Money* included in its press release and commonly referred to in several reviews reads: '[w]hile the young captains lead the revolution in the streets, the people of Fontainhas search for Ventura, lost in the woods'. This synopsis gives hints as to what may trigger the plot of the film, as well as to its possible historical setting (the 1974 Revolution and its immediate aftermath). This summary is as suggestive as it is deceptive. Such limited information circumvents any explanation of the overlapping of the different temporal settings re-enacted by Ventura. As Edmundo Cordeiro argues (in his appropriately titled essay 'A character's mental landscape as history'), Ventura is a 'stratigraphic' character; he is a result of the 'confrontation between fictional and documentary powers which permanently shift' between the actor and the (invented) character depicted in Costa's films (2017: 35). Ventura the character gives clear signs of being trapped in different tenses. He mediates between subjective and chronological past and present and, more confusingly, re-enacts actions which at times merge the factual with the imaginary.

To negotiate between the different narrative moments structuring *Horse Money*, Costa resorts to stylistic devices which are similar to those previously deployed in *Colossal Youth*. Different scene sequences are grouped together without conventional plot referents or stylistic tropes; what can be considered a flashback becomes a narrative unit in an atemporal and fragmented timeline. Similarly, settings and characters become characterised as atemporal and figurative, taking further the narrative fragmentation structuring the film. The central setting used in *Horse Money* is a maze-like hospital or psychiatric institution to which Ventura is confined and from which he occasionally seems to be able to escape. The changing nature of this location evokes different chronological times. It also conveys the psychological nuances experienced by Ventura during different narrative episodes. In some of the daytime scenes, the hospital is presented as a sanitised and dehumanised space. Mostly, however, the plot of the film takes place in its dark and spatially constricted areas, resembling a subterranean medieval prison. This is the stage to which Ventura comes to summon spectral figures. The occasional appearance of these ghosts gives density to his own narrative, while also illustrating difficult experiences lived by other Cape Verdeans in Lisbon. The reworking of the filmic space observed in *Horse Money* finds a correspondence in the treatment of Ventura's *dramatis persona*, as well as the different characters he meets over the course of the film. While mostly confined (physically) to this pivotal space, Ventura nonetheless manages to transport himself to other locations. The actual ruins of the workshops of a construction company are used to re-enact the work issues faced by Ventura in the 1970s. The same setting is also used by Ventura to summon the presence of his godson and previous co-worker, Benvindo (played by Benvindo Tavares). Benvindo informs Ventura of the bankruptcy of the construction company and the fate of their other former work colleagues.

The characters' relationship with the settings calls our attention to the atemporal characterisation initially emerging in *Colossal Youth*. As Costa explains in an interview with Mark Peranson, *Horse Money* is a film 'always in the present' (Peranson 2014). Ventura the stratigraphic character relies on the aged figure of Ventura the actor, even when he re-enacts moments clearly set in the past. Similarly, the film portrays many of the remaining characters as having a figurative function. Early in the film we are introduced to different characters who come to visit Ventura in his hospital bed. These characters are denied a literal presence and their oneiric quality is clear. They are mostly ghostly appearances invoked by Ventura's memories: family members and friends who met their death as a result of the miserable living conditions and harsh work routines lived by migrant workers populating the building sites in Lisbon. This trope was initially conferred on Lento (Alberto Barros) and Alfredo (Alfredo Mendes); the former a character in *Colossal Youth* (also appearing briefly in *Horse Money*), the latter featuring in the three short films directed by Costa between 2007 and 2010 (see Chapter 5). As ghostly evocations, these hospital visitors are only embodied in the filmic space and time occupied by Ventura.

The subjective treatment of filmic time is also reflected in Ventura's hospital internment. Early in *Horse Money* we are provided with clues that this internment may have taken place around the mid-1970s, in the aftermath of a knife fight between Ventura and another Cape Verdean immigrant, Joaquim (played by Tito Furtado). Though it may be only a memory, this incident also provides clues to its possible temporal setting. This period corresponds to the troubled historical time in Portugal after the 1974 Revolution. When questioned by a doctor, Ventura claims that he was found and brought to the hospital by soldiers belonging to the Armed Forces Movement. These are soldiers who initiated the revolution and who later prevented a right-wing counter-coup in 1975. This initial understanding of the chronological time, however, soon becomes countered by the introduction of another character, Vitalina (played by Vitalina Varela). Meeting Ventura at the hospital, Vitalina narrates her ordeal when travelling from Cape Verde to Lisbon to attend to her husband's funeral. It took place on 27 June 2013, three days before her arrival. It becomes clear that Ventura lives in a reality which is as much atemporal as it is imagined. This continuous oneiric timeline is also perceived through the constant reappearance of Ventura's rival, Joaquim, who persistently haunts him. His interpellations are pacified only after Ventura's cathartic experience in the elevator. In the same vein, Ventura's oneiric state allows for momentary confluence between characters: Vitalina impersonates the doctor assisting Ventura; similarly, Ventura's former rival Joaquim is understood as also being Vitalina's husband. This overlapping is clearly manifested when Ventura contradicts Vitalina's account about her husband's death and claims that Joaquim is interned at the hospital, recovering from a nervous condition similar to the one he is currently experiencing.

It is worth underscoring once again that the filmic treatment of time, space and characters in *Horse Money* constitutes a refining of the stylistic devices initially adopted in *Colossal Youth*. These convey Ventura's fragmented memories, independently of their factual or fictitious nature. The narrative of both films merges personal stories with historical events to offer a critique, albeit not explicitly represented, of the inadequate living conditions suffered over the years by many of the actors featured in these two films. Many of these actors are either the members or the offspring of a workforce that, throughout several decades, built many of Lisbon's infrastructures (see Arenas 2011: 168; Jorge 2014: 52). Providing context to this connection between Ventura's personal stories and its historical setting, as well as between his past and present condition, film critic Aaron Cutler observes:

> Throughout the course of [*Horse Money*], Ventura's mind keeps returning to the Carnation Revolution and its aftermath. He fixates [. . .] on his terrified acts of fleeing and hiding from soldiers who wandered the woods in search of possible dissidents. He relives his receiving a severe wound from a knife fight on March 11th, 1975, the same day as a failed countercoup that led to government restrictions. Ventura's life has not improved since then, a fact that the film underlines when he tells a doctor his current age: nineteen years and three months. He registers as a person stuck in time. (Cutler 2015)

A film review penned by Michael Guarneri offers a similar understanding of Ventura's continuous temporal confinement. As Guarneri argues, Ventura's personal conditions reflect social issues which have not been resolved by the historical process initiated by the 1974 Revolution:

> [b]y casting sixty-something Ventura to play twenty-year-old Ventura during Portugal's revolutionary period [. . .], and by having him wander between medieval and present-day Lisbon, *Horse Money* clearly shows that nothing has really changed for him and his people. Ventura emigrated to the Portuguese Empire's capital city in August 1972 and, in spite of the 1974 Carnation Revolution putting an end to 48 years of fascist dictatorship in Portugal and to hundreds of years of Portuguese colonial rule in Africa, he kept on working as a slave, building rich people's banks and museums in Lisbon for a ridiculous salary, and living in the clandestine slum of Fontainhas until the late 1990s. (Guarneri 2015b)

These readings of the film call our attention to how stylistic devices, such as narrative ellipses and achronological filmic time, are used to organise a historical reflection on the past and present condition of Costa's collaborators. There is a clear connection between the historical contours suggested in *Horse Money* and Ventura's personal story. The film offers clues to possible subjective readings of historical narratives. Marcia Landy argues that contemporary film makes possible 'an expanded and altered understanding of what constitutes historical thinking' (2015: ix). As Landy contends, cinema offers a form of 'counter-history' as it can represent subjective narratives that historiography may disregard. This being said, I should point out that *Horse Money* is not a historical narrative, although such an idea is surely appealing.[2]

Instead, its filmic artifice calls our attention to the clear Deleuzian contours animating Landy's concept: 'indiscernibility of the real and the imaginary, or of the present and the past'; also, as needs to be stressed, the indiscernibility 'of the actual and the virtual' (Deleuze 1989: 69; Landy 2015: xvii; see also Rushton 2012: 89).

Costa seems aware of the ambiguities of historical recreation when asserting that it is impossible to 're-create the past' in his films, as the past 'is always unfolding in the present' (Cutler 2015). The historical resonances observed in *Horse Money* are dispensed through stylistic artificiality and temporal incongruence. This is so even when, in the film, we perceive some engagement with historical recreation. One instance of this is presented in the scene depicting Ventura being seized by revolutionary soldiers. Some of these soldiers approach Ventura in a Chaimite armoured vehicle, widely used by the Portuguese Army during the African Colonial/Independence War(s); it was also the main form of transportation during the 25 April 1974 coup (Figure 7.1).[3] There are both clear historical and symbolic resonances in this scene. Yet any of its verisimilitude is somehow questioned by its stylised depiction and temporal incongruity.

Figure 7.1 Still from *Horse Money* (2014): the appearance of the iconic Chaimite armoured vehicle serves as a narrative device both for a historical setting and for Ventura's achronological subjective condition

A 'DOCUMENT OF DOCUMENTS' 137

INTERTEXTUALITY AND THE PERSONAL ARCHIVE

The filmic universe created by Costa and Ventura negotiates between individual stories that are dramatically intertwined with a historical past. This is particularly evident when considering both the postcolonial condition alluded to in *Colossal Youth* and *Horse Money* and the social exclusion and inadequate living conditions experienced by the actor. The different filmic works starring Ventura are structured around the universe of (mostly male) immigrants in Lisbon and surrounding areas. *Colossal Youth*, for instance, either unveils or alludes to personal stories of backbreaking low-paid jobs, precarious everyday conditions and solitude, caused by social exclusion and the absence of wife and offspring left on Cape Verde. *Horse Money* adds detail to this context, particularly through the interactions between Ventura and Vitalina. In the long dialogue between the two characters, soon after meeting for the first time, Vitalina adds further depth to Ventura's condition as an immigrant by telling him of the life left behind in Cape Verde. During this scene, Vitalina asks Ventura about the wedding dowry he brought to his wife. Later, Vitalina informs him that his house in Cape Verde is now a ruin. She tells Ventura that vultures attacked his horse, Dinheiro (Money). There are clear links between Vitalina's condition and the female-centred thematic animating Costa's second feature film, *Casa de Lava*. Vitalina's personal story reflects the other side of Cape Verdean migration, one that concerns the women left behind and who, perhaps, will one day join their husbands.

Moreover, *Casa de Lava*, *Colossal Youth* and *Horse Money* convey Costa's attention to documents. Among other items, these films depict personal letters, photos, oral recollections, songs, certificates and other official proof of identity. The inclusion of these documents elucidates to us the multi-layered intertextuality of Costa's cinema. Firstly, these items prompt textual correlations between the three films; secondly, they create figurative associations between personal stories and historical events, as well as between their overlapping social and political contexts. An example of the first characteristic is the inclusion of letters in all three films. *Casa de Lava* and *Colossal Youth*, for instance, include the same epistolary prop, a letter written in Kriolu (Cape Verdean creole). This document is an adaptation of a letter-poem that French poet Robert Desnos wrote to his wife Youki (née Lucie Badoud) from the Buchenwald concentration camp, a few months after his arrest by the Gestapo in February 1944.[4] In *Casa de Lava*, Mariana (played by Inês de Medeiros) steals the letter from Edite's lodgings (Edith Scob); later, its contents are partially read aloud by one of the local teenagers whom Mariana befriended, played by Sandra do Canto Brandão (Figure 7.2). In *Colossal Youth*, the contents of this letter are repeatedly recited by Ventura to his illiterate friend Lento, who asked him to write it so he could send it to his wife in Cape Verde.

138 THE FILMS OF PEDRO COSTA

Figures 7.2 and 7.3 The epistolary device as narrative juxtaposition between films: Mariana (Inês de Medeiros) reads the letter destined for Edite (Edith Scob) in *Casa de Lava* (1994); Vitalina (Vitalina Varela) reads the letter penned by Ventura in *Horse Money* (2014)

In all instances, the letter (in both films, as well as in Desnos's original) draws on a (hypothetical) list of presents which the writer will give to their loved one when they meet again. The analogy between political repression and its historical context (Desnos was a member of the French Resistance) and the perpetual condition of the immigrants featured in both of Costa's films is clear (Rancière 2014: 135; also Jorge 2014: 53; Cordeiro 2017: 35). In *Horse Money* we also see Ventura writing a letter. While its contents are never disclosed, it can be assumed that this is a message to a loved one, perhaps Ventura's wife. Later in the film Ventura gives the letter to Vitalina, claiming that her late husband has written it (Figure 7.3). Ventura's intentions are not clear, yet their symbolic value is not lost; the letter provides Vitalina with a final connection to the deceased husband. This epistolary device may also offer a textual juxtaposition with *Colossal Youth*. In *Horse Money* Ventura finally fulfils his role as a scribe of a letter which was neither written nor delivered in the previous film.

As shown above, textual correlations are one of the aesthetic tropes adopted by Costa to merge different narrative moments, and to provide a thematic and narrative unity to his films. A clear example of the layered nature of these correlations in *Horse Money* is the initial sequence of the film. In it are presented twelve photographs taken by Jacob Riis portraying the precarious everyday life of New York migrants in the late nineteenth century. Later in the film, this group of photographs is mirrored by a musical sequence using as soundtrack Os Tubarões' 'Alto Cutelo', a song that narrates the miserable life of Cape Verdean immigration in Lisbon. This sequence shows several people in their dwelling or in narrow streets, depicted in most instances individually and occupying the filmic space in a stationary manner. There is a stylistic and thematic rapport between these *tableaux vivants* shot in the early twenty-first century and Riis's photographs. The alleys and living dwellings shot by Costa echo the tenement alleys, lodging houses and drinking dives photographed by Riis. Both instances document people with the same or similar precarious living conditions; 'very little has changed', Costa argues in an interview with Michael Guarneri (2015a).

The correlation between two filmic moments in *Horse Money* alludes to the notion of persistence of a perpetual present which brings the narrative of the film together. In Costa's cinema, such correlations are not confined within the duration of a particular work. As Jacques Rancière asserts in his analysis of *Horse Money*, there is a striking similarity between Riis's photographs and some scenes included in *Colossal Youth* (2015: 50). And Jonathan Rosenbaum points out that the inclusion of these images at the beginning of *Horse Money* matches, structurally, the 'heroic portraiture of Cape Verdeans at the start of' *Casa de Lava* (2015: 130). Costa acknowledges the presence of textual juxtapositions in and between the different films he directs, suggesting that this is one of the characteristics of his ongoing collaborative creative process with Ventura and, more recently, with Vitalina Varela. As he explains in the interview with Mark Peranson already cited, the letter penned by Ventura during *Horse Money*

> will be in another film. This is how I get my scripts. I am very fortunate to get the scripts written by the actors during the shooting. Ventura wrote a little bit what I should do in the near future. (Peranson 2014)

Costa may be hinting at the beginning of the creative process which gave origin to a filmic project initiated soon after the theatrical release of *Horse Money*. At the time of writing, this project, titled *Vitalina Varela*, is in the final stages of post-production. More assertively, the above quote indicates the importance given by Costa to the inclusion of (material and immaterial) objects provided by his collaborators in the creative process. *Horse Money* is exemplary in this sense. Its narrative is structured around the oral recollections of several events lived by Ventura and Vitalina Varela and, even more pertinently, around several documents and objects that the latter actor brought into the film set. Some scenes in the film are structured around Varela's personal belongings: her passport and plane tickets and ornaments such as necklaces (Figure 7.4). These objects highlight both the actor's performance and her lived experiences. The use of official documents sourced from Vitalina's personal archive provides

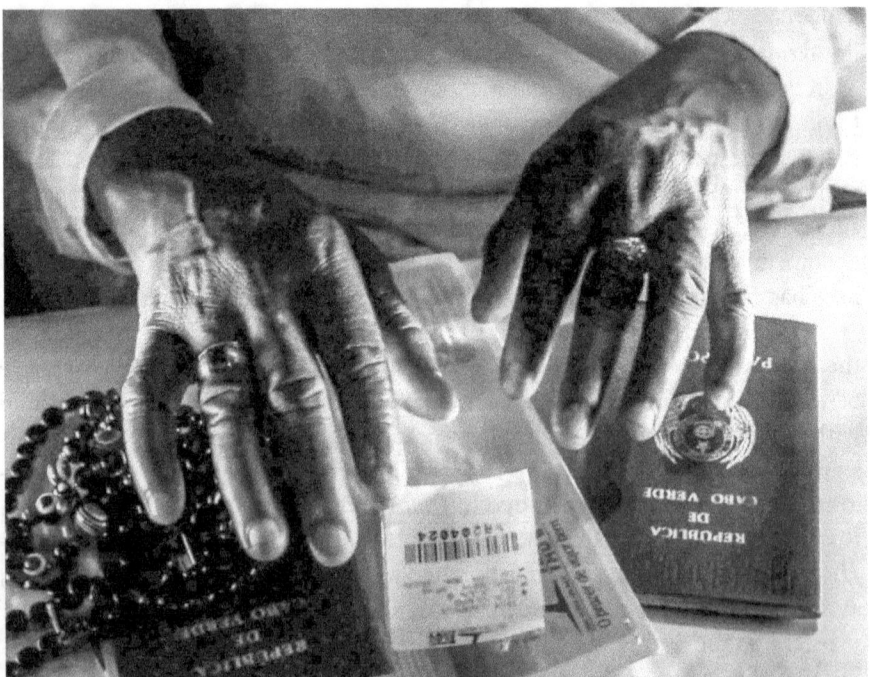

Figure 7.4 Still from *Horse Money* (2014): Vitalina Varela's off-screen personal documents and objects are used as filmic props to reinstate her identity on screen

further depth to her characterisation. Vitalina is seen reciting, though with some small omissions, her own and her husband's birth and marriage records, official memos from the Cape Verde embassy, and her husband's death certificate. As with all of her dialogue lines in the film, Varela whispers the formally written information contained in these documents. While her body posture is contained, there is a clear emotional display in her delivery. This information provides factual consistency to her personal biography, while also alerting us to the bureaucratic brutality which Varela has been subjected to as an immigrant. As in the letters used in *Casa de Lava* and *Colossal Youth*, Varela's documents in the film serve as a form of resistance against oblivion and invisibility.

Vitalina Varela's participation in *Horse Money* deserves contextualisation, as it elucidates both her personal circumstances, alluded to in the film, as well as her performance. Interviews with Costa are, once again, useful to trace the authorial process around Varela's contribution. As he explains to the Belgian-based film publication Sabzian:

> [the] first time I met Vitalina, I asked her if I could film in her house, just inside the house [the scene is included in the sequence featuring the song by Os Tubarões]. She said yes, and later we started talking and she kept whispering all the time and I had to ask her to repeat her phrases; she doesn't speak Portuguese and even for me it's hard because her creole accent is very tough. But I also think she was whispering not just because of some natural shyness, but because she was suspicious of me: she was afraid, being a stranger in a strange land and not having all her legal papers yet.
>
> [. . .] We all know that people on the margins of society [. . .] immediately lower their voices when confronted with the authorities; they whisper not to be caught; they spend their existence in hiding; she's coming from far away and her whispering is almost a voice without a body or a body with a strange, broken, faded identity. [. . .]
>
> I think we did well in materializing a social, political violence through this form, through this metaphor of a plaintive *sotto voce*. (Ramstedt and Grennberger 2015; italics in the original)

In the interview with Peranson already cited, Costa provides further explanation of how Varela's personal documents came to be included in the film:

> When we met she said, 'Come in, come in, let me show you something.' And she showed me all of the papers, she had a pile . . . it's very important for immigrants, papers are fundamental, a dossier. It's going to the embassy, they spend hours and months and days in queues, they think about that. She reads the real stuff. I didn't expect her to do what she does, to be so emotional. (Peranson 2014)

These considerations call our attention to the repressive rendering of Costa collaborators' identities through bureaucracy. Vitalina's form of translating her living conditions, through a particular form of delivery, transmits the political context contained in *Horse Money*. This underlines, once again, the importance of personal sources – either material, such as Varela's documents, or immaterial, such as Ventura's oral stories – as a narrative strategy to activate links between the personal and the political.

THE POLITICS OF REPRESENTATION: CRITICAL RECEPTION OF *HORSE MONEY*

The political reading made possible by the use of an assemblage of documents in *Horse Money* is, however, ambiguous. The political aspects present in Costa's cinema are suggested by the participation of non-professional actors and their contribution to the creative process. Yet any political stance seems to be veiled by a representational mode which does not translate any formal commentary. As Jacques Rancière asserts, politics and art construct fictions, '*material* rearrangements of signs and images, relationships between what is seen and what is said, between what is done and what can be done' (2005: 39; emphasis in the original). Over the years, this relationship between representation and meaning came to characterise Costa's authorial process (see Chapter 2). The political ambiguity in Costa's cinema is more acutely scrutinised in the critical discourses around *Horse Money*.

Conversely, and with regards to *Horse Money*, possible manifestations of the political emerge from the intertextual nature of the film. This characteristic links *Horse Money* to other works previously directed by Costa, organising an articulated filmic universe which is increasingly more complex. This being said, *Horse Money* also reflects the further stage of a constantly evolving filmic style, which is informed by protracted creative collaborations and the use of digital video. The inclusion of different sources in the film is deployed through an aestheticised treatment of filmic space and time, and in the characters' ambiguous presence. With regard to the stylistic treatment of filmic space, Chris Fujiwara asserts:

> *Horse Money* confirms the heightening of a Mannerist treatment of space in Costa's films. The images are more oblique than ever, foregrounding a certain degree of effort involved in seeing, and the shadows that fall across the spaces assume a greater independence and force; at the same time, within the increasing fragmentation of the filmic space, the ability of the human figures to hold on and survive assumes an ever purer significance. (Fujiwara 2016: 4)

Jonathan Rosenbaum, reviewing the film for *Artforum*, offers further understanding of this intensification in Costa's filmic style. He argues that *Horse Money* is a 'sharp departure' from previous works, in which 'the long takes' structuring Costa's earlier feature films 'now accede to a privileging of traumatic memory and consciousness – and all the narrative fragmentation this entails – over any sustained continuity of space or chronology' (2015: 129).

Critical responses to *Horse Money* emphasise this ambiguous relation between film style and possible political readings conveyed by its narrative. In the understanding of many film critics, a central characteristic of this ambiguity is the lack of narrative clarity. Film reviews almost unanimously emphasise the fragmented and intangible narrative of the film. Mark Peranson addresses such intangibility in an exemplary manner: '[every] review of this film is guaranteed to get at least one detail wrong; after seeing it three times the film remains intangible to me' (2014). Jonathan Romney's review in *Film Comment* similarly points out that its narrative 'discontinuity is unsettling' (2015a). Some critics add to this narrative intangibility the possible elusiveness of its thematic context. Portuguese film critic Jorge Mourinha, for example, contends that the film's subjective references to a 'Portuguese historical past' may prevent its full understanding by international audiences (2014: 7).

Costa is somehow responsive to these critiques concerning lack of intelligibility. As he confides in an interview to *Filmmaker*, *Horse Money* is 'a film that no one understands' (Barker and Porterfield 2015). The filmmaker, however, also defends the film from such an indictment by maintaining that: '[perhaps] this may annoy some people, but there are no mysteries or artist secrets to be revealed. All I can say is that everything is on screen' (Cutler 2015). Costa's views on the lack of intelligibility are, perhaps, inconclusive. Yet these views also transmit his personal stance, commonly observed during interviews, in eschewing commentary on the textual meaning of his films. Contrastingly, and as noted in the numerous interviews cited so far, Costa is eager to offer generous explanations of the collaborative creative process of *Horse Money*. Equally, he also stresses how his collaborators' personal contexts strongly inform his authorial process. This stance is just as revealing, as it is part of a discourse maintained by the filmmaker. Information conveyed by Costa surely assists tracing the different contexts gaining expression in the film. It also, however, discloses a narrative of production emphasising detachment from normative industrial filmmaking practices.

Inevitably, Costa's narrative of production expresses a political stance which intertwines film style with the conditions of production of the films he directs. Such a stance helps shape the consumption of *Horse Money*. While adding new layers to the production context of the film, it also leaves possible textual readings open to different interpretations. This ambiguity seems to be appealing to some audiences. Appropriately, critical responses to *Horse*

Money also make a connection between its cryptic narrative and the public to which Costa's cinema commonly caters. Reviewing the film in *Variety*, Scott Foundas points out that, albeit more accessible than Costa's previous works, *Horse Money* 'still lacks a traditional narrative structure and demands a patient, inquisitive audience' (2014). Brandon Judell's review in the *Huffington Post* (US) similarly asserts that the film (which he classifies as an 'unnecessary addition to the Fontainhas trilogy') mostly suits audiences which are receptive to 'self-indulgent befuddlement' (2015). Perhaps because of the ambiguous narrative of the film, some of the critical literature around *Horse Money* concentrates its attention on its elaborate visuals. Similarly, some film critics resort to approximate it to different cinema traditions and genres. The filmic style of *Horse Money* has been characterised, for instance, as reflecting aesthetics close to German expressionism and horror genres (see Romney 2015a; Rosenbaum 2015: 130). Other film critics see in the film the influence of classic filmmakers commonly mentioned when discussing Costa's cinema, among others Jacques Tourneur, Edgar G. Ulmer and Val Lewton (see, for example, Cronk 2015).

Some of the reviews above place Costa's cinema in general, and *Horse Money* in particular, as works mostly conveying political dilettantism and exploitation of poverty for the enjoyment of a cinephile fringe. Offering further criticism of Costa's filmic style and his audience, Geoffrey Cheshire argues that

> Costa is a darling of many critics and festivals for reasons that strike me as mostly dubious: his films feature heavily aestheticized surfaces lacquered over fashionable political subjects and attitudes. Like the rock band that only you and 12 other people like, he preaches to a like-minded coterie. (Cheshire 2014)

These accusations are not new. Over the years, Costa has received extensive criticism of his aesthetic approach. One of his harshest detractors is the American cultural critic Armond White. Commenting on the three films included in the DVD boxed set released by Criterion in 2010 (*Bones*, *In Vanda's Room* and *Colossal Youth*), White accuses Costa of 'perversely' distorting the misery lived by the collaborators in these films to fit his 'art-cinema etudes':

> The political indifference that prevails in contemporary film culture is [. . .] indulged by Costa's artiness. His style – long takes, chiaroscuro compositions, minimal movement – is a highly refined decadence. It allows guilt-free detachment from the reality of his characters and the many non-professional actors he enlists. (White 2010)

Such accusations of decadent artistic pretentiousness and political indifference reveal the problematic contours of a filmic style which, while enthusiastically received by some cinephiles, does not convey a clear political message concerning the lived conditions of its characters or actors. White's unfavourable view of Costa echoes the criticism around different filmic trends thriving at certain film festivals – for example, the European 'miserabilist' art film and world cinema 'poverty porn' (see Quandt 2006: 356 and Ross 2011: 262, respectively). This is so even if Costa's filmic style differs from the explicit and graphic depictions seen in works of, for example, the controversial Filipino filmmaker Brillante Mendoza (see Gonzaga 2017: 113).

The criticism of Costa's cinema, of which White's article is perhaps the most articulate example, finds contrasts in the critique offered by Jacques Rancière. Over the years, the French philosopher has devoted attention to Costa's work in both scholarly and non-scholarly literature, centring its analysis on the problematic relation between aesthetics and politics. Contrary to the analysis offered by critics such as White, Rancière understands Costa's stylised representational mode as a sincere form of connecting with his collaborators. This filmic representation, Rancière agues, offers a political stance rendered through a filmic sensory perception favouring contemplation. This quality conveys a form of 'politics through aesthetics', which circumvents 'explanations' and condescending feelings towards the characters depicted in Costa's films (Rancière [2008] 2009a: 80; 2009b; see also Baumbach 2013: 31). Elaborating on this understanding, Rancière argues that Costa's filmic style is informed by a close attention to the lives of these characters and, consequently, the non-professional actors performing them. This quality offers, again according to Rancière, a possible answer to the dilemma of the aesthetic representation of poverty; it neither engages with an 'indiscreet aestheticism' unconcerned with the situation of these characters nor with the 'populism' offered by a simplistic denunciation of what caused their social condition (2014: 130; see also Rancière 2009b).

Rancière takes this point further in his article about *Horse Money*, published in the October 2015 edition of British film magazine *Sight & Sound*. The inclusion of Riis's photographs at the beginning of the film causes Rancière to ask if it does not translate an effort by Costa to 'claim' some of the 'militant engagement' that characterised the Danish-American photographer and social reformer (2015: 49). Costa categorically denies such intent, pointing out that 'what Riis did is not possible anymore'; instead, he argues, these photographs are used to claim back some of the 'emotional' substance which they originally may have conveyed (Guarneri 2015a). Rancière recognises, however, that the use of these images and other sources in the film come to reaffirm: 'the true measure of the violence inflicted on all those who had to come and throw their lives away amidst the construction sites and shanty towns of Capital's metropolises' (2015: 50). Rancière's argument echoes observations offered by Chris Fujiwara and Jonathan Rosenbaum. Both writers suggest that *Horse Money* could be considered a refinement of a filmic style that now further expresses political contours once only alluded to in previous films. It is noteworthy that Armond White, when reviewing the film in 2015, offers a similar reading of such possible aesthetic development. As White asserts:

> *Horse Money* differs from Costa's usual poverty porn because he finally lets his victim-actors become expressive. [. . .] By finding the humanity in these figures, Costa goes beyond what makes them pathological and discovers their universality. [. . .] Costa is not a Neorealist analyzing the political circumstances that affect poor people's lives [. . .] but his formalist story structures and stylized vision of depredation finally, in *Horse Money*, pierce their sociological surface and attain an almost spiritual and *political clarity*. (White 2015; emphasis added)

The debates emerging around the critical reception of *Horse Money* are still divided and to some extent inconclusive. Some critics read the film as a continuation of Costa's aesthetic preoccupations, more concerned with a marked stylisation of the lives of the non-professional actors collaborating in the film than in conveying narrative clarity and political intent. As some of these critiques reveal, however, the film also transmits a development in the way of addressing the multiple contexts – historical, political and personal – lived by these actors over the years.

More conclusively, these different perceptions around the film bring to the fore the increasing importance of the collaborative authoring of the films directed by Costa. This authorial practice is translated into an attentive use of documents – material and immaterial – to convey both emotion and meaning to these fictionalised filmic narratives. As a document of documents, *Horse Money* illustrates the constant dialogue between the textual and contextual in such collaborative authorship. A possible textual analysis of the film, such as the one attempted in some sections of this chapter, is greatly informed by the factual and emotional information provided by the documental items featured in it. This analysis also becomes influenced by the extra-textual information disclosed by Costa in several published interviews. This type of public address provides yet another layer of intertextuality to the film, which transcends its textual boundaries and helps organise its reception.

It is never redundant to point out that *Horse Money* is the latest instalment of a filmic universe that transcends several works, as are the collaborative practices that sustained its making. As discussed here, though, the film also presents evolving characteristics in aesthetic and narrative terms which come to reflect changes in Costa's authorial process. As the filmmaker implies, *Horse Money* may be the 'final' film structured around Ventura's recollections; 'if we do something else', Costa suggestively argues, 'we have to do something different'

(Peranson 2014). Adding to this understanding, the inclusion of Vitalina Varela in the film also points to the beginning of another creative collaboration. The information released by OPTEC Filmes about Costa's upcoming feature film leads to the understanding that its narrative is centred in the personal story of Varela. As already mentioned, at the time of writing the project goes by the revealing title of *Vitalina Varela*. Like the layers of understanding of the authorial process giving shape to *Horse Money*, this recent evidence contributes further to a central assertion made here: the films of Pedro Costa are animated, in equal measure, by an evolving aesthetic, narrative and thematic coherence, as well as by constantly developing collaborative practices which support both their production and their consumption.

NOTES

1. It can also be pointed out that this production blueprint maintained by OPTEC Filmes is extended to other film projects. As with *Horse Money*, other films produced by the company rely on micro-budgets, with the company assuming the technical side of production and post-production. Recent examples of this approach are the Portuguese feature film *Verão Danado* (*Damned Summer*, dir. Pedro Cabeleira, 2017) and the short film *Farpões Baldios* (*Barbs, Wastelands*, dir. Marta Mateus, also 2017), the latter produced in partnership with Lisbon-based production company C.R.I.M.
2. For possible readings of *Horse Money* as a historical narrative, see Preto (2017: 32–3).
3. For production details about this scene sequence, which had the collaboration of the Portuguese Army, see Costa's interviews with Neil Bahadur (2015) and Patrick Holzapfel (2014).
4. An English translation of Desnos's letter, as used in *Colossal Youth*, is reproduced in the catalogue of Costa's film retrospective that took place at the Jeonju International Film Festival in 2010.

Conclusion

In 2015, two seminal works of the Portuguese *Cinema Novo*, *Os Verdes Anos (Green Years*, 1963) and *Mudar de Vida (Change One's Life*, 1966), were re-released for the Portuguese commercial cinema and home cinema circuits. Exhibited and circulating for decades through poor-quality theatrical and VHS copies, the two feature films, both directed by Paulo Rocha, were subjected to a prolonged and careful digital restoration of image and sound initiated in 2011 and supervised by Pedro Costa. The restoration work of Rocha's films was only completed after his death, in December 2012. The process, nonetheless, illustrates the aesthetic complicity shared, and relation of trust established, between the two filmmakers over the years.[1]

The working process around the restoration of Rocha's films provides us with clues as to how Costa's creative and technical competence is not merely confined to the films he authored and directed over the last three decades. As examined in Chapter 6, Costa's filmmaking activities also include the recuperation of his own works, as the re-mastering processes of *Blood* and *Casa de Lava* demonstrate. During the last decade, such expertise has also been extended to films of other filmmakers who were an influence on both his work and professional attitude. This aspect of Costa as a 'recuperation' agent, it should be noted, started earlier when he took the initiative to help recover and restore Jean Eustache's documentary *Numéro Zéro* (1971), which was considered lost until 2003.[2] These activities around film recuperation, moreover, are extended to exhibition and circulation. Costa's active role in film promotion encompasses both his films but also, for instance, the championing of the cinema of António Reis and Margarida Cordeiro within international cinephile circles in which his own work commonly circulates. In similar terms, Costa also participated in promotional activities of Rocha's posthumously-released

Se Eu Fosse Ladrão . . . Roubava (2013), premiered at the 2013 Locarno International Film Festival.

These recent activities around the restoration of Rocha's films and the promotion of the cinema of Reis and Cordeiro provide yet another layer to Costa's manifold production and consumption contexts. These particular undertakings are integrated within an articulated professional agency which allows different intersecting roles – director, author and artist – as well as a creative and commercial agent with significant authority in the production and promotion of his films. As discussed across this book these different roles reflect a narrative of production, maintained through different collaborative practices and sustained by interconnected networks of film production and cultural consumption. What transpires in this role of recuperation agent, moreover, is the management of a rich cinema legacy which informs Costa's films. Once confined to visible stylistic allusions and homages, this legacy seems to be managed through some of the consumption practices maintained by Costa. In the case of Rocha's two films, such agency is also extended to technical procedures that were once confined to his own films.

More broadly, and with exhibition and circulation still in mind, the management of a legacy around the filmic works of Pedro Costa gains visible expression in numerous initiatives curated with the help of the Portuguese filmmaker. Among others, the film retrospective *The School of Reis*, held in 2012 at different venues in the USA (mentioned in Chapter 1), and the film cycle curated by Costa at the Portuguese Cinematheque in January 2015 (mentioned in Chapter 5), serve as examples of how his work has come to be commonly positioned side by side with already canonised art cinema. This curatorial agency – yet another of Costa's possible roles – gains further countenance in the 2018 exhibition *Company*, discussed at the beginning of Chapter 7. These and other initiatives helped to resituate the work of different filmmakers within Costa's own filmic universe, as well as include them in the authorial practices that animate it.

As also discussed across this book, Costa's cinema shows reverence for a constellation of canonised filmmakers – Tourneur, Ozu, Straub and Huillet, Bresson . . . Inevitably, such reverence is also manifested through a discourse transmitted in public disclosures. These and other filmmakers are commonly referred to by Costa as being models, both for the aesthetics of his films and for his filmmaking practices. Concerning the latter, these influences are mediated through a personal narrative maintained by Costa, who depicts them as able to somehow escape imposed restrictions of the film industry and, instead, become meticulous and obstinate highly-skilled cinema artisans. Consistently and over the years, film criticism and fan commentary use these same qualities to describe Costa's austere filmmaking practices. It can be argued, even if only tentatively, that Costa himself became a model for young film directors whose works have recently started to circulate on the art-house and festival international circuits. Costa's consistent presence at the international film festival and his promotional activities over this and the past decade, created awareness of his work among different international cinephile communities outside Europe – communities whose constituencies also include different film professionals. As Kazuyuki Yano pointed out to me, both Costa's film aesthetics and filmmaking practices have been influential to a new generation of Japanese filmmakers working within low-budget frameworks. Among others, he mentions the emerging filmmakers Kei Shichiri and Katsuya Tomita (Yano 2014).

This exposure seems to have generated a similar effect in Latin America. Since 2014, *Horse Money* has circulated through film festivals in Argentina, Brazil, Chile, Colombia and Mexico, and has had theatrical releases in Argentina and Ecuador. Among several Latin American filmmakers citing Costa as an influence, both aesthetically and in terms of filmmaking practice, are José Luis Torres Leiva (Chile), Yulene Olaizola (Mexico), Matias Piñedo (Argentina) and Argentina-based Spanish director Hermes Paralluelo. It is pertinent to point out that Leiva's *El cielo, la tierra, y la lluvia* (*Sky, The Earth and the Rain*, 2008), Paralluelo's *Todo no es vigilia* (*Not All Is Vigil*, 2014), and Olaizola's *Paraísos Artificiales* (*Artificial Paradises*, 2011) and *Fogo* (2012) are stylistically close to Costa's films shot in digital video. This aesthetic approximation is extended to works produced outside this particular geographical region. Among others, Costa's (assumed or only noted) influence expands to films such as *Putty Hill* (dir. Matthew Porterfield, USA, 2010), *Nana* (dir. Valérie Massadian, France, 2011), *Cilaos* (directed by Paris-based Colombian filmmaker Camilo Restrepo, 2016), as well as to the work of Portuguese filmmaker João Salaviza. It is problematic, of course, to maintain that these different works may present a coherent filmic sensibility or a filmmaking style which links them to Costa. In the same vein, it is difficult to contend that Costa's influence may be revealed in the same way as, for instance, the inspiration provided by António Reis to a group of Portuguese filmmakers emerging in the 1980s. However it can be argued that, in recent years, Costa's cinema provides both an aesthetic and a filmmaking blueprint for young filmmakers working with low budgets and using digital video.

The dialogue between aesthetics and technique, central in such an influential digital video blueprint, is also carried further in academic-related activities maintained by Pedro Costa during the present decade. As explained in Chapter 6, Costa maintains regular activities in university-related venues, such as master classes and lectures. These activities are often integrated into dissemination practices, and offer an opportunity for Costa to articulate aesthetic preoccupations and to dispense technical competence with regard to his approach to digital video. This pedagogic facet became further visible in 2013 when Costa collaborated at the intensive doctoral level (DLA) programme of Film.Factory. This course in filmmaking was a collaborative effort between Hungarian filmmaker Béla Tarr, the University of Sarajevo School of Science and Technology and the Sarajevo Film Academy. As an invited lecturer, Costa participated in a curriculum which included both theoretical and practical modules, delivered by the actor Tilda Swinton, the filmmakers Gael García Bernal, Fred Kelemen, Carlos Reygadas, Apichatpong Weerasethakul, and film critics and scholars Jonathan Rosenbaum and Jean-Michel Frodon, among others.

These different practices undertaken by, and concentrated around, Pedro Costa offer further understanding of the complex mechanisms operated by the manifold art cinema institutional formations. The end of Chapter 7 hints at possible new characteristics in Costa's narrative of production, and these will surely animate future discussions about the Portuguese filmmaker. Overall, I aimed to provide, instead, a comprehensive understanding of this evolving narrative over the last three decades. As discussed across this book, Costa's professional agency elucidates the multiple forms in which specific filmmaking, authorial, exhibition and reception practices are sustained by both cultural discourses and industrial and commercial processes. Some of the evidence presented in this book may tend to suggest that there is a need to emphasise the centrality of production and consumption practices in scholarly discussions about contemporary art film. More conclusively the aims of the book have been to unpack the social, cultural and political contexts within which such production and consumption practices take place. As such, the films of Pedro Costa served here to illustrate some of the multifaceted and constantly changing practices which underpin our understanding of contemporary art cinema.

NOTES

1. Costa provides a detailed account of the restoration process of Rocha's films in Lisboa (2019).
2. Costa became aware of *Numéro Zéro* through a conversation with Jean-Marie Straub in 2001. With the help of filmmaker and producer Thierry Lounas, Costa was able to contact Eustache's son, who provided a working print of the film. This print was restored by the Portuguese Cinematheque and later used to produce the exhibition copies used to commercially re-release the film in 2003 (for details and anecdotes concerning the finding Eustache's film see, for example, Morain 2003).

Filmography

AS DIRECTOR

'As Cartas da Júlia', Portugal, 1984 (?). Twelve co-directed episodes for television commissioned by RTP. 16mm, colour, length unknown. Considered lost.
O *Sangue/Blood*, Portugal, 1989. Feature film, 35mm, b&w, 95 min.
Casa de Lava (aka *Down to Earth*), Portugal, France, Germany, 1994. Feature film, 35mm, colour, 110 min.
Ossos/Bones, Portugal, France, Denmark, 1997. Feature film, 35mm, colour, 94 min.
No Quarto da Vanda/In Vanda's Room, Portugal, Germany, Switzerland, 2000. Feature film, DV, colour, 170 min.
'Danièle Huillet/Jean-Marie Straub: Où gît votre sourire enfoui?' Included in the TV series 'Cinéma, de notre temps' (1988–), La Sept-Arte. France, 2001. Television documentary, DV, colour, 72 min.
Où gît votre sourire enfoui?/Where Does Your Hidden Smile Lie?, Portugal, France, 2001. Documentary, DV, colour, 104 min.
6 Bagatelas. Outtakes from *Where Does Your Hidden Smile Lie?* Portugal, France, 2001. Documentary short, DV, colour, 18 min.
Ne Change Rien, Portugal, 2005. Documentary short, HD DV, b&w, 12 min.
Juventude em Marcha/Colossal Youth, Portugal, France, Switzerland, 2006. Feature film, HD DV, colour, 155 min.
A Caça ao Coelho com Pau/The Rabbit Hunters. Included in the omnibus film *Memories*. South Korea, 2007. Short film, HD DV, colour, 22 min.
Tarrafal. Included in the omnibus film *State of the World*. Portugal, 2007. Short film, HD DV, colour, 16 min.
Ne Change Rien/Change Nothing, Portugal, France, 2009. Documentary, HD DV, b&w, 100 min.
O Nosso Homem/Our Man, Portugal, 2010. Short film, HD DV, colour, 23 min.
Lamento da Vida Jovem/Sweet Exorcism. Included in the omnibus film *Centro Histórico*. Portugal, 2012. Short film, HD DV, colour, 23 min.
Cavalo Dinheiro/Horse Money, Portugal, 2014. Feature film, HD DV, colour, 103 min.
Vitalina Varela, Portugal, 2019. Feature film, HD DV, colour, 124 min.

AS ASSISTANT DIRECTOR

Do outro lado do espelho (aka *Atlântida*). Directed by Daniel Del-Negro. Portugal, 1985. Feature film, 16mm, 100 min.
Um Adeus Português/A Portuguese Farewell. Directed by João Botelho. Portugal, 1986. Feature film, 35mm, colour, 85 min.
Uma Rapariga no Verão/A Girl in Summer. Directed by Vítor Gonçalves. Portugal, 1986. Feature film, 16mm, 80 min.
Duma Vez por Todas. Directed by Joaquim Leitão. Portugal, 1987. Feature film, 35mm, 99 min.
Agosto/August. Directed by Jorge Silva Melo. Portugal, France, 1988. Feature film, 35mm, colour, 97 min.

VIDEO INSTALLATIONS

Untitled (2001). Single screen installation, 60 min.
The End of a Love Affair (2003). Single screen installation, 16 min.
Benfica, Colina do Sol e Pontinha (2005). Double screen installation, 12 min.
Casal da Boba (2005). Single screen installation, 475 min.
Fontaínhas (2005). Single screen installation, 5 min.
Minino Macho, Minino Fêmea/Little Boy Male, Little Girl Female (2005). Double screen installation, 37 min.
Filhas do Fogo/Daughters of Fire (2013). Double screen installation, 4 min.

DOCUMENTARIES ABOUT PEDRO COSTA

Tout refleurit: Pedro Costa, cinéaste/All Blossoms Again: Pedro Costa, Director. Directed by Aurélien Gerbault. France, 2006, 78 min.
Finding the Criminal. Directed by Craig Keller. UK, 2010, 118 min.
Sacavém. Directed by Júlio Alves. Portugal, 2018, 65 min.

Bibliography

Álvarez, Iván Villarmea (2016), 'Mudar de Perspetiva: A Dimensão Transnacional do Cinema Português Contemporâneo', *Aniki*, 3:1, pp. 101–20.
Alves, Laurinda (1990), 'Pedro e o Segredo', *O Independente*, supplement *Vida3*, 30 November, pp. 28–9.
Andersen, Thom (2010), 'Ghost Stories', in Yoo Un-Seong (ed.), *The Cinema of Pedro Costa*, Jeonju: Jeonju International Film Festival, pp. 246–54.
Andrews, David (2013), *Theorizing Art Cinemas: Foreign, Cult, Avant-Garde, and Beyond*, Austin: University of Texas Press.
Antunes, João (1990), 'Os Filmes da Prateleira', *Se7e*, 11 October, p. 15.
APORDOC (2002), *Livro de debates Doc's Kingdom 2000*, Lisbon: APORDOC.
Arenas, Fernando (2011), *Lusophone Africa: Beyond Independence*, Minneapolis: University of Minnesota Press.
Atalanta Filmes (1990), 'O Sangue', press release, np.
Azoury, Philippe (2009), 'Órfãos', in *O Sangue*, DVD extras, Lisbon: Midas Filmes.
Bahadur, Neil (2015), 'Interview: Pedro Costa', *Film Comment*, blog, 21 July 2015, <https://www.filmcomment.com/blog/interview-pedro-costa> (accessed 17 July 2018).
Balsom, Erika (2013), *Exhibiting Cinema in Contemporary Art*, Amsterdam: Amsterdam University Press.
Baptista, Tiago (2010), 'Nationally Correct: The Invention of Portuguese Cinema', *P: Portuguese Cultural Studies*, 3:1 (Spring), pp. 3–18.
Barker, David and Matthew Porterfield (2015), 'Standing on Opposite Sides of the Road: Pedro Costa on Horse Money', *Filmmaker*, 24 July, <http://filmmakermagazine.com/95049-standing-on-opposite-sides-of-the-road-pedro-costa-on-horse-money> (accessed 11 January 2019).
Barroso, Bárbara and Daniel Ribas (2008), 'No Cinema Português – Continuidades e Rupturas em Pedro Costa', *Revista Devires*, 5:1 (January–June), pp. 136–59.
Barwick, Chris (2014), Email interview with the author, 27 May.
Baumbach, Nico (2013), 'What Does It Mean to Call Film an Art?', in Paul Bowman (ed.), *Rancière and Film*, Edinburgh: Edinburgh University Press, pp. 20–33.
Bellour, Raymond (2012), *La Querelle des Dispositifs: Cinéma, Installations, Expositions*, Paris: Éditions P.O.L.
Berlakovich, Jürgen (2005), '"V"-Interview: Pedro Costa – The Film Is Rolling Like the Earth Is Rolling', *V'Blog* – Vienna International Film Festival, available at *Pedro Costa Herói*,

<http://pedrocosta-heroi.blogspot.co.uk/2008/02/i-dont-have-ideas-to-make-films-i-just.html> (accessed 23 May 2018).
Berry, Chris, Lu Xinyu and Lisa Rofel (eds) (2010), *The New Chinese Documentary Film Movement: For the Public Record*, Hong Kong: Hong Kong University Press.
Betz, Mark (2003), 'Art, Exploitation, Underground', in Mark Jancovich, Antonio Lazaro Reboll, Julian Stringer and Andrew Willis (eds), *Defining Cult Movies: The Cultural Politics of Oppositional Taste*, Manchester: Manchester University Press, pp. 202–22.
Betz, Mark (2010), 'Beyond Europe: On Parametric Transcendence', in Rosalind Galt and Karl Schoonover (eds), *Global Art Cinema: New Theories and Histories*, Oxford: Oxford University Press, pp. 31–47.
Bonnaud, Frédéric (2001), '*The Captive Lover* – An Interview with Jacques Rivette', *Senses of Cinema*, 79 (September), <http://sensesofcinema.com/2001/jacques-rivette/rivette-2> (accessed 12 June 2018).
Boozer, Jack (2008), 'The Screenplay and Authorship in Adaptation', in Jack Boozer (ed.), *Authorship in Film Adaptation*, Austin: University of Texas Press, pp. 1–30.
Bordwell, David (1985), *Narration in the Fiction Film*, London: Routledge.
Bordwell, David [1979] (2002a), 'The Art Cinema as a Mode of Film Practice', in Catherine Fowler (ed.), *The European Cinema Reader*, New York: Routledge, pp. 94–102.
Bordwell, David (2002b), 'Intensified Continuity: Visual Style in Contemporary American Film', *Film Quarterly*, 55:3 (Spring), pp. 16–28.
Bordwell, David and Kristin Thompson (2011), 'Good and Good for You', *Observations on Film Art*, 10 July, <http://www.davidbordwell.net/blog/2011/07/10/good-and-good-for-you> (accessed 24 May 2018).
Borges, Pedro (2014), Email interview with the author, 29 July.
Bourdieu, Pierre (1980), 'The Production of Belief: Contribution to an Economy of Symbolic Goods', trans. Richard Nice, *Media Culture Society*, 2:3 (July), pp. 261–93.
Bourdieu, Pierre (2010), *Distinction: A Social Critique of the Judgement of Taste*, trans. Richard Nice, London: Routledge.
Bradshaw, Peter (2009), 'Pedro Costa, the Samuel Beckett of Cinema', *The Guardian Film Blog*, 17 September, <http://www.theguardian.com/film/filmblog/2009/sep/17/pedro-costa-tate-retrospective> (accessed 7 May 2018).
Brady, Martin (2016), '"The attitude of smoking and observing": Slow Film and Politics in the Cinema of Jean-Marie Straub and Danièle Huillet', in Tiago de Luca and Nuno Barradas Jorge (eds), *Slow Cinema*, Edinburgh: Edinburgh University Press, pp. 71–84.
Brás, António (1990), 'Não é vermelho, é sangue', *A Grande Ilusão*, December, pp. 51–2.
Burdeau, Emmanuel (1999), 'Seul le cinéma – Pedro Costa tourne Dans la Chambre de Vanda', *Cahiers du Cinéma*, 536 (June), pp. 60–2.
Çağlayan, Emre (2018), *Poetics of Slow Cinema: Nostalgia, Absurdism, Boredom*, Basingstoke: Palgrave Macmillan.
Caldwell, John (2008), *Production Culture: Industrial Reflexivity and Critical Practice in Film and Television*, Durham, NC: Duke University Press.
Câmara, Vasco (1995), 'Convalescer na ilha dos mortos', *Público*, 10 February, p. 3.
Campany, David (2008), *Photography and Cinema*, London: Reaktion.
Carmo, Ana Teresa (2014), 'Como Nova Iorque inspirou o novo filme de Pedro Costa', *Público*, supplement *Ípsilon*, 9 October, <http://www.publico.pt/2014/10/09/culturaipsilon/noticia/pedro-costa-1672346> (accessed 17 October 2018).
Carmo, Teresa (1991), 'A Primeira Vez', *Se7e*, 9 May, pp. 25–9.
Chaves, Abel Ribeiro (2018), Email interview with the author, 7 June.
Cheshire, Geoffrey (2014), 'NYFF 2014: "Eden," "Horse Money" Use Fest to Build Stateside Buzz', *RogerEbert.com*, 5 October, <https://www.rogerebert.com/festivals-and-awards/

nyff-2014-eden-horse-money-use-fest-as-platform-to-build-stateside-buzz> (accessed 10 January 2019).

Cordeiro, Edmundo (2017), 'Ventura: A Character's Mental Landscape as History', *International Journal of Film and Media Arts*, 2:1, pp. 32–41.

Corless, Kieron (2008), 'Ace Ventura: King of the Quarter', *Sight & Sound*, 18:5 (May), p. 12.

Corless, Kieron (2009), 'Crossing the Threshold: Interview with Pedro Costa', *Sight & Sound*, 19:10 (October), pp. 28–31.

Corrigan, Timothy (1991), *A Cinema without Walls: Movies and Culture after Vietnam*, London: Routledge.

Costa, Pedro (2005), 'A Closed Door that Leaves Us Guessing', address at the Tokyo Film School, March 2004, trans. Downing Roberts, <http://www.rouge.com.au/10/costa_seminar.html> (accessed 13 March 2018).

Costa, Pedro (2006), 'Juventude em Marcha', promotional leaflet, np.

Costa, Pedro (2012), Personal interview with the author, Lisbon, 2 July.

Costa, Pedro (2013), Personal interview with the author, Lisbon, 22 February.

Costa, Pedro and Rui Chafes (2015), 'Pedro Costa e Rui Chafes à Conversa', Portuguese Cinematheque, 15 January, <http://youtu.be/KaYxUlgzSQg> (accessed 13 June 2018).

Costa, Pedro and Jean-Pierre Gorin (2010), 'Video Conversation', in *Letters From Fontainhas*, DVD supplements, New York: Criterion Collection.

Costa, Pedro, Cyril Neyrat and Andy Rector (2012), *Um Melro Dourado, um Ramo de Flores, uma Colher de Prata. Conversa com Pedro Costa*, Lisbon: Midas Filmes/Orfeu Negro.

Coutinho, Isabel (2009), 'Pedro, Inês e os fantasmas', *Público*, supplement *Ípsilon*, 25 September, pp. 9–11.

Cowie, Elisabeth (1999), 'The Spectacle of Actuality', in Jane M. Gaines and Michael Renov (eds), *Collecting Visible Evidence*, Minneapolis: University of Minnesota Press, pp. 19–45.

Crespo, Nuno (2012), 'O fascínio de Pedro Costa explicado pelos japoneses ao mundo', *Público*, 21 December, <http://www.publico.pt/n1578285> (accessed 15 June 2018).

Cronk, Jordan (2015), 'Horse Money', *Little White Lies*, 17 September, <http://lwlies.com/reviews/horse-money> (accessed 10 January 2019).

Cutler, Aaron (2015), 'Horse Money: An Interview with Pedro Costa', *Cineaste*, XL:3 (Summer), <http://www.cineaste.com/summer2015/horse-money-pedro-costa-aaron-cutler> (accessed 11 June 2018).

da Costa, João Bénard (1990), 'Sangue antigo e sangue novo', *Revista K*, November, p. 117.

da Costa, João Bénard (1996), *O Cinema Português Nunca Existiu*, Lisbon: CTT.

da Costa, João Bénard (2001), 'Os filmes que nos veem/os olhos que nos filmam: No Quarto da Vanda', *O Independente*, 2 March, p. 56.

da Costa, João Bénard (2009), 'O Negro é uma Cor ou o cinema de Pedro Costa', in Ricardo Matos Cabo (ed.), *Cem mil cigarros: os filmes de Pedro Costa*, Lisbon: Orfeu Negro, pp. 16–28.

da Silva, Rodrigues (1995a), 'O Rosto dos Verdes Anos: entrevista com Pedro Hestnes', *JN: Jornal de Letras e Ideias*, 1 March, pp. 5–7.

da Silva, Rodrigues (1995b), 'Públicos: o direito à diferença', *JN: Jornal de Letras e Ideias*, 15 March, p. 15.

da Silva, Rodrigues (1997), 'Malhas que o Império Tece(u)', *JL: Jornal de Letras e Ideias*, 5 November, p. 28.

Dargis, Manohla and A. O. Scott (2011), 'In Defense of the Slow and the Boring', *New York Times*, 3 June, <http://www.nytimes.com/2011/06/05/movies/films-in-defense-of-slow-and-boring.html> (accessed 23 May 2018).

Darke, Chris (2001), 'DV – Déjà vu, sobre o cinema digital', in Dário Oliveira (ed.), *Ciclo de Cinema, Instalação e Performance*, Porto: Porto 2001, pp. 44–51.

David, Catherine, Chris Dercon and Pedro Costa (2007), 'From the Black Box to the White Cube', *Jan van Eyck Video Weekend*, 26 May, <http://www.minch.org/jve/0_4_6_text_files/David_Dercon_Costa.html> (accessed 12 July 2018).

de Luca, Tiago and Nuno Barradas Jorge (2016), 'Introduction: From Slow Cinema to Slow Cinemas', in Tiago de Luca and Nuno Barradas Jorge (eds), *Slow Cinema*, Edinburgh: Edinburgh University Press, pp. 1–21.

de Pina, Luís (1986), *História do Cinema Português*, Mem-Martins: Publicações Europa-América.

de Valck, Marijke (2007), *Film Festivals: From European Geopolitics to Global Cinephilia*, Amsterdam: Amsterdam University Press.

Deleuze, Gilles (1989), *Cinema 2: The Time Image*, trans. Hugh Tomlinson and Robert Galeta, London: Athlone Press.

Del-Negro, Daniel (2012), Email interview with the author, 28 July.

Dercon, Chris (2002), 'Gleaning the Future', *Vertigo*, 2:2 (Spring), <http://www.closeupfilmcentre.com/vertigo_magazine/volume-2-issue-2-spring-2002/gleaning-the-future> (accessed 13 June 2018).

Ebert, Roger (2006), 'Cannes #10: Guessing Games', *Rogerebert.com*, 29 May, <https://www.rogerebert.com/festivals-and-awards/cannes-10-guessing-games> (accessed 4 May 2018).

Eisenschitz, Bernard (2009), 'O Que Conta Este Filme(s)?', in Ricardo Matos Cabo (ed.), *Cem mil cigarros: os filmes de Pedro Costa*, Lisbon: Orfeu Negro, pp. 237–9.

Elsaesser, Thomas (2005), *European Cinema: Face to Face with Hollywood*, Amsterdam: Amsterdam University Press.

Elsaesser, Thomas (2011), 'Stop/Motion', in Eivind Rossack (ed.), *Between Stillness and Movement: Film Photography Algorithms*, Amsterdam: Amsterdam University Press, pp. 109–22.

Elwes, Catherine (2004), *Video Art, a Guided Tour*, London: I. B. Tauris.

Emerson, Jim (2011), 'Into the Great Big Boring', *Scanners*, 9 June, <http://www.rogerebert.com/scanners/into-the-great-big-boring> (accessed 29 May 2018).

English, James F. (2005), *The Economy of Prestige: Prizes, Awards, and the Circulation of Cultural Value*, Cambridge, MA: Harvard University Press.

Ferreira, Carlos Melo (1995), 'Melancolicamente', *Cinema*, 24 (August–October), p. 6.

Ferreira, Francisco (2006), 'Guarda a minha fala para sempre', *Expresso*, 25 November, pp. 14–17.

Ferreira, Francisco (2010), 'Photomaton & Vox: An Interview with Pedro Costa about *Ne Change Rien*', in Yoo Un-Seong (ed.), *Pedro Costa*, Jeonju: Jeonju International Film Festival, pp. 157–64.

Figueirinhas, Rita do Carmo (2011), 'Bairro, identidade, interacção: Um olhar etnográfico sobre o Centro Social do Bairro 6 de Maio', unpublished Master's dissertation, Lisbon: ISCTE, Instituto Universitário de Lisboa.

Filipovic, Elena (2005), 'The Global White Cube', in Barbara Vanderlinden and Elena Filipovic (eds), *The Manifesta Decade*, Cambridge, MA: MIT Press, pp. 63–84.

Flanagan, Matthew (2008), 'Towards an Aesthetic of Slow in Contemporary Cinema', *16-9*, 29 (November), <http://www.16-9.dk/2008-11/side11_inenglish.htm> (accessed 13 February 2014).

Foundas, Scott (2006), '2006 Toronto Film Festival: Vote for Pedro (and Larry)', *LA Weekly Blog*, 16 September, <http://blogs.laweekly.com/foundas/2006/09/vote_for_pedro_and_larry.php> (accessed 8 May 2018).

Foundas, Scott (2014), 'Film Review: "Horse Money"', *Variety*, 15 August, <http://variety.com/2014/film/reviews/film-review-horse-money-1201283386> (accessed 11 June 2018).

Frohne, Ursula (2008), 'Dissolution of the Frame: Immersion and Participation in Video Installations', in Tanya Leighton (ed.), *Art and the Moving Image: A Critical Reader*, London: Tate Publishing, pp. 355–70.
Fujiwara, Chris (1998), *Jacques Tourneur: The Cinema of Nightfall*, Jefferson, MD: Johns Hopkins University Press.
Fujiwara, Chris (2010), 'The Mystery of Music: *Ne Change Rien*', in Yoo Un-Seong (ed.), *Pedro Costa*, Jeonju: Jeonju International Film Festival, pp. 313–18.
Fujiwara, Chris (2016), 'The Road to Perdition: Pedro Costa's Horse Money', in *Horse Money*, DVD booklet, New York: The Cinema Guild, pp. 1–4.
Fundação Calouste Gulbenkian (2012), 'Informações sobre o financiamento do filme "O Sangue" de Pedro Costa', email communication with the author, 3 August.
Furtado, José Afonso (1995), 'Regresso e Chegada', *Público*, 10 February, p. 6.
Gallagher, Mark (2013), *Another Steven Soderbergh Experience: Authorship and Contemporary Hollywood*, Austin: University of Texas Press.
Gallagher, Tag (2007), 'Straub Anti-Straub', *Senses of Cinema*, 43 (May), <http://sensesofcinema.com/2007/feature-articles/costa-straub-huillet> (accessed 25 May 2014).
Galt, Rosalind and Karl Schoonover (2010), 'Introduction: The Impurity of Art Cinema', in Rosalind Galt and Karl Schoonover (eds), *Global Art Cinema: New Theories and Histories*, New York and Oxford: Oxford University Press, pp. 3–27.
Gandolfi, Loreta (2013), 'Lights Off On Pedro Costa', *Take One*, 23 March, <http://www.takeonecff.com/2013/lamour-nexiste-pas-lights-off-on-pedro-costa> (accessed 9 February 2015).
Gibson-Graham, J. K. (2006), *A Postcapitalist Politics*, Minneapolis: University of Minnesota Press.
Gomes, Miguel (2009), 'Serenity', *Sight & Sound*, 25 September, <http://www.bfi.org.uk/news-opinion/sight-sound-magazine/comment/serenity-pedro-costa-s-fontainhas-trilogy> (accessed 16 May 2018).
Gonzaga, Elmo (2017), 'The Cinematography Unconscious of Slum Voyeurism', *Cinema Journal*, 56:4 (Summer), pp. 102–25.
Gorin, Jean-Pierre (2009), 'Nove notas sobre *Onde Jaz o Teu Sorriso?*', in Ricardo Matos Cabo (ed.), *Cem mil cigarros: os filmes de Pedro Costa*, Lisbon: Orfeu Negro, pp. 249–57.
Graça, André Rui (2016), 'O conceito de "Cinema Artesanal"', in Frederico Lopes, Paulo Cunha and Manuela Penafria (eds), *Cinema em Português – IX Jornadas*, Covilhã: Universidade da Beira Interior, pp. 93–104.
Grainge, Paul (2002), *Monochrome Memories: Nostalgia and Style in Retro America*, Westport, CT: Praeger Press.
Granja, Paulo (2010), 'Paulo Rocha *Os Verdes Anos* (1962) and the New Portuguese Cinema', *P: Portuguese Cultural Studies*, 3:1 (Spring), pp. 61–8.
Grant, Catherine (2008), 'Auteur Machines? Auteurism and the DVD', in Tom Brown (ed.), *Film and Television after DVD*, London: Routledge, pp. 101–15.
Grieb, Margit and Will Lehman (2007), 'Screen Wars: German National Cinema in the Age of Television', in Dorota Ostrowska and Graham Roberts (eds), *European Cinema in the Television Age*, Edinburgh: Edinburgh University Press, pp. 71–86.
Grilo, João Mário (2006), *O Cinema da Não-ilusão*, Lisbon: Livros Horizonte.
Guarneri, Michael (2015a), 'Pedro Costa: Documentary, Realism, and Life on the Margins', *BOMB – Artists in Conversation*, 16 July, <http://bombmagazine.org/article/5506714/pedro-costa> (accessed 7 August 2015).
Guarneri, Michael (2015b), 'Colossal Youth and Horse Money, Pedro Costa. Where Now Are the Dreams of Youth?', *Débordements*, 3 September, <http://www.debordements.fr/Colossal-Youth-and-Horse-Money-Pedro-Costa> (accessed 11 June 2018).

Hagener, Malte and Marijke de Valck (2008), 'Cinephilia in Transition', in Jaap Kooijman, Patricia Pisters and Wanda Strauven (eds), *Mind the Screen: Media Concepts According to Thomas Elsaesser*, Amsterdam: Amsterdam University Press, pp. 19–31.

Hagman, Hampus (2007), '"Every Cannes needs its scandal": Between Art and Exploitation in Contemporary French Film', *Film International*, 5:5, pp. 32–41.

Harbord, Janet (2002), *Film Cultures*, London: Sage.

Hjort, Mette (2010), 'On the Plurality of Cinematic Transnationalism', in Nataša Ďurovičová and Kathleen Newman (eds), *World Cinemas, Transnational Perspectives*, New York and London: Routledge, pp. 12–33.

Hjort, Mette and Scott MacKenzie (2003), 'Dogma 95 Manifesto and Progeny', in Mette Hjort and Scott MacKenzie (eds), *Purity and Provocation: Dogma 95*, London: BFI, pp. 199–200.

Holzapfel, Patrick (2014), 'Viennale 2014: Filmmaking on High Seas: An Interview with Pedro Costa', *ScreenAnarchy*, 3 November, <http://screenanarchy.com/2014/11/viennale-2014-filmmaking-on-high-seas-an-interview-with-pedro-costa.html> (accessed 11 June 2018).

Hong, Sung-nam (2010), 'Constant Confrontation, and a Love Story', in Yoo Un-Seong (ed.), *Pedro Costa*, Jeonju: Jeonju International Film Festival, pp. 208–12.

Hughes, Darren (2008), 'Pedro Costa's "Vanda Trilogy" and the Limits of Narrative Cinema as a Contemplative Art', in Kenneth R. Morefield (ed.), *Faith and Spirituality in Masters of World Cinema*, Newcastle upon Tyne: Cambridge Scholars Publishing, pp. 160–74.

Iles, Chrissie (2001), 'Between the Still and the Moving Image', in *Into the Light: The Projected Image in American Art 1964–1977*, New York: Whitney Museum of American Art, pp. 33–69.

Ingawanij, May Adadol and Benjamin McKay (eds) (2012), *Glimpses of Freedom: Independent Cinema in Southeast Asia*, Ithaca, NY: Southeast Asia Program, Cornell University.

Iordanova, Dina (2009), 'The Film Festival Circuit', in Dina Iordanova and Ragan Rhyne (eds), *Film Festival Yearbook 1: The Festival Circuit*, St Andrews: St Andrews Film Studies, pp. 23–39.

Iordanova, Dina (2012), 'Digital Disruption: Technological Innovation and Global Film Circulation', in Dina Iordanova and Stuart Cunningham (eds), *Digital Disruption: Cinema Moves On-line*, St Andrews: St Andrews Film Studies, pp. 1–31.

Jäckel, Anne (2003), *European Film Industries*, London: British Film Institute.

Jaffe, Ira (2014), *Slow Movies: Countering the Cinema of Action*, New York: Wallflower Press.

James, David E. (2005), *The Most Typical Avant-Garde: History and Geography of Minor Cinemas in Los Angeles*, Berkeley and Los Angeles: University of California Press.

James, Nick (2010), 'Passive Aggressive', *Sight & Sound*, 20:4 (April), p. 5.

Jorge, João Miguel Fernandes (2009), 'Ossos', in Ricardo Matos Cabo (ed.), *Cem mil cigarros: os filmes de Pedro Costa*, Lisbon: Orfeu Negro, pp. 157–9.

Jorge, Nuno Barradas (2014), 'Thinking of Portugal, Looking at Cape Verde: Notes on Representation of Immigrants in the Films of Pedro Costa', in Cacilda Rêgo and Marcus Brasileiro (eds), *Migration in Lusophone Cinema*, New York: Palgrave Macmillan, pp. 41–57.

Judell, Brandon (2015), 'Pedro Costa: The "Unknown" Auteur Deals Out Horse Money', *Huffington Post*, 30 July, <http://www.huffingtonpost.com/brandon-judell/pedro-costa-the-unknown-a_b_7888774.html> (accessed 10 January 2019).

Keller, Craig (2014), Email interview with the author, 17 April.

Kim, Jihoon (2010), 'Between Auditorium and Gallery: Perception in Apichatpong Weerasethakul's Films and Installations', in Rosalind Galt and Karl Schoonover (eds), *Global Art Cinema: New Theories and Histories*, Oxford: Oxford University Press, pp. 125–41.

King, Geoff (2014), *Indie 2.0: Change and Continuity in Contemporary American Indie Film*, London: I. B. Tauris.

Kois, Dan (2011), 'Eating Your Cultural Vegetables', *New York Times*, 29 April, <http://www.nytimes.com/2011/05/01/magazine/mag-01Riff-t.html> (accessed 23 May 2018).
Kovács, András Bálint (2007), *Screening Modernism: European Art Cinema, 1950–1980*, Chicago: University of Chicago Press.
Landy, Marcia (2015), *Cinema and Counter-History*, Bloomington: Indiana University Press.
Lefebvre, Martin (2006), 'Between Setting and Landscape in the Cinema', in Martin Lefebvre (ed.), *Landscape and Film*, London: Routledge, pp. 19–59.
Lemière, Jacques (2006), '"Um centro na margem": o caso do cinema português', *Análise Social*, 41:180, pp. 731–65.
Lemière, Jacques (2009), 'Terra a Terra: O Portugal e o Cabo Verde de Pedro Costa', in Ricardo Matos Cabo (ed.), *Cem mil cigarros: os filmes de Pedro Costa*, Lisbon: Orfeu Negro, pp. 99–111.
Lim, Dennis (2007), 'Director's Quest for Truth among the Downtrodden', *New York Times*, 29 July, <http://www.nytimes.com/2007/07/29/movies/29lim.html> (accessed 15 May 2018).
Lim, Dennis (2012), 'Under the Influence', *Artforum*, 50:10 (Summer), pp. 101–2.
Lim, Song Hwee (2014), *Tsai Ming-liang and a Cinema of Slowness*, Hawaii: University of Hawai'i Press.
Lisboa, Ricardo Vieira (2019), '"Talvez fosse uma loucura, talvez começasse a escavar outro filme nesse filme . . .". Entrevista com Pedro Costa sobre o restauro de *Os Verdes Anos* e *Mudar de Vida*, de Paulo Rocha', *Aniki*, 6:1, pp. 149–65.
Liz, Mariana (2018a), 'Introduction: Framing the Global Appeal of Contemporary Portuguese Cinema', in Mariana Liz (ed.), *Portugal's Global Cinema: Industry, History and Culture*, London: I. B. Tauris, pp. 1–14.
Liz, Mariana (2018b), 'Cinema and the City in European Portugal', in Mariana Liz (ed.), *Portugal's Global Cinema: Industry, History and Culture*, London: I. B. Tauris, pp. 115–33.
Luz, Nuno H. (1990), 'De Pedro Costa', *Revista Semanário*, December, pp. 28–9.
Luz, Nuno H. (1994), 'Estou desgostado com Portugal', *Diário de Notícias*, 22 May, p. 29.
McGilligan, Patrick (2010), '"Letters from Fontainhas": Interview with Pedro Costa', *Film International*, 8:3, pp. 82–3.
Machuel, Emmanuel (2012), 'Interview', in *Casa de Lava*, DVD extras, London: Second Run.
Madragoa Filmes (1991), *Quando Ninguém Olhar Por Mim, de Pedro Costa*, unpublished film treatment, np.
Madragoa Filmes (1992), *Down to Earth*, unpublished film treatment, np.
Maimon, Vered (2012), 'Beyond Representation. Abbas Kiarostami's and Pedro Costa's Minor Cinema', *Third Text*, 26:3 (May), pp. 331–44.
Martin, Adrian (2008), 'What's Cult Got to Do with It?: In Defense of Cinephile Elitism', *Cineaste*, 34:1 (Winter), pp. 39–42.
Martin, Adrian (2009), 'The Inner Life of a Film', in *Blood*, DVD booklet, London: Second Run, pp. 3–7.
Martins, Susana (2001), 'No Palco da Vida', *JL: Jornal de Letras e Ideias*, 7 March, p. 9.
Meigh-Andrews, Chris (2006), *A History of Video Art: The Development of Form and Function*, Oxford: Berg.
Meintel, Deirdre (1984), *Race, Culture, and Portuguese Colonialism in Cabo Verde*, Foreign and Comparative Studies/African Series no. 41, Syracuse, NY: Maxwell School of Citizenship and Public Affairs, Syracuse University.
Mendes, Pedro Boucherie (1997), 'Cine-negócios', *O Independente*, 22 August, p. 45.
Morain, Jean-Baptiste (2003), 'Inedit Jean Eustache: Numéro zéro', *Les Inrockuptibles*, 1 January, <http://www.lesinrocks.com/cinema/films-a-l-affiche/inedit-jean-eustache-numero-zero> (accessed 21 May 2015).

Mourinha, Jorge (2009), 'Geração Perdida', *Público*, supplement *Ípsilon*, 25 September, pp. 11–12.
Mourinha, Jorge (2014), 'Cineasta, do nosso tempo', *Público*, supplement *Ípsilon*, 5 December, pp. 6–8.
Moutinho, Anabela (1996), *Os bons da fita: depoimentos inéditos de realizadores portugueses*, Faro: Cineclube de Faro/INATEL.
Moutinho, Anabela and Maria da Graça Lobo (1997), *António Reis e Margarida Cordeiro: A Poesia da Terra*, Faro: Cineclube de Faro.
Naficy, Hamid (2001), *An Accented Cinema: Exilic and Diasporic Filmmaking*, Princeton, NJ: Princeton University Press.
Neale, Steve (1981), 'Art Cinema as Institution', *Screen*, 22:1 (Spring), pp. 11–39.
Neyrat, Cyril (2010), 'Rooms for the Living and the Dead', in *Letters from Fontainhas*, DVD booklet, New York: Criterion Collection, pp. 10–17.
Nisa, João (2007), 'O Cinema no Museu: A partir de *Une visite au Louvre*, de Jean-Marie Straub and Danièle Huillet', *Docs.pt*, 6 (December), pp. 68–74.
Nisa, João (2009), 'Do Filme à Exposição: As Instalações Vídeo de Pedro Costa', in Ricardo Matos Cabo (ed.), *Cem mil cigarros: os filmes de Pedro Costa*, Lisbon: Orfeu Negro, pp. 301–13.
Oliveira, Luís Miguel (1995), 'A Pureza Ferida', *Público*, supplement *Zoom*, 10 February, p. 5.
Oliveira, Luís Miguel (2000), 'A malta do bairro', *Público*, 15 October, p. 27.
Oliveira, Luís Miguel (2009), 'Uma pequena avalanche', *Público*, supplement *Ípsilon*, 25 September, pp. 8–9.
O'Neill, Paul (2012), *The Culture of Curating and the Curating of Culture(s)*, Cambridge, MA: MIT Press.
Oumano, Elena (2010), *Cinema Today: A Conversation with Thirty-Nine Filmmakers from Around the World*, New Brunswick, NJ: Rutgers University Press.
Owen, Hilary (2018), 'White Faces/Black Masks: The White Woman's Burden in Pedro Costa's *Down to Earth*', in Mariana Liz (ed.), *Portugal's Global Cinema: Industry, History and Culture*, London: I. B. Tauris, pp. 185–204.
Pantenburg, Volker (2008), '"Post Cinema?" Movies, Museums, Mutations', *Site Magazine*, 24, pp. 4–5.
Pantenburg, Volker (2010), 'Realism, Not Reality: Pedro Costa's Digital Testimonies', *Afterall*, 24 (Summer), pp. 54–61.
Paradelo, Martin and Xiana Arias (2012), '"Eu acho que há cineastas que não têm a coragem de não fazer filmes"', *Cineclube de Compostela*, 6 December, <http://cineclubedecompostela.blogaliza.org/files/2012/12/entrevista-Costa.pdf> (accessed 13 January 2015).
Pardue, Derek (2014) '*Outros Bairros* and the Challenges of Place in Postcolonial Portugal', in Cacilda Rêgo and Marcus Brasileiro (eds), *Migration in Lusophone Cinema*, New York: Palgrave Macmillan, pp. 59–76.
Parente, André and Victa de Carvalho (2008), 'Cinema as *dispositif*: Between Cinema and Contemporary Art', *Cinémas: Journal of Film Studies*, 19:1, pp. 37–55.
Peranson, Mark (2010), 'Pedro Costa: An Introduction', in Yoo Un-Seong (ed.), *Pedro Costa*, Jeonju: Jeonju International Film Festival, pp. 125–46.
Peranson, Mark (2014), 'L'avventura: Pedro Costa on Horse Money', *Cinema Scope*, 60, <http://cinema-scope.com/cinema-scope-magazine/tiff-2014-horse-money-pedro-costa-portugal-wavelengths> (accessed 17 July 2018).
Preto, António (2017), 'Notes on a Certain Trend in Portuguese Cinema', *Journal of Lusophone Studies*, 2:1 (Spring), pp. 32–40.
Quandt, James (2006), 'Still Lives', *Artforum International*, 45:1 (September), pp. 354–9.
Quintana, Àngel (2009), 'Hacia un hiperrealismo de la imagen digital', *Cahiers du Cinéma España*, 6 (May), pp. 24–5.

Quintín (2009), 'The Second Story', *Sight & Sound*, 19:10 (October), pp. 31–3.
Ramstedt, Stefan and Martin Grennberger (2015), 'In the Shadows of Catacombs, A Conversation with Pedro Costa', *Sabzian*, 26 October, <http://www.sabzian.be/article/in-the-shadows-of-catacombs> (accessed 19 December 2018).
Rancière, Jacques (2005), *The Politics of Aesthetics*, 2nd edn, New York: Continuum.
Rancière, Jacques [2008] (2009a), *The Emancipated Spectator*, London: Verso.
Rancière, Jacques (2009b), 'The Politics of Pedro Costa', in *Retrospective Pedro Costa*, booklet, London: Tate Modern, np.
Rancière, Jacques (2014), *The Intervals of Cinema*, trans. John Howe, London: Verso.
Rancière, Jacques (2015), 'The Ghost Road', *Sight & Sound*, 25:10 (October), pp. 48–52.
Rapfogel, Jared (2010), 'The 11th Jeonju International Film Festival', *Cineaste*, 35:4, <http://www.cineaste.com/fall2010/the-11th-jeonju-international-film-festival> (accessed 4 September 2018).
Rato, Vanessa (2008), 'Pedro Costa deverá representar Portugal na Bienal de Veneza de 2009', *Público*, 6 November, <http://www.publico.pt/2008/11/06/culturaipsilon/noticia/pedro-costa-devera-representar-portugal-na-bienal-de-veneza-de-2009-1349096> (accessed 11 July 2018).
Ribas, Daniel (2009), 'Nova Geração?: a geração curtas chega às longas', in Frederico Lopes (ed.), *Cinema em Português: Actas das II Jornadas*, Covilhã: Labcom, pp. 93–101.
Robert, David (2001), 'O Lugar de Pedro', in Dário Oliveira (ed.), *Porto 2001: Ciclo de Cinema, Instalação e Performance*, Porto: Porto 2001, pp. 90–2.
Robinson, Luke (2013), *Independent Chinese Documentary: From the Studio to the Street*, Basingstoke: Palgrave Macmillan.
Rombes, Nicholas (2009), *Cinema in the Digital Age*, London: Wallflower Press.
Romney, Jonathan (2000), 'Are You Sitting Comfortably?', *The Guardian*, 7 October, <http://www.theguardian.com/film/2000/oct/07/books.guardianreview> (accessed 13 May 2014).
Romney, Jonathan (2008), 'Exile and the Kingdom', *Sight & Sound*, 17:6 (June), pp. 46–7.
Romney, Jonathan (2010), 'In Search of the Lost Time', *Sight & Sound*, 20:2 (February), pp. 43–4.
Romney, Jonathan (2015a), 'Film of the Week: Horse Money', *Film Comment*, 16 July, <http://www.filmcomment.com/blog/film-of-the-week-horse-money> (accessed 11 January 2019).
Romney, Jonathan (2015b), 'Pedro Costa: Portuguese Director Who Fashioned Gil Scott-Heron's Film Prayer', *The Guardian*, 17 September, <http://www.theguardian.com/film/2015/sep/17/pedro-costa-director-horse-money-cavalo-dinheiro-gil-scott-heron-interview> (accessed 11 June 2018).
Rosado, Pedro Garcia (1990), 'Anemia Ficcional', *JL: Jornal de Letras e Ideias*, 11 December, p. 22.
Rosenbaum, Jonathan (2010a), 'Finding Oneself in the Dark: The Mysterious Cinema of Pedro Costa', in Yoo Un-Seong (ed.), *Pedro Costa*, Jeonju: Jeonju International Film Festival, pp. 189–200.
Rosenbaum, Jonathan (2010b), 'Cinema of the Future: Still Lives, the Films of Pedro Costa', in *Goodbye Cinema, Hello Cinephilia: Film Culture in Transition*, Chicago: University of Chicago Press, pp. 204–6.
Rosenbaum, Jonathan (2012), 'Eruptions and Disruptions in the House of Lava', in *Casa de Lava*, DVD booklet, London: Second Run, pp. 3–8.
Rosenbaum, Jonathan (2015), 'Pedro Costa's *Horse Money*', *Artforum International*, 53:10 (Summer), pp. 129–30.
Ross, Miriam (2011), 'The Film Festival as Producer: Latin American Films and the Rotterdam's Hubert Bals Fund', *Screen*, 52:2 (Summer), pp. 261–7.

Rothermel, Dennis (2009), 'Slow Food, Slow Film', *Quarterly Review of Film and Video*, 26:4, pp. 265–79.
Rushton, Richard (2012), *Cinema after Deleuze*, London: Continnum.
Sampaio, Sofia (2013), '"Nós não precisamos de ajuda": materialidade e ética em *O Sangue*, de Pedro Costa', in Tiago Baptista and Adriana Martins (eds), *Atas do II Encontro Anual da AIM*, Lisboa: AIM, pp. 474–86.
Sante, Luc (2010), 'The Space Between', in *Letters from Fontainhas*, DVD Booklet, New York: Criterion Collection, pp. 22–5.
Saramago, Patrícia (2013), Email interview with the author, 23 July.
Sayad, Cecilia (2014), *Performing Authorship: Self-Inscription and Corporeality in Cinema*, London: I. B. Tauris.
Schneider, Jörg (2013), Email interview with the author, 26 July.
Schober, Anna (2013), *The Cinema Makers*, Bristol: Intellect.
Scott, A. O., Manohla Dargis and Dan Kois (2011), 'Sometimes a Vegetable Is Just a Vegetable', *New York Times*, 17 July, <http://www.nytimes.com/2011/06/19/movies/critics-discuss-cinema-thats-good-for-you.html> (accessed 23 May 2018).
Seabra, Augusto M. (1987), 'Exibidores precisam-se', *Expresso*, 31 October, p. 130.
Seabra, Augusto M. (1990), 'Verdes Anos', *Público*, 1 December, p. 18.
Shaviro, Steve (2010), 'Slow Cinema vs Fast Films', *The Pinocchio Theory*, 12 May, <http://www.shaviro.com/Blog/?p=891> (accessed 23 May 2018).
Smith, Barbara Herrnstein (1991), *Contingencies of Value*, Cambridge, MA, and London: Harvard University Press.
Staiger, Janet (2003), 'Authorship approaches', in David A. Gerstner and Janet Staiger (eds), *Authorship and Film*, New York and London: Routledge, pp. 27–57.
Stanbrook, Alan (1989), 'Hard Times for Portuguese Cinema', *Sight & Sound*, 58:2 (Spring), pp. 118–21.
Stringer, Julian (2001), 'Global Cities and the International Film Festival Economy', in Mark Shiel and Tony Fitzmaurice (eds), *Cinema and the City: Film and Urban Societies in a Global Context*, Oxford: Blackwell, pp. 134–44.
Tarrant, Patrick (2013), 'Montage in the Portrait Film: Where Does the Hidden Time Lie?', *Alphaville: Journal of Film and Screen Media*, 5 (Summer), <http://www.alphavillejournal.com/Issue5/PDFs/ArticleTarrant.pdf> (accessed 14 October 2018).
Tavares, João Miguel (2001), 'Relato de um mundo em queda', *Diário de Notícias*, 2 March, p. 42.
Tomaz, Cláudia (2013), Email interview with the author, 20 May.
Tuttle, Harry (2010), 'Slow Films, Easy Life (Sight&Sound)', 5 December, <http://unspokencinema.blogspot.co.uk/2010/05/slow-films-easy-life-sight.html> (accessed 23 May 2018).
Uroskie, Andrew V. (2014), *Between the Black Box and the White Cube: Expanded Cinema and Postwar Art*, Chicago: University of Chicago Press.
Villa-Lobos, Francisco (2013), Personal interview with the author, Cascais, 11 February.
Villa-Lobos, Francisco (2018), Email communication with the author, 18 September.
Villaverde, Teresa (2012), Personal interview with the author, Lisbon, 28 June.
Wall, Jeff (2009), 'A Propósito de *Ossos*', in Ricardo Matos Cabo (ed.), *Cem mil cigarros: os filmes de Pedro Costa*, Lisbon: Orfeu Negro, pp. 151–5.
Wall, Jeff (2010), 'Video Essay', in *Letters From Fontainhas*, *Ossos* DVD supplements, New York: Criterion Collection.
Walsh, Martin (1981), *The Brechtian Aspect of Radical Cinema*, London: BFI.
Wasson, Haidee (2005), *Museum Movies: The Museum of Modern Art and the Birth of Art Cinema*, Berkeley: University of California Press.

White, Armond (2010), 'Portrait of a Black Man', *New York Press*, 13 April, <http://nypress.com/portrait-of-a-black-man> (accessed 17 January 2014).

White, Armond (2015), 'Paying Attention to Black Lives', *The National Review*, 24 July, <http://www.nationalreview.com/2015/07/do-black-lives-matter-movies> (accessed 12 January 2019).

Wilinsky, Barbara (2001), *Sure Seaters: The Emergence of Art House Cinema*, Minneapolis: University of Minnesota Press.

Wong, Cindy Hing-Yuk (2011), *Film Festivals: Culture, People, and Power on the Global Screen*, London: Rutgers University Press.

Yano, Kazuyuki (2014), Email communication with the author, 1 August.

Index

Note: Page numbers in *italics* refer to illustrations.

6 *Bagatelas*, 76
25 of April Revolution 1973, 3, 8, 17, 18, 78, 132, 134, 135, 136

A Comédia de Deus (1995), 49
À Flor do Mar (1986), 22
A Idade Maior (1991), 13
Abraham, Ayisha, 101
Agosto (1988), 22
Akerman, Chantal, 54, 55, 90, 94, 101
Akomfrah, John, 86
Alonso, Lisandro, 79, 81, 82, 85
Alves, Cristiano Andrade, 35
Ana (1985), 20, 44
Andersen, Thom, 61, 63
Angelopoulos, Theo, 83
Arenas, Fernando, 41, 42, 45
art cinema, 3, 5–6, 54, 55, 151
  circuits, 5, 6, 117
  and digital video, 55, 58; *see also* digital video
  as institution *see* Neale, Steve
  Portuguese art cinema, 13, 27, 29, 56
  production, 65, 67; *see also* co-production
  and symbolic value, 70, 71, 108
  taxonomies, 70, 79, 81, 82; *see also* Slow Cinema
'Art Cinema as Institution' (Neale), 6
'The Art Cinema as a Mode of Film Practice' (Bordwell), 6
artisanal filmmaking, 9, 54, 55, 56
Atalanta Filmes, 12, 27, 116
Atlântida (1985), 22, 23
auteur, 7
AV Festival, 82
Azul, 22, 23

Balibar, Jeanne, 113, 114, 121
Balsom, Erika, 92, 98
Baptista, Tiago, 19, 56, 67
Barros, Alberto 'Lento', 78, 104, 134
Barroso, Bárbara, 20, 21
Bartas, Sharunas, 74
Barwick, Chris, 8, 123, 124, 125, 126; *see also* Second Run

Baumgartner, Karl, 66
Bazar do Video *see* OPTEC Filmes
Bazin, André, 92
Bedlam (1946), 129
Benfica, Colina do Sol e Pontinha (video installation, 2005), 93
Benning, James, 58, 82, 86, 120
Berit Films, 36
Berry, Chris, 55
Betz, Mark, 79, 85
Birdsong (2008), 81
'black box', 5, 10, 92, 97, 98, 99–100
Blood (1989), 3, 8, 38, 114
   aesthetic influences, 12, 14, *15*
   budget, 24
   cinematography, 24–5, 26, 28
   domestic reception, 28, 30
   domestic release, 12, 27
   DVD releases, 110, 123, 124, 126
   film script, 24
   marketing campaign, 28, *29*
   shooting, 25, 26
   synopsis, 14, 15–16
Bogalheiro, José, 19, 22
Bones (1997), 4, 9, 32, 34, 44, 47
   DVD releases, 122
   politics, 47, 48
   production, 49
   script, 45–6
   shooting, 50, 62
   synopsis, 46
Boozer, Jack, 37
Bordwell, David, 6, 79, 81
Borges, Pedro, 8, 27, 116
Botelho, João, 22, 24, 49
Bourdieu, Pierre, 6, 70, 71, 84, 108
Bradshaw, Peter, 73
Branco, Paulo, 4, 9, 21, 27, 34, 38, 39, 45, 49, 54, 67, 112, 113, 116, 117, 122

Brandão, Sandra do Canto, 35
Bresson, Robert, 3, 12, 14, 18, 19, 32, 36, 48, 79, 128, 149
Burdeau, Emmanuel, 53, 64

Cabo, Ricardo Matos, 2, 117
Caça ao Coelho com Pau see The Rabbit Hunters
Çağlayan, Emre, 82
Cahiers du Cinéma, 53, 64
Caldas, Pedro, 22
Calouste Gulbenkian Foundation, 17–18, 21, 22, 24, 101, 105, 108
Câmara, Vasco, 34, 42
Canijo, João, 13, 21, 24
Cannes Film Festival, 42, 69, 71, 72, 73, 124
Canto e Castro, Henrique, 14
Cape Verde, 32, 35, 39, 41, 42, 43, 44
Cardoso, Isabel, 104
Cardoso, Lucinda, 102
Carmo, Teresa, 21
Cartas à Júlia, 23, 31n
Casa de Lava (1994), 4, 9, 32, 34, 90, 98, 137, *138*
   DVD releases, 122, 123, 124, 126
   film script, 37–8, 40
   funding, 37, 38–9
   politics, 42, 43
   postcolonial context, 35, 36, 41, 42, 43, 44
   production, 38, 39
   shooting, 39, 40
   synopsis, 35, 36, 40–1
Casa de Lava (notebook), 43–4
Casal da Boba, 78, 86, 100, 114
Casal da Boba (video installation, 2005), 93, 100
Cavaco Silva, Aníbal, 42
Cavalo Dinheiro see Horse Money
Centro Histórico (2012), 103–4
Ceylan, Nuri Bilge, 85

Chafes, Rui, 5, 93, 105, 107, 108, 128
Change Nothing (2005, 2009), 4, 10, 110, 112
  DVD releases, 122, 123, 127n
  funding, 115
  Japanese theatrical release, 121, 127n
  production, 113–14
  synopsis, 114
Chaves, Abel Ribeiro, 8, 113, 130, 131; *see also* OPTEC Filmes
The Chronicle of Anna Magdalena Bach (1968), 129
Cilaos (2016), 150
Cinema Novo, 19, 30
Cinema Scope, 74
Cinemateca Portuguesa *see* Portuguese Cinematheque
'cinematic' (trend), 92, 93–6, 98
Cinematrix, 115, 120, 121, 127n
cinephilia, 8, 12, 13, 16, 28, 73, 121
Cintra, Luís Miguel, 14, 24, 26
CNC (Centre national du cinéma et de l'image animée), 39
Colossal Youth (2006), 4, 9, 69, 86, 93, 98, 104, 112, 129, 137, 139
  aesthetics, 77
  at Cannes Film Festival, 69, 72
  distribution, 113
  DVD releases, 122, 124
  production, 127n
  shooting 87
  synopsis, 78
  at Toronto Film Festival, 74
  co-production, 4, 9, 21, 49, 54, 56, 65, 67, 115, 130
Companhia see Company
Company (exhibition), 128–9
'contemplative contemporary cinema' (Tuttle) *see* Tuttle, Harry

'contemporary parametric film' (Betz), 79, 85
Contracosta Produções, 54, 66, 112, 113, 115; *see also* Villa-Lobos, Francisco
copyright (of Costa's films), 115–16
Cordeiro, Edmundo, 132, 139
Cordeiro, Margarida, 20, 26, 32, 44, 56, 128, 148
Corless, Kieron, 47, 57, 61, 69, 77
Cowie, Elizabeth, 59–60
The Criterion Collection, 110
Cutler, Aaron, 132, 135, 136, 143

da Costa, João Bénard, 16, 18, 21, 28, 55
Dans la Ville Blanche (1983), 26
Dargis, Manohla, 84
Darke, Chris, 55, 57
Das Kleine Fernsehspiel (DKF), 66, 68n
Daughters of Fire (video installation), 90, *91*, 98
David, Catherine, 93, 94, 97, 103, 107, 108
de Almeida, Acácio, 26
De Bankolé, Isaach, 35, 39, 40
de Carvalho, Victa, 99, 100
de Castro, Isabel, 24
de Luca, Tiago, 58, 80
de Medeiros, Inês, 14, 23–4, 28, 29, 35, 38, 39, 46, 49, 137, 138
de Pina, Luís, 17, 21
de Valck, Marijke, 12, 70, 71, 126
Deleuze, Gilles, 136
Del-Negro, Daniel, 19, 22, 23
Dercon, Chris, 92, 96
Desnos, Robert, 128, 137, 139
Diaz, Lav, 58, 82, 85, 86
'digital realism' (Pantenburg), 58–9, 63–4

digital video, 4, 54, 55, 56, 57, 58, 61, 64, 87, 95
  in artistic practices, 94–5
  Portuguese context, 56
disintermediation, 111, 112, 116, 126
Docufiction, 32, 44, 57, 78, 59–60, 78
Documenta X, 94
Dogme 95, 49
Down to Earth (film) *see Casa de Lava*
Down to Earth (script treatment, 1992), 37, 39, 40
Duarte, Vanda, 45, 46, 49, 51, 59, 63, 64, 66, 78, 83, 98, 100, 114
Duarte, Zita, 45, 48, 49, 59, 63, 64, 66, 98
Duma Vez Por Todas (1986), 22
Dumas, Richard, 76, 77
Dumont, Bruno, 47, 79
DVD extras, 125

'economy of prestige' (English), 70
Egoyan, Atom, 90
Eisenschitz, Bernard, 103
El cant dels ocells see Birdsong
El cielo, la tierra, y la lluvia (*Sky, The Earth and the Rain*, 2008), 150
Elsaesser, Thomas, 47, 65, 71, 80, 81, 100, 105
Elwes, Catherine, 95
The End of the Love Affair (video installation, 2003), 100, *101*
epistolary device, 137, *138*, 139
Équation, 113, 122
Erice, Víctor, 90, 104
Escalante, Amat, 85
Escola Portuguesa, 19, 56
Escola Superior de Teatro e Cinema *see* Lisbon Theatre and Film School

Eureka! *see* Masters of Cinema
Eurimages, 49
European Union, 27, 42–3, 47

Família (exhibition), 93
fandom of Costa, 69, 73, 74, 118
  in Japan, 121
  at JIFF, 120
Farocki, Harun, 86
Fernandes, João Miguel, 46
Ferraz, Vicente, 101
Ferreira, Francisco, 78, 113
Ferreira, Nuno, 14, 24, 38
Festen (1998), 55
Fiadeiro, João, 100, 105
Filhas do Fogo see Daughters of Fire
Filipovic, Elena, 106
film festivals, 7, 9, 71, 56, 85, 118
  as film producers, 85, 86, 87
Film.Factory, 151
Filmic deceleration 4, 58, 81, 96, 97, 99
  in Costa's films, 54, 83
Finding the Criminal (2010), 125
Flanagan, Matthew, 81
Fogo (2012), 150
Fontainhas, 4, 32, 44, 45, 46, 48, 50, 53, 59, 62, 76, 83, 99
Fontainhas (video installation, 2005), 93
Fora!/Out! (exhibition), 93
Ford, John, 18, 128
Franju, Georges, 38
Frohne, Ursula, 95, 96
Fujiwara, Chris, 34, 114, 142
Fulton, Hamish, 82
Fundação Calouste Gulbenkian *see* Calouste Gulbenkian Foundation
Fundação de Serralves *see* Serralves Foundation

G.E.R. (Grupo de Estudos e Realizações), 22
Gallagher, Mark, 13–14
Garrel, Philippe, 74
Gemini Films, 39, 122
Géricault, Théodore, 129
Godard, Jean-Luc, 18, 19, 90, 94
Gomes, Miguel, 1, 75
Gomes, Rita Azevedo, 21
Gonçalves, Vítor, 20, 22
Gordon, Douglas, 96
Gorin, Jean-Pierre, 45, 66, 76
Granja, Paulo, 29, 30
Grant, Catherine, 111
Green, Eugène, 86
Guimarães, Ana Luísa, 13, 22, 23

Hagener, Malte, 3, 12, 126
Harbord, Janet, 6
Hestnes, Pedro, 14, 22, 23–4, 28, 29, 35, 38, 39
History Lessons (1972), 130
Hodgkinson, Tom, 80
Horse Money (2014), 4, 10–11, 104, 114, 117, 128, 129, 130, *138*
  authorial process, 131–2
  comparisons with *Colossal Youth*, 132–3, 134, 139
  critical reception, 143, 144, 145
  DVD releases, 123
  funding, 130–1
  historical context, 134, 135, 136
  intertextual qualities, 129, 137, 139, 140–1, 142, 146
  politics, 130, 135, 142, 144–5, 146
  postcolonial context, 137, 139
  production, 130–1
  stylistic characteristics, 133, 136, 142–3
  synopsis, 132, 133, 137
Hou Hsiao-hsien, 79
Hubert Bals Fund (HBF), 85

Hughes, Darren, 79
Huillet, Danièle *see* Straub and Huillet

I Walked with a Zombie (1943), 32, 34, 35, 36, 37, 38, 40, 43
ICA *see* IPC
ICAM *see* IPC
The Idler, 80
In Vanda's Room (2000), 4, 9, 20, 45, 53, 54, 93, 98, 114
  cinematography, 61
  digital video, 61
  docufiction, 59–60
  DVD releases, 122, 123, 127n
  editing, 66–7
  funding, 65–6, 67
  at Locarno Film Festival, 72
  long take, 59, 61
  production, 64–5
  shooting, 53, 62–3
  sound, 63, 66
  synopsis, 59
'industrial reflexivity' (Caldwell), 8
Ingawanij, May Adadol, 55
'intensified continuity' (Bordwell), 81
interstitial production 4, 9, 54, 56, 64, 65, 67, 108
Iordanova, Dina, 69, 111, 124
IPC (Instituto Português de Cinema), 21, 65, 130
Ishii, Sogo, 86

Jaffe, Ira, 60
Jaime (1974), 20
James, Nick, 84, 85
Jensen, Kris, 114
Jensen, Peter Aalbæk, 49
Jeonju Digital Project (JDP), 10, 71, 85
Jeonju International Film Festival (JIFF), 85, 101, 105, 118, 120

Jia Zhangke, 58, 79, 86
Jorge, Nuno Barradas, 42, 58, 80, 85, 135, 139
Juventude em Marcha see Colossal Youth

Kaurismäki, Aki, 104
Kawase, Naomi, 86
Kelemen, Fred, 74
Keller, Craig, 8, 124, 125; *see also* Masters of Cinema
Kiarostami, Abbas, 90
Kim, Jihoon, 97
King, Geoff, 55
Kings of the Road (1976), 25
Kois, Dan, 84

La Haine (1995), 47
La Promesse (1996), 47
La vie de Jésus (1997), 47
La Ville des Pirates (1983), 26
Lamento da Vida Jovem see Sweet Exorcism
Lanban, Pedro, 64
Landy, Marcia, 135
Lang, Fritz, 18, 34, 128
L'avventura (1960), 69
Le Quattro Volte (2010), 84
Lefebvre, Martin, 32
Leitão, Joaquim, 22, 31n
Leiva, José Luis Torres, 150
Lemière, Jacques, 2, 19, 21, 43, 56
Les glaneurs et la glaneuse (2000), 55
Les Yeux Sans Visage (1960), 38, 44
Let Us Now Praise Famous Men: The Films of Pedro Costa, 117
Letters from Fontainhas, 110
Lewton, Val, 34
Lim, Dennis, 20, 44, 72, 73, 74, 80
Lipkina, Mariya, 46, 49, 51
Lisbon Story (1994), 45

Lisbon Theatre and Film School, 3, 18, 19, 20
Little Boy Male, Little Girl Female (video installation, 2005), 93, 98–9, 99
Liz, Mariana, 45, 56, 57
Locarno Film Festival, 66, 71, 72, 149
Lockhart, Sharon, 96
long take, 4, 47, 59, 61, 77, 79, 80, 81, 99, 143, 144
Lounas, Thierry, 53, 75
Lusomundo, 26, 116

Machuel, Emmanuel, 49, 50, 51, 61, 68n
McKay, Benjamin, 55
McQueen, Steve, 96
Madragoa Filmes, 39, 49, 116
Maïkoff, Henri, 49, 50
Martin, Adrian, 2, 16–17, 73, 74
Massadian, Valérie, 150
Masters of Cinema, 123, 124
Materialist film, 96
Medeia Filmes, 27, 116
Meek's Cutoff (2010), 84
Meigh-Andrews, Chris, 95
Meintel, Deirdre, 41–2
Memories (2007), 86
Mendes, Alfredo, 102, 103
Mendoza, Brillante, 145
MFA (Armed Forces Movement), 134, *136*
Midas Filmes, 122–3
Minino macho, minino fêmea see Little Boy Male, Little Girl Female
Monteiro, João César, 1, 29, 49, 52, 116
Morel, Philippe, 63
Mouchette (1967), 14
Mourinha, Jorge, 21, 23, 143
Mozos, Manuel, 13, 20–1

MU (exhibition), 93
Mudar de Vida (1966), 148
Müller, Marco, 66
Müller, Robby, 25

Naderi, Amir, 54
Naficy, Hamid, 54
Nana (2011), 150
narrative of production, 7, 8, 11, 57, 68, 75, 87, 108, 119, 143
Ne Change Rien see Change Nothing
Neale, Steve, 6
Neyrat, Cyril, 18, 59, 62, 64, 122
Night of the Demon (1957), 102
Night of the Hunter (1955), 14, 15
Nisa, João, 100
No Quarto da Vanda see In Vanda's Room
Noites (2001), 47, 52n, 63
Non, ou A Vã Glória de Mandar (1990), 27
NOS *see* Lusomundo
Not Reconciled (1965), 129
Número Zéro (1971), 148, 151n
Nuvem (1992), 13, 22

O Desejado (1987), 24
O Estado do Mundo (2007), 101
O Nosso Homem see Our Man
O Sangue see Blood
Olaizola, Yulene, 150
Oliveira, Luís Miguel, 36, 54, 118, 121
Oliveira, Manoel de, 1, 21, 24, 26, 27, 29, 104
OPTEC Filmes, 10, 111, 112, 113, 115, 130, 131, 147n
Os Filhos do Tejo, 108
Os Mutantes (1998), 47, 52n
Os Verdes Anos (1963), 30, 148
Ossos see Bones

Où gît votre sourire enfoui? see Where Does Your Hidden Smile Lie?
Our Man (2010), 10, 92, 103, 105, 129
Owen, Hilary, 42, 43
Ozu, Yasujirō, 18, 61, 74, 79, 149

Pandora Films *see* Baumgartner, Karl
Pantenburg, Volker, 58, 64, 94
Paraísos Artificiales (*Artificial Paradises*, 2011), 150
Paralluelo, Hermes, 150
'parametric narration' (Bordwell), 79
Parente, André, 99, 100
Peranson, Mark, 24, 40, 63, 74, 129, 133, 140, 141, 143, 146
Perez, Gilberto, 129
Petit, Christopher, 25, 55
Piñedo, Matias, 150
Pinto, Joaquim, 13, 20, 27, 49
Portuguese Cinematheque, 17–18, 20, 21, 105, 121, 149
Putty Hill (2010), 150

Quando Ninguém Olhar Por Mim (script treatment, 1991), 37–8
Quandt, James, 2, 48, 60, 72, 74, 77, 145
Quintana, Àngel, 58
Quintín, 75

The Rabbit Hunters (2007), 10, 86, 87, 92, 101, 102, 103, 104
Radio On (1979), 25
Rancière, Jacques, 2, 60, 77, 79, 139, 142, 145
Ray, Nicholas, 12, 14, 15, 24
Recordações da Casa Amarela (1989), 27
Rector, Andy, 125
'recycling' (Balsom), 98

Reis, António
  as a filmmaker, 20, 31n, 32, 44, 48, 56, 128, 148
  The School of Reis, 20, 149
  as a teacher, 19
Resnais, Alain, 79
retrospectives, 10, 116–18, 119, 120–1, 126
Reygadas, Carlos, 79, 81, 85, 151
Ribas, Daniel, 20, 21, 56
Ribeiro, Orlando, 32, *33*, 52n
Riis, Jacob, 128, 129, 139, 145
Rivette, Jacques, 2, 74
RKO Radio Pictures, 34, 36, 102
Robinson, Luke, 55
Rocha, Paulo, 24, 26, 30, 148
Rodrigues, João Pedro, 1, 20
Rombes, Nicholas, 57
Romney, Jonathan, 60, 79, 81, 82, 132, 144
Roque, Elso, 26
Rosa de Areia (1989), 20
Rosenbaum, Jonathan, 2, 16, 36, 38, 139, 143, 144, 151
Rosetta (1999), 47
Ross, Miriam, 85
Rossellini, Roberto, 18, 36
RTP (Rádio e Televisão de Portugal), 21, 23, 24, 38, 39, 49, 52n, 156
Ruiz, Raúl, 22, 26, 90
Ruth, Isabel, 46, 49, *51*

Salaviza, João, 150
Sampaio, Sofia, 12–13
Santos, António, 104, 132
Santos, Luís, 14
Sapinho, Joaquim, 20
Saramago, Patrícia, 8, 66, 67, 114
Schäfer, Martin, 25, 26, 28

Schneider, Jörg, 8, 66
The School of Reis, *see* Reis, António
Schroeter, Werner, 22
Scob, Edith, 35, 38, 39, 137
Scott, A. O., 84
Scott-Heron, Gil, 131, 132
Se Eu Fosse Ladrão . . . Roubava (2013), 149
Seabra, Augusto, M., 21, 26, 30
Second Run, 110, 123, 124, 125
Semedo, António, 78, 104
Serralves Foundation, 93, 100, 105, 128
The Seventh Victim (1943), 129
Shaviro, Steven, 84
Shichiri, Kei, 150
Sicilia! (1999), 75, 103
Sight & Sound, 61, 81, 84, 145
Silent Night (2007), 81
Silva, José Alberto, 102
Siodmak, Curt, 34, 40
slow (movements), 80
Slow Cinema, 9, 70, 79, 80, 81–4, 88, 96–7
Smith, Barbara Herrnstein, 7
Sokurov, Aleksandr, 79
Solaris (1972), 84
Stars in My Crown (1950), 129
The State of Things (1982), 22, 25
Stellet Licht see Silent Night
Still Lives: The Films of Pedro Costa, 117, 119, 127n
still-life, 60, 77
Straub, Jean-Marie *see* Straub and Huillet
Straub and Huillet, 2, 10, 18, 70, 73, 74, 75, 76, *77*, 78–9, 103, 128, 129, 149
Stromboli (aka *Stromboli, terra di Dio*, 1950), 36, 38

Structural film, 96
Sud (1999), 55
Suleiman, Elia, 54
Sumpta, Gustavo, 100, *101*
Suwa, Nobuhiro, 121
Sweet Exorcism (2012), 10, 92, 103–4, 129, 132
symbolic value, 70, 71, 72, 73, 87, 88, 106; *see also* Bourdieu, Pierre

Tableau Vivant, 77, 104, 139; *see also* still-life
Tanner, Alain, 22, 26
Tarkovsky, Andrei, 83, 84
Tarr, Bela, 74, 79, 82, 151
Tarrafal (2007), 10, 92, 101–2, *102*, 103, 129
Tarrafal (prison camp), 35, 42, 44
Tarrant, Patrick, 76
Tavares, Benvindo, 133
Tavares, João Miguel, 55
Tempos Difíceis (1987), 24
Temps d'Images, 100
They Live by Night (1948), 14, 15
Todo no es vigilia (*Not All Is Vigil*, 2014), 150
Tomaz, Cláudia, 8, 47, 63
Tomita, Katsuya, 150
Tourneur, Jacques, 3, 12, 15, 32
Tráfico (1998), 49
'translation' (Balsom), 98
Trás-os-Montes (1976), 20, 44
Três Menos Eu (1988), 13, 24
Trier, Lars von, 49
Trópico Filmes, 22, 23, 24
Tsai Ming-liang, 86
Tsukamoto, Shinya, 86
Tubarões, Os, 129, 139, 141
Tuttle, Harry, 84

Um Adeus Português (*A Portuguese Farwell*, 1986), 22
Uma Pedra no Bolso (*Tall Stories*, 1988), 13, 27
Uma Rapariga no Verão (*A Girl in Summer*, 1986), 22, 23, 24, 31n
Unspoken Cinema (blog) *see* Tuttle, Harry
Untitled (video installation, 2001), 93

Varela, Vitalina, 5, 129, 134, 137, 140, 141, 147
Vasconcelos, Joana, 106
Vaz, Nuno, 46, 49
Ventura, 5, 77, 78, 86, 101, 103, 104, 129, 131, 132
   as a character, 78, 101, 103, 104, 132, 133, 134, 137
Viana, Henrique, 14
Villa-Lobos, Francisco, 8, 10, 54, 65, 66, 67, 72, 76, 88, 111, 112, 113, 115, 117, 122
Villaverde, Teresa, 13, 18, 21
Vitalina Varela (2019), 5, 140

Wall, Jeff, 48, 50, 128
Wallace, Inez, 34
Wang Bing, 58, 101
Warhol, Andy, 96
Weerasethakul, Apichatpong, 58, 79, 82, 85, 86, 90, 97, 101, 125, 151
Wenders, Wim, 22, 25, 28, 45
Where Does Your Hidden Smile Lie? (2001), 4, 9–10, 103, 112, 114, 127n
   DVD releases, 122, 123
   shooting and production details, 75–6

'white cube', 5, 10, 92, 94,
    95, 97, 98, 99–100,
    106
Wray, Ardel, 34, 40

Xavier (1992), 13
Xavier, Waldir, 66

Yano, Kazuyuki, 8, 120, 121, 124,
    150; *see also* Cinematrix
youth cultures (Lisbon),18, 20, 21

Zentropa, 49
ZON *see* Lusomundo
Zona J (1998), 47, 52n

EU representative:
Easy Access System Europe
Mustamäe tee 50, 10621 Tallinn, Estonia
Gpsr.requests@easproject.com

www.ingramcontent.com/pod-product-compliance
Lightning Source LLC
Chambersburg PA
CBHW070358240426
43671CB00013BA/2556